PRESCRIPTION GAMES

Also by Jeffrey Robinson

– Fiction –

A True and Perfect Knight
The Monk's Disciples
The Margin of the Bulls
The Ginger Jar
Pietrov and Other Games

– Non-Fiction –

The Merger
The Manipulators
The Hotel
The Laundrymen
Bardot – Two Lives
The End of the American Century
The Risk Takers – Five Years On
Rainier and Grace
Yamani – The Inside Story
Minus Millionaires
The Risk Takers
Teamwork
Bette Davis

PRESCRIPTION GAMES

MONEY, EGO AND POWER INSIDE
THE GLOBAL PHARMACEUTICAL INDUSTRY

JEFFREY ROBINSON

SIMON & SCHUSTER
A VIACOM COMPANY

First published in Great Britain by Simon & Schuster UK Ltd, 2001
A Viacom Company

1 3 5 7 9 10 8 6 4 2

Simon & Schuster UK Ltd
Africa House
64–78 Kingsway
London WC2B 6AH

Simon & Schuster Australia
Sydney

A CIP catalogue record for this book is available
from the British Library

ISBN 0-684-85837-1

Typeset by Palimpsest Book Production Limited,
Polmont, Stirlingshire
Printed and bound in Great Britain by
Butler & Tanner Ltd, Frome, Somerset

To

Meg Lefever

and Dr Robert Lefever

with enormous affection

Contents

CHAPTER ONE

Big Pharma

Bĭg Făf-mă, *n*. term used to describe the global collective of
research-based pharmaceutical companies, of which there
are an estimated 75–100

Brenda never lived to see her daughter's first communion.

Diagnosed with ovarian cancer at the age of thirty-one, she
could have had her life extended by 12–14 months with drugs
– which would have been long enough so that she could watch
her only child receive God's blessing – but she couldn't afford
to pay more than $2,300 (£1,500) every three weeks for her
treatment, and no one else in the United States was willing
to pay.

This, at a time of unprecedented corporate prosperity.

The drug she needed, Taxol, had been developed by the
US government with the taxpayers' money and handed as
a gift to Bristol-Myers Squibb to exploit commercially as a
prescription drug. The year Brenda died, BMS's worldwide
sales on Taxol came to $1.27 billion (£820 million).

Several thousand miles away in sub-Saharan Africa, more
than 23 million people are HIV positive. That's 70 per cent
of the total HIV-infected population on the planet. Until

the summer of 2000, Big Pharma had flatly turned its back on those people. Its collective excuse had been that the Africans didn't have an infrastructure through which the pharmaceutical companies could work and, if the Africans wanted help, they had to begin by doing what they could for themselves.

When an AIDS conference in South Africa convinced the world's media to spotlight Big Pharma's intransigence, the industry's legions of press and public relations managers went to work mopping up this messy affair. Almost in unison they said, of course we're willing to do something, we've always been willing to help, but what's really required is patent protection in the Third World and more respect for intellectual property rights because without that, if we give our drugs away for free, they'll only wind up being sold on the black market back in the West.

The media laid on more heat.

Glaxo Wellcome was first to blink. The company announced that, as a gesture of genuine concern, it would reduce the daily price of its AIDS drug, Combivir, from $16.50 (£10.75) – which is the retail price in the USA – to a mere $2 (£1.30), which is presumably at, or just above, cost. Could that be an inadvertent admission that drug companies work on an 800 per cent markup?

Still, $2 worth of drugs a day wasn't going to help a lot of those people, most of whom were living in countries where the total annual healthcare expenditure per person was under $10 (£6).

Several thousand miles away, in New York, *Fortune Magazine* was rating thirty-eight industries in several different commercial categories. Big Pharma was placed first in return on revenues, first in return on assets, and first in return on equity. It rated fifth for profit growth, sixth for total return to investors over one year, and fourth for total return to investors over ten years.

For much of the final decade of the twentieth century, and now into the twenty-first century, the pharmaceutical industry has continued to pay shareholders a higher percentage of revenues than any other sector. Drug companies have surpassed almost all other Fortune 500 companies in profit rates, outperforming the Standard and Poor's 500 index by 90 per cent and averaging profits more than three times those of the other Fortune 500 industries in the survey. Pharmaceuticals have been rated either first or second in the list of the most profitable sectors for more than thirty of the past forty years.

A very deep and very wide philosophical canyon runs through the centre of this industry, and nowhere has this divide been more plainly visible than in Basle, Switzerland.

In the days before the two Swiss pharma-giants Ciba-Geigy and Sandoz merged to form Novartis – now the seventh-largest drug company in the world – Ciba was already a major international player. The company's headquarters were spread out along the Rhine in a most telling way. Research and Development had its own building. That's where the scientists were. Corporate affairs were dealt with down the block. That's where the commercial people were. The top floor of that building was for executive offices, the legal department and a group of strategic planners called the Pharma-Policy Unit. Those were the people who drove the corporation towards what they intended would be ever-increasing profits. Below them was Medical, the doctors who evaluated the commercial aspects of R&D and oversaw regulatory reporting requirements. Below them was Sales and Marketing, the people whose only role in this was to move product. They were close enough to the chief executive to be under his thumb, but purposely far away from the scientists.

In other big pharmaceutical companies, even when Marketing and R&D are not separated by a few streets, they are still kept miles apart. The reason why is fundamental to the industry – scientists should not worry about marketing, and marketing people must never confuse their own issues with medicine and science. The first group is soberly dedicated to changing the world, to finding that one molecule which might, somehow, cure the incurable. The second group is about making money for the company. If a drug cures the incurable but doesn't sell, it may be great science but it's lousy business. If a drug sells but doesn't cure much of anything, it's still good business.

This elementary principle – call it Big Pharma's theme song – drives the commercial side.

We need to make a lot of money in order to pay for the research that will produce the next blockbuster drug that will provide a lot of people with a lot of benefit.

It's a tune that Wall Street happily whistles with them. But *'a lot of people'* doesn't inevitably mean patients, and *'a lot of benefit'* doesn't automatically mean better health. Typically, 'the people' are shareholders and, customarily, 'the benefit' is financial reward. That isn't, in and of itself, sinister. Except when it results in such a massive energy force that commercial velocity nourishes group-think, which then feeds off itself by rewarding ruthlessness. Sometimes referred to as the tyranny of the bottom line – *small evils occasionally happen so that, in the end, there is a something worthwhile* – it is how and why corporations in general, and the pharmaceutical industry in particular, can wind up making good people do bad things.

For Dr Peter Mansfield, it is, in one way, akin to marriage. 'You accept the faults of your partner so that you can get the benefits.'

Mansfield is an Australian GP who runs a non-profit pharmaceutical industry watchdog group called MaLAM – the Medical Lobby for Appropriate Marketing. In 1981, as a

4

young medical student, he'd travelled to Bangladesh where he was appalled to see drug companies promoting anabolic steroids and glucose solutions for children with slow growth, tetracycline syrups for children, and breastmilk substitutes, all of which his training told him perverted the objectives of scientific medicine. He created MaLAM on a shoestring, hoping to pressure the industry into more ethical behaviour by bringing together 53 equally concerned healthcare professionals.

It was 1986 when the group had its first significant success. It had challenged a manufacturer's promotion of an anti-stress concoction – a mixture of arsenic, strychnine, vitamins and alcohol – and got it withdrawn. Over the next five years, MaLAM forced drug companies to yank a total of 11 similarly inappropriate medicines off the market, including the top-selling over-the-counter product for diarrhoea in the Philippines. Around the same time, MaLAM began publicly attacking the quality of the evidence used by pharmaceutical companies to justify efficacy claims.

Today MaLAM has 6,000 subscribers in thirty countries and it has well earned its place as a constant thorn in Big Pharma's side.

'To understand the way the commercial people in this industry think,' Mansfield begins, 'you need to consider the nature of the beast. These are huge corporations and the people working for them, just like the corporations themselves, are trying to survive and prosper. To avoid discord, people don't express their concerns. So, you've got a drug that's very important for the survival of the company and also for everybody's year-end bonus, and maybe there's a little bit of concern about that drug, but nobody expresses it. Instead, they prefer to talk about the good things, to reinforce the positive view of the drug. To promote it they need to believe in it, so they convince themselves that their drug is superior to the competition, even if the evidence shows otherwise. They trust the company's information. They accentuate the positive and if there are negatives, they talk about how those negatives could be benefits. If a drug causes sedation, for instance, then they point out that it helps you sleep.'

Adding to commercial pressures is the turmoil created in this industry by almost two decades of consolidation.

'They're called mergers,' Mansfield says, 'but in a sense they're really the takeover of the weaker company by the dominant company. Underlying it is a tone of bitterness. It's an environment of uncertainty. There is a driving need to perform better, to sell more. If you're a drug company representative and your job is at risk, forgetting to tell a doctor about a contraindication which might worry him is easily rationalized away. You think to yourself, the literature spells out the contraindication, let him read the literature, my job is at stake. Let's face it, in a high-paid, job-insecure atmosphere, people aren't going to say things that will upset their boss or cost a sale.'

He sees it as a consequence of evolution. 'If you've got an environment where survival relies on getting the leaves at the top of the trees, then you're going to produce giraffes. If you've got an environment where you're only going to sur- vive by producing increased sales at the end of every quarter, then this is the kind of creature you're going to get.'

In any other field of business, all this might not matter so much. If you don't like Coke, you can drink Pepsi. If the jeans don't fit, you can take them back and get another pair. If you want to buy a television, you go into the store, look at the different brands, compare values and buy what you think is the best value for your money. If one television has some little gadget that's been patented that's different from another television, that doesn't automatically mean the manufacturer can charge more than it's worth. Having a patent isn't a licence for extortion.

But that's not the way life works in the pharmaceutical

industry. The products are not interchangeable at the level of the consumer unless they are exactly the same product, unless they're the same compound, the same molecule. What's more, the person who pays for the product is not the person who chooses the product. We go to a doctor and the prescription we get represents someone else making a purchasing choice for us. Nor is there any discussion of price. The product must be paid for by us, or through an insurance plan, or out of government coffers. And yet a cost consideration is hardly ever made when the product is chosen. Doctors may well ponder several similar drugs and, all things being equal, deliberately prescribe the least expensive. Yet it's a rare doctor who actually discusses the price of a drug with a patient before writing that prescription, especially when the bill for it falls on the National Health Service. The question of cost may, at least in theory, be pertinent when you're standing at the pharmacy counter and there's the possibility of substituting a less expensive, bio-equivalent generic drug. But it's a rare patient who, before accepting a prescription from a doctor, is in the least concerned with how much the drug is going to cost the NHS.

The industry is unique.

That's partially because there is a certain inevitability about prescription medicines. Many people go through life without soft drinks, automobiles and jeans, but everybody, at some point, needs medication. Frequently, life itself depends on it.

Stephen Schondelmeyer, doctor of pharmacology and director of the Prime Institute at the College of Pharmacy, University of Minnesota, staunchly believes that drugs are 'public goods', in much the same way that public utilities are, or should be.

'Drugs are in limited supply. That's why we, as a society, grant patents to the companies that discover new drugs because we want to encourage and stimulate innovation. To some degree, patents do that. But, if I have a debilitating disease that affects the length of my life, I need that drug. If it's in limited supply because that company has a patent, which means no one else can manufacture it, and if I can't afford it, because they have no competition and can charge whatever they want, then the result is that I have a shortened life. I argue that drugs meet that criteria of a public good. There is universal demand. There is limited supply. There is limited access to the product. It is essential to the health of the population.'

But that's not how the Big Pharma marketing people see it.

'To these guys, drugs are just commodities,' notes Dr Larry Sasich, a pharmacologist with the Health Research Group of the watchdog organization Public Citizen in Washington DC. 'They don't look at drugs as something people need in order to live or to make their lives better when they face a disease. For them, drugs are just like a pair of shoes or a tennis racket.'

It is that attitude which leads Sasich to use the word 'amoral'. 'Not immoral but amoral, even if some people inside the industry may act in immoral ways when faced with stiff competition. The public's general view of the industry is that it exists for the public's best interest. And I think the industry has done a great PR job in portraying this image. What the public doesn't know is a lot of the background, about what goes on inside, about information that's withheld, about the spin that's put on drugs that aren't very effective, about how people get hurt. The public doesn't think of pharmaceutical companies as being amoral because the PR people have made certain that they don't hear about things like that.'

Research and development is the nucleus of the pharmaceutical business and also the rationale the industry uses to justify much of what it does.

The process begins with the discovery of new molecules – the most minute particule forming the basis of any element or compound – and the subsequent determination of whether or not any specific molecule has a pharmaceutical application. This screening and discovery phase generally takes two to four years, and in many cases even longer. Once a molecule is suspected of having some medicinal powers, the extremely complicated and very expensive chore of turning it into a drug can take eight–twelve years. Included in the maze of hurdles that must be surmounted are an average of six–eight years of clinical testing. The final cost of bringing a molecule to market as a drug can run as high as $300–500 million (£195–325 million).

Making the venture even more high risk for Big Pharma is the fact that, for every 4,000–7,000 molecules looked at, only one winds up as a drug in a package on a pharmacist's shelf.

That's not to say that only one drug is possible out of every 4,000–7,000 molecules. It's likely that dozens, if not hundreds, could be developed. But only one molecule out of those 4,000–7,000 actually emerges as a saleable pharmaceutical product.

And therein lies one of the massive contradictions that underscores this industry: the development of drugs that are needed versus the need to develop drugs that sell.

The World Health Organization has maintained for years, 'There is an inherent conflict of interest between the legitimate business goals of manufacturers and the social, medical and economic needs of providers and the public to select and use drugs in the most rational way.'

Not surprisingly, the industry sees it differently. Its battle-cry is: 'Innovation has a price.' And while no argument is possible with that basic premise, legitimate questions remain, such as, how much? And, what do we get for it?

Big Pharma's answer to the first is, very little; to the second, quite a lot.

The increasing cost of drugs is a topic that won't go away,

despite Big Pharma's extensive efforts to downplay it. Don't look at the cost, they urge, look at how much innovative drugs can save. For example, drug therapy to treat coronary artery disease costs around $1,000 (£650) a year, which is considerably less than the $25,000–41,000 (£16,000–27,000) that it costs for bypass surgery. And the cost of drugs to treat depression is $5,000 (£3,250) a year, whereas the cost of keeping someone in an institution is $75,000 (£48,750) a year. Of course, the treatment of illness, like most things in life, is hardly ever an either–or situation. A bottle of aspirin costs much less than brain surgery, but no one is seriously going to accept the argument that brain surgery is the best way to cure a headache, any more than someone might suggest aspirin is the best way to treat brain tumours. Then too, if all the drugs on the market were as cost effective as Big Pharma insists they are, healthcare expenditures would be going down. But that's not the case. Not in Britain. Not in Australia. Not in New Zealand. Not in any of the EU member states. Not in Canada, where drugs now cost HealthCanada more money every year than doctors. Not in the United States, where three out of every four people over the age of sixty-five rely daily on prescription drugs and where, today, some 5 million people in that age category are forced to choose between medicine and food.

Not in any country.

Drug company spin doctors would also have the public believe that drug costs reflect the competitive nature of science. They are fast to point out that pharmaceuticals is an industry where breakthrough drugs soon find rivals, and generic alternatives take a growing share of the market. The cost of innovation, they justify, must include those factors.

Both arguments are, at best, only half-true.

Breakthrough drugs eventually do find competitors, but that's largely because the industry itself continues to sink limited R&D funds into breakthrough imitations. When one company has a huge success in a major market, the commercial people make a bottom-line calculation to decide how much of that market they can pry loose. If it isn't big enough for a second or third competing drug, they don't bother. But if it is, they develop what is known as a 'me-too' drug. Because it's an imitation and not an exact copy, me-toos require separate patents and separate clinical testing and separate regulatory approval. It's an expensive gamble, especially since me-toos also have to be heavily marketed. When Searle launched Celebrex in early 1999, the company expected its 'Cox-2 inhibitor' – a new class of arthritis treatment – to enjoy unparalleled market share. But Merck was right behind with Vioxx. Warner-Lambert thought much the same when it launched its disastrous diabetes treatment, Rezulin. SmithKline was right behind with Avandia and Eli Lilly showed up with Actos. Me-toos traditionally take a back seat to the first drug entering the market, but it's not for want of trying, and competition gets fierce. So for any company to complain about breakthrough competition, when everyone is doing it, is nothing more than bitching about what Big Pharma inflicts on itself.

The second contention, referring to generic competition, simply contravenes the rules of the game. It's as if one football team were to argue that the only reason they can't score against another team is because the other team is still on the field.

Patent protection is for a limited time only. Everybody understands that from the start. Once it's over, the market is open to anyone. To fight that, Big Pharma spends tens of millions lobbying politicians to move the goalposts, and hundreds of millions developing what are known as 'line extensions'. Those are variations on their originally patented drug which allow them to get new patents and, basically, to re-exploit their original market.

Eli Lilly, for example, has spent several hundred million

dollars defending Prozac from patent expiration. Arguably the most successful drug in history – with the possible exceptions of aspirin and penicillin – Prozac has been taken by nearly 40 million people worldwide since it came onto the market in 1988. Never out of the top ten of most-prescribed drugs, more than 10 million new prescriptions were written for it in 1999. Sales exceeded $2.5 billion (£1.62 billion). Needless to say, it's a cash cow that Eli Lilly does not want to give up easily. What it's done is to develop a once-a-week version and patent that. By the time the original patents have expired on the old daily Prozac, Lilly will have moved that market on to the patent-protected weekly pill and kept the cash registers ringing.

What Big Pharma is essentially saying about generic competition when patents expire is, where our profits are at stake, we'll pull every rabbit we can out of the hat and, by the way, that's included in the price of innovation, too. What Big Pharma is not saying is that me-toos and line extensions typically take up around 80 per cent of R&D spending.

Granted, it's an extremely competitive world. But commercial aggression is not unique to the pharmaceutical industry. It is, however, a uniquely fragmented market. No single company commands a very large share. A combined Glaxo SmithKline will top the list with 7 per cent. Pfizer with Warner-Lambert is next with 6.9 per cent. Then come Merck and AstraZeneca (tied with 4.4 per cent) and Bristol-Myers Squibb (4 per cent). The next five companies – Aventis, Novartis, Johnson & Johnson, American Home Products and Pharmacia & Upjohn – are all in the 3 per cent range. But these are slightly misleading figures because they imply that drug companies compete in all areas. In fact, they don't. The commercial powers pick and choose the fields where they want to compete and, there, the market is anything but splintered.

It's called 'disease management'.

Disease is a business and disease management is both a

marketing technique to make that business profitable and a philosophy to make that marketing technique businesslike.

Drug companies view healthcare illness by illness, which allows them to examine the interrelated elements of any specific disease, to establish a distinct pattern of cost elements unique to each illness, and then to create treatments that will, in effect, give the company a start-to-finish market. This is not about modelling R&D to fit the needs of the patient, it is about roping off territory in which they stake a claim to controlling rights. Once a company has a dominant share of the drugs for any particular disease, competition recedes because moving in on it becomes prohibitively costly.

Glaxo SmithKline may only hold 7 per cent of the overall market, but it will control an estimated 46 per cent of the anti-migraine market. Warner-Lambert controls nearly half of the market for drugs in the cholesterol-lowering category. Schering-Plough, which isn't even a top-ten company in terms of sales, controls about 40 per cent of the anti-allergy market just with its drug Claritin.

Enter now the financial markets and great expectations.

The bigger these companies become, the more marketing clout they amass. Smaller companies are either taken over by the bigger ones or forced to retreat into smaller markets. In turn, the bigger companies must spend ever-increasing sums to protect their established positions. The real battleground now becomes the stock market.

It is possible that there is a CEO at a top-twenty-five drug company who doesn't keep one eye permanently on his share price. But, even if you found one who said he doesn't, chances are you'd be able to catch him peeking. After all, his business life depends on it. Share price values the company and a company's market value is a report card on the CEO's stewardship. But several factors determine share price and one of them is expectations – where the market believes the company is heading.

The yardstick used to determine expectations is the company's pipeline. Those are the drugs in various stages of development, all of which the company hopes will come onto the market over the course of the next ten years. In reality, most of them will fail. The trick is to figure out as early as possible which ones will reach the market and what impact they'll have. Good analysts who get that right can make a lot of money for investors. Touting a strong pipeline can also boost the share price of a company. Those same analysts, casting doubts about a pipeline, can drive share prices down.

Expectations come into play at least every quarter when results are announced. If the analysts' expectations are lower than the results, the share price usually rises. If, on the other hand, the company has led analysts to believe that the results will be good and the 'whisper price' is higher than the results, expectations take their revenge.

Maintaining a pipeline full of promise – and eventually delivering on expectations – is one way that savvy CEOs keep a company from becoming a takeover target. With survival at stake, it's not surprising that CEOs' instincts tell them to bet on marketing and not on science. Which is why survival in the pharmaceutical industry is not about curing the incurable – if that happens, it's a fortunate and happy coincidence – instead it is about blockbusters.

In 1990, a blockbuster drug was defined as one with $500 million (£325 million) annual sales. Ten years later, the figure was up to $1 billion (£650 million) and there were already twenty-three drugs on the list. By 2005 the figure will probably be $2.5 billion (£1.62 billion), and as many as fifty drugs are expected to make that list.

The top-selling blockbusters at the turn of the millennium were Zocor (lipid-lowering, anti-cholesterol treatment; manufactured by Merck, with sales of £3.16 billion); Losec (ulcer/gastric distress drug; AstraZeneca, £2.88 billion); Prozac (anti-depressant; Eli Lilly, £1.68 billion); Norvasc (calcium channel blocker used to treat heart problems; Pfizer, £1.5 billion); and Lipitor (lipid-lowering, anti-cholesterol drug; Warner-Lambert, £1.23 billion), which was also the first drug to hit the $1 billion mark within a year of coming on the market.

To understand how blockbusters shape the industry, you have to realize that not every therapeutic category lends itself to blockbuster potential. Blockbusters are harvested out of chronic illnesses, as opposed to acute illnesses, because the real money is in drugs that must be taken every day for years and not in one-pill miracles. You also need very large disease populations located in countries where sufferers have the money to pay for expensive drugs.

Chief among the categories that meet those criteria are cancer, hypertension, psychiatric disorders, osteoporosis, rheumatoid arthritis and thrombosis. Also included is almost anything that alleviates constant pain and treatments that lower cholesterol. And then there are lifestyle medications, the drugs people take because they want to, which includes diet drugs, sexual enhancers – Viagra, launched in sixty countries in its first year, is the prime example – and stuff that grows hair.

Big Pharma openly admits that's what everyone is after. But by directing R&D budgets to target blockbusters – approximately four-fifths of Big Pharma's total R&D budget is aimed at providing such drugs for one-fifth of the world's population – research on less profitable diseases is simply discarded. Drug companies are more and more financially captive to blockbusters. Dependence on billion dollar drugs requires more billion dollar drugs to support that dependence. The next big drug has to outsell the last big drug or the quarterly results will start to go backwards. Consequently, somewhere, somehow, someone has to determine the 'floor', a quantifiable figure for projected sales below which the company will simply refuse to develop a drug.

A report from corporate analysts Standard and Poor's suggests: 'Most companies' primary strategy is to focus on products with minimum peak sales potentials of $500 million (£325 million) per year.' Another floor number informally bandied about is $200 million (£130 million). Whatever the number is, the thinking remains that, if a drug is going to sell less than that, the money is better invested elsewhere. Oddly, six phone calls to six Big Pharma press spokespersons, posing the question 'Is there a quantifiable amount that a drug must sell before you put it onto the market?' prompted these responses: No; Absolutely not; Don't be daft; It doesn't work that way; Anybody who says there is doesn't understand how this business works; and No.

Except, there is all sorts of anecdotal evidence that floors definitely exist. At some point, someone has to make a decision about whether or not their company is going to proceed with the development of a drug and, at that point, commercial considerations include projected sales. It's hardly surprising that, according to several people inside the industry, commercial priorities always win out over scientific priorities.

'Board meetings', noted one company executive, 'are not about science, they're about shareholder value.'

In well-run companies it almost never gets to the point where someone in a board meeting has to say, here's this drug for which we have no market, now what? The decision is very clinical and happens long before a drug can become either a public relations disaster or a profit drain. It happens as early in gestation as possible – the commercial equivalent of an abortion. R&D is simply stopped before too many people can find out about it.

In January 2000, the CIA put together a National Intelligence Estimate entitled 'The Global Infectious Disease Threat and Its Implications for the United States'. The gist of it was that twenty well-known diseases – including malaria, TB, cholera and dengue – are fast reaching epidemic levels, are spreading to new regions and are deadlier than ever before.

And no one is doing much about them.

The seven infectious diseases which the CIA credited with the highest number of deaths in 1998 were HIV/AIDS, TB, malaria, hepatitis B and C, lower respiratory infections, diarrhoeal diseases and measles.

Each of them remains a threat well into the twenty-first century.

As the CIA report noted, 'Almost all research and development funds allocated by developed country governments and pharmaceutical companies, moreover, are focused on advancing therapies and drugs relevant to developed country maladies, and those that are relevant to developing country needs usually are beyond their financial reach.'

Advanced sleeping sickness, which scientists believed had been wiped out half a century ago, is on the rise again – estimated to be killing 150,000 people a year. The only drug currently available to treat it is a seventy-year-old mixture of melarsen oxide and propylene glycol that has been likened to arsenic in antifreeze. The treatment itself kills 5 per cent of the people who are injected with it.

There used to be alternatives, made by Aventis and Bayer, but both companies are backing away from producing them. In the meantime, one strain of sleeping sickness is becoming resistant to that only drug left on the market and no major pharmaceutical company reports new research on the disease.

Again, the numbers tell the story and point to a floor.

North America, Western Europe and Japan represent 80 per cent of the world's drug market. Africa is 1 per cent. The industry claims to invest $27 billion (£17.5 billion) a year in R&D. What it does with that money is what any business does with any investment – it goes where the consumer power is and caters to the market. The sad thing is that even if companies

17

spent their budgets proportionately, and dedicated 1 per cent of their R&D to finding solutions for problems in Africa, that would put only $270 million (£175 million) in the pot, about half the money it takes these days to develop just one new drug.

When you ask about a 'floor', they say it doesn't exist. That's because the term they use is 'cost-effective illnesses'.

Explains Prime Institute's Schondelmeyer, 'When it's cost effective, they find a cure. The opposite, non-cost effective illnesses, is where there is no economic inventive for anyone to go find a cure. Where you have rare diseases in developed countries with resources, they're likely to get taken care of. But if you have diseases, even with large populations in Africa, but no resources, people die.'

Sasich at Public Citizen agrees. 'Just look at the drugs that are being developed for malaria.' He points to Glaxo's Malarone, which won approval in Europe in mid-2000. The first new anti-malarial developed by a drug company in forty years – the others had all come from institutions – Malarone is preventative, meaning that its main market is the estimated 7 million tourists, business people and military personnel who travel annually into malaria-affected regions. 'They're marketed to treat travellers from rich western nations going to sub-Saharan Africa,' he goes on, 'not to deal with malaria in Africa. New anti-malarials could probably be used to treat the problem in Africa but those people don't have any money. So they don't get the drugs.'

Even though Glaxo has announced that it would be donating some quantities of Malarone to Kenya and Uganda, malaria is the perfect example of Big Pharma's cost-effective neglect.

Malaria is one of the most ancient diseases known to man. It was named by the Romans, who believed it came from evil air – hence, *mal aria* – it is transmitted by mosquitoes. In the past it was contained by spraying swamps to kill the mosquitoes and had been widely treated with quinine compounds. But several strains have become resistant to standard drugs – largely through the indiscriminate use of those older anti-malarials – and today, with approximately 500 million cases around the world, 3,000 children are dying of the disease in Africa every day.

It has taken several gifts from the Bill & Melinda Gates Foundation to offer some real hope to those people in Africa. First there was $50 million (£32.5 million) given to the Malaria Vaccine Initiative, then $25 million (£16.2 million) for the Medicines for Malaria Venture. In July 2000, $40 million (£26 million) was offered to the London School of Hygiene and Tropical Medicine. That money will be spent on insecticides, vaccines to treat the disease and the development of new drugs to prevent it.

Sadly, malaria is far from the only disease adversely affected by the cost-effective equation.

Bacterial meningitis was once treated cheaply and easily with something called 'Chloramphenicol in oil'. The drug was manufactured by Roussel Uclaf – later merged into the Hoechst group to become HMR – but in 1995 Roussel stopped making it. Now, no one does.

A disease called leishmaniosis comes from a parasite and causes severe skin lesions and, sometimes, death. The treatment for it is said to exist in a drug company laboratory. None of the companies suspected of holding the cure will admit to it. But all of them say that they have no plans to market any such drug.

The Nobel Peace Prize winning group Médecins sans Frontières – international physicians who travel the globe to treat the untreated – says that somewhere in the world, someone dies of tuberculosis every 10 seconds. The group also points out that, of the more than 1,200 molecules brought to market by Big Pharma in the twenty-two-year period 1975–97, a mere thirteen wound up in trials for the treatment of tropical diseases. However, nine of the thirteen had nothing to do with Big Pharma and human disease R&D. Five came out of veterinary research – to cure animal illnesses, which is a hugely profitable business – while the other four came out of US Army research during the Vietnam War.

In other words, if you suffer from erectile dysfunction in the industrialized West, Big Pharma is there to help you out with Viagra. If you suffer from malaria, diarrhoea or measles in Africa, it's likely that you will die.

Kurt Briner was fed up.

As CEO of the Swiss pharmaceutical company Sanofi, he didn't like criticism aimed at Big Pharma. He took it personally. So he used his keynote address at a management conference in Paris to lash back at the critics. Where others saw conflicts of interest – such as between the needs of drug companies to satisfy the stock market and the needs of the public for better, cheaper and more accessible drugs – Briner assured his audience that they simply didn't exist. 'It is an insult to our industry, an insult to our ethics as healthcare professionals and an expression of utter contempt for the numerous legal obligations by which we are bound by our ethical practice.'

Bernard Lemoine was also fed up.

As director-general of France's National Pharmaceutical Industry Association, he had a real problem with anyone who refused to understand that the pharmaceutical business was just that, a business. 'I don't see why special effort should be demanded from the pharmaceutical industry. Nobody asks Renault to give cars to people who haven't got one.'

That same year Big Pharma – despite all its bragging about science and innovation – spent more money on marketing to sell its drugs than it did on research and development to find new drugs.

And so it has ever since.

CHAPTER TWO

The Third Wave

Ego may have played some role.
                    (One man present at merger talks between
                    Glaxo Wellcome and SmithKline Beecham)

For most of man's history on Earth, the best that the science of medicine could achieve was to make patients more comfortable. Pain could be relieved and some illnesses could be treated, but pain relief was temporary and most illnesses ran their course regardless, or led to more serious complications and eventually death.

Historically, it could be argued, the turning point came in 1928. Until then, the greatest single advancement to the overall well-being of mankind – the one innovation that so significantly impacted on disease that it extended the human lifespan – was neither medical nor particularly scientific. It was indoor plumbing – running water brought into homes and waste taken out.

Then, a 47-year-old Scottish bacteriologist working at St Mary's Hospital in Paddington, London, changed the world.

Alexander Fleming had been studying the antibacterial qualities of nasal mucus, trying to determine how it affected

Staphylococcus bacteria when, in September 1928, he went on holiday. He left a bacteria-smeared culture plate on a table that, somehow, while he was away, became contaminated with a spore. By the time he returned, the plate was covered with a yellow–green mould surrounded by a clear halo. The mould, he expected. But the clear halo excited him, because it meant that some sort of substance from the contaminating spore had stopped the bacteria's growth.

That was penicillin.

Fleming published a few papers on what he'd discovered, but within three years he had turned his attention to other matters. Those papers remained relatively obscure until 1939, when a pair of Oxford University researchers – Australian-born physiologist Howard Florey and German refugee chemist Ernst Boris Chain – took a fresh look at Fleming's discovery. With a grant from the Rockefeller Foundation, they were able to isolate and purify penicillin. By 1941, the drug was being widely used in an injectable form. By the end of World War II it was universally considered one of the greatest discoveries of all time.

Work on bio-synthetic penicillins, formed through mould fermentation, led to work on semi-synthetic penicillins. This led to the science of antibiotics, which altered the way the medical profession dealt with illness. And, as science changed, the nature of the pharmaceutical business changed, too.

For much of the first half of the twentieth century, the industry was a by-product of the big German and Swiss chemical corporations. The companies supplied bulk chemicals to pharmacists, who then compounded those chemicals – mixed them right there on a bench in front of the customer – into finished drugs. But the war destroyed the German factories and, at the same time, required so many drugs, especially penicillin, that the US government backed American companies to assure production for the army. Once the war was over, those American companies, and a host of European companies too, filled the vacuum left by the destruction of German industry and gradually moved away from bulk chemical supply to become manufacturers and distributors of finished drugs.

This set the stage for the second wave, somewhere around the end of the 1960s, which saw science shift from chemical-based research towards what would be called bio-pharmaceutical research. By learning how to clone proteins which can kill bacteria and otherwise reinforce the body's natural ability to fight disease, and by learning how to produce what are called monoclonal antibodies – which prevent bacteria from releasing poisons into the body – the industry opened the door to doctors to treat conditions that had once been considered untreatable and to prevent illnesses that had once been considered inevitable killers.

Superimposed on this were the earth-shattering social and economic ramifications of jet travel, satellite communications and, before long, the Internet.

Within a quarter of a century, the planet would shrink into two distinct markets: the industrialized online First World, no corner of which is, today, any further away than the price of a local phone call; and the so-called developing markets, or Third World, which comprises the fragmented have-nots in the process of being left behind.

Computers got faster, became more powerful and were better able to complete enormously complicated tasks in nanoseconds. Libraries of molecules were now easily stored, easily analysed and just as easily referenced. Databases were moved between laboratories with the click of a mouse. Disease models that once took years to create in test tubes or in living organisms were efficiently recreated on a desktop. Chemistry by robotics, and other microprocessor-controlled approaches, created a vast increase in the number of compounds that could be tested each year.

Out of this came the biotech sector, companies whose only assets were, often, whatever money shareholders poured into them. In a modern version of the California Gold Rush, suddenly every punter in tech stocks was betting that five scientists crammed into an office in Cambridge – England or Massachusetts – were on the verge of coming up with a breakthrough molecule that some drug company would pay handsomely for.

In the midst of this frenzy, the human genome was being mapped.

James Watson's and Francis Crick's discovery of the structure of DNA in 1952–3 spurred the most dramatic transformation the pharmaceutical industry might ever see. Even though it would take nearly half a century before the final pieces in the map of the molecule of life could be put into place – it was officially declared complete in Spring 2000 – the excitement and the promise generated by the project rival any in science.

Even as recently as the early 1990s, the quest for new drugs saw the same companies chasing the same molecule because that was the limit of science and medicine at the time. Genomics dramatically changed that by expanding exponentially the number of molecular targets available. By understanding the basic mechanisms of disease, scientists realized they had the keys to unlock the cures to human disease. Whatever blockbuster gene-based therapies that would soon follow guaranteed Big Pharma's prosperity for decades.

But none of this was without cost.

The pharmaceutical industry unexpectedly found itself a prisoner of these new technologies, and in much the same position that the automobile industry had found itself when Henry Ford invented the assembly line. There were a lot of other people making cars in those days, but this more proficient, cheaper way forced the automobile industry into massive consolidation, until only three or four top players were left.

Now, what began as a trickle of drug company mergers

in the early to mid-1980s, turned into a flood by the mid-1990s.

Wyeth and Ayerst combined and then became part of American Home Products, Bristol-Myers linked up with Squibb, and Smith, Kline & French merged first with Beckman and then with Beecham to become SmithKline Beecham.

Marion Laboratories merged with Merrell Dow Pharmaceuticals, Hoechst purchased Roussel Uclaf, then acquired Marion Merrell Dow and began to operate as HMR. Rhône-Poulenc took over Rorer, Rhône-Poulenc Rorer grabbed Fisons, and then the two merged their life sciences business with Hoechst to form Aventis.

Sanofi merged with Winthrop then took over Synthelabo, Pharmacia merged with Upjohn, and Glaxo took over Wellcome. Ciba-Geigy teamed up with Sandoz to create Novartis, Alliance Santé merged with Unichem, and the Swedish Astra joined forces with the British Zeneca to become AstraZeneca.

Amalgamation raged to the point where, in just three months – November 1999 to January 2000 – four major deals were put on the table worth $223.3 billion (£145 billion). Warner-Lambert tried to merge with American Home Products ($54.3 billion/£35 billion). Pfizer stepped in to grab Warner-Lambert ($70 billion/£45.5 billion) – 'We look at every merger to see if we should have done it or whether we should try to screw it up,' Bill Steere, Pfizer's Chairman and Chief Executive, said at the time – Pharmacia & Upjohn went into talks with Monsanto ($23.3 billion/£15 billion), SmithKline Beecham began the initial phase of a merger with Glaxo Wellcome ($75.7 billion/£49.2 billion).

For many observers, these mergers were a solid indication that the companies could no longer expect organic growth.

Dr P. Roy Vagelos, former Chairman and CEO of the pharmaceutical giant Merck, is one of them. 'This is often what happens when drugs are running out of patent protection and a company doesn't have adequate new products coming through their own pipeline. They merge to fill holes in pipelines. And, of course, to cut costs. One could work with much smaller manufacturing capacity, perhaps make R&D more efficient, and make sales and marketing organizations more efficient by putting more drugs in the hands of smaller numbers of people. All of that has driven the industry to consolidation.'

So has, he acknowledges, the 'biggest lion in the jungle' syndrome – the animal that doesn't eat gets eaten. 'Yes, there's a little bit of that going on, too. When I left Merck, we were number one in the world for prescription drugs with something like 5.5 per cent. The share we had of the US market was something like 10.5 per cent. This, at a time when market leaders in other industries could enjoy shares ranging from 20 per cent to 30 per cent. We were significantly larger than the number two drug company but not very large in overall market share. Because it is such a very fragmented market, for many companies, consolidation was always likely to follow.'

Occasionally, though, the shrewdest companies are the ones resisting mergers. In May 2000, Schering-Plough – which had been mentioned as an obvious takeover target in several analyst reports – struck a deal with Vagelos' own Merck, arguably the biggest merger target of all. The two got together to develop a pair of drugs in which they had mutual interests.

Schering's allergy drug Claritin was tottering on the brink of patent expiration. A $2.7 billion (£1.75 billion) market was at risk. To protect it, Schering had been working on a new-generation Claritin, supposedly more potent and faster than regular Claritin. At the same time, Merck has an asthma drug called Singulair, which wouldn't lose patent protection for another ten years. Schering realized that, if they could somehow combine this new-generation Claritin with Singulair, the new drug would essentially protect Claritin's patent for another decade and maintain a large share of its market.

The notion appealed to Merck because it was looking at a comparable problem with its cholesterol-lowering blockbuster, Zocor. Once the leader in the field with $4.5 billion (£2.9 billion) in worldwide sales, Zocor had been overtaken by Warner-Lambert's Lipitor. Now, facing a combined Pfizer–Warner-Lambert, Merck recognized a heightened threat to Zocor. Schering-Plough had an experimental drug in development that might meld with Zocor and therefore boost Merck's chances of taking back the lead in the cholesterol-lowering drugs.

If they pull it off, both companies would be that much more takeover proof, although there has been speculation that these deals were really just the first step in yet another industry consolidation.

Even when companies as seemingly solid as Merck are mentioned, investment analysts suggest that, in order to maintain 'acceptable growth expectations', each of the top-twelve drug companies needs to come up with three major new drugs per year. Plainly, that's not going to happen. And once a board of directors accepts that the company will fall short – in so doing, possibly antagonizing the investment community – the company become susceptible to a deal aimed at keeping Wall Street happy.

Which brings into play the often overlooked role of the investment banks themselves. As a group, they make absolute fortunes out of midwifing mergers. The carrots they dangle are huge payoffs for the board members who won't be in the new company, and huge salaries and bonuses for the board members who stay on. While board members are not supposed to put their personal interests before the interests of the shareholders, with so much at stake it's not all that difficult to find shareholder value somewhere.

One of those places is yet another force that seems to be propelling mergers – the reshaped markets.

Merged companies are always crowing that they now have

more money to spend on R&D. But when *Business Week* looked at the Big Pharma mergers of the 1990s, the magazine was left to conclude that few of them had actually delivered on that original promise. 'Big budgets do allow companies to conduct cutting-edge research, but there is little evidence that massive research spending leads to a better record in developing hot new drugs.'

None of the Big Pharma mergers since 1980 – for example, Glaxo plus Wellcome, and Ciba-Geigy plus Sandoz – produced the promised long-term growth. Nor were there any real increases in productivity. In fact, almost every merger since 1970 has led to a subsequent loss in market share. In the end, what many of these mergers become is a substitute for capital investment. The combined companies have more to spend on marketing and, critically, a clearer field in which to market. In 1995, twenty-five companies controlled more than half of the global drug market. Five years later, 53 per cent of the market is in the hands of fifteen companies. The top four alone account for just over 20 per cent.

Simply put, mergers are a lot better for the industry and for investors than they are for consumers because they make for diminished competition.

In 1980, there were approximately eighty major pharmaceutical houses in the world. Twenty years later, the largest companies were whittled down to thirty-five. By 2010, it is reasonably expected there could be as few as twelve. In just the two-year period 1997–9, more than half of the top-twenty-five drug companies were involved in some sort of merger. Seven of the ten largest drug companies in the year 2000 started the previous decade with a different name.

It took a lot of people who never knew they'd ever meet to form what would one day become the nucleus of the British pharmaceutical industry, and it took two men, who, deep down, didn't appear to like each other much, to almost save it.

Britain, 1842. A chemist, druggist and tea dealer named Thomas Beecham invented a laxative which he called Beecham's Pills. It became so successful that he named his company after it. By 1913, 1 million Beecham's Pills were sold every day – they're still sold today – which was when he added Beecham's Powders to the product list, a cough and cold remedy that has brought relief to every generation in the UK since.

Philadelphia, 1865. A pharmacist named John Smith hired a 19-year-old bookkeeper named Mahlon Kline to help him run the wholesale side of a business that manufactured extracts, elixirs, syrups and tablets, dispensed drugs and also sold paint and varnish. Within a few years, Kline saw the advantage of moving more into pharmaceuticals and within ten years the company was called Smith, Kline & Co.

New Zealand, 1873. Joseph Nathan created a general trading company he called Glaxo. It wasn't until 1924 that the company got into pharmaceuticals by producing a vitamin D preparation.

Britain, 1890. Two American pharmacists – Henry Wellcome and Silas Burroughs – arrived in London to establish a company that bore their name, and began by making compressed tablets. The word they invented and registered to describe their tablets was tabloids.

By the mid-1880s, Smith, Kline & Co. was operating a full-blown pharmaceutical laboratory and in 1891 it acquired a consumer brands company called French, Richards & Company. The company's name was changed to Smith, Kline & French and soon went down in pharmaceutical industry history as the first company to send drug samples to physicians.

Henry Wellcome died in 1926. The shares he'd owned in Burroughs Wellcome formed the basis of a medical research charity called the Wellcome Trust. A few years later, Glaxo

Laboratories, the pharmaceutical arm of the trading company, established itself in Britain and went head to head against Burroughs Wellcome. The two companies remained competitors for sixty years, until Glaxo launched a hostile $14 billion (£9 billion) bid for Wellcome and in September 1995 they named themselves Glaxo Wellcome. That takeover created one of the largest research-based pharmaceutical companies in the world.

Following World War II, Beecham's Pills came up with Lucozade, a drink so unbelievably successful that the management decided they could now afford to make some heavy investments in pharmaceutical research. Thanks to the profits from Lucozade, the company produced a new generation of penicillins, and also amoxycillin, one of the world's most widely used antibiotics.

Maintaining its headquarters in Philadelphia, Smith, Kline & French expanded around the world, developed the time-release capsule and marketed it to huge success with the cold remedy Contac. In 1982, the company acquired a diagnostic and measurement instrument firm called Beckman, and became SmithKline Beckman. By this time it had hit really big with the first drug ever to sell $1 billion (£650 million) in one year – the ulcer treatment Tagamet. But by 1989, the management at SmithKline Beckman began to have serious concerns about the year 1994. That's when Tagamet would come off patent, when generic competition would jump in and when a huge chunk of its annual sales would simply fly out of the door. The pipeline was not strong enough to sustain such a heavy loss. The company needed to make increased investments in R&D right away, but management conceded it would take a partner to help them.

Beecham has offices in the States and was considered a successful business. But the management in Britain were starting to think that the company was not properly positioned for what they saw as a global marketplace.

The CEO at SmithKline knew the senior man in Beecham US, and spoke to him about possibly melding one unit. From there, talk turned into a full-blown merger. In July 1989, SmithKline Beecham became the first transnational pharmaceutical company.

By 1997, Glaxo Wellcome was spending £1.2 billion ($2 billion) on research and development but still had less than 5 per cent of the world market in prescription medicines.

In the meantime, SmithKline Beecham was not in the best of shape. As soon as Tagamet was gone, sales slipped from over $1 billion a year to around $200 million (£130 million). The company also had a kind of split personality. It was being run by a Dane – the former professional tennis player Jan Leschly – and 65 per cent of SmithKline's shares were held in the UK. It was, undoubtedly, the most European minded of any American drug company. But it was still, fundamentally and culturally, very much an American company.

Enter here another Philadelphia company, American Home Products (AHP).

SmithKline Beecham's uniqueness made it an extremely attractive target for AHP, a pharmaceutical holding company very much in the market for a partner. It's made up of prescription drug manufacturer Wyeth-Ayerst, over-the-counter drug manufacturer Whitehall-Robins, a cancer research arm and a veterinarian medicine manufacturer. The group had a strong pipeline which appeared to complement SmithKline's and the two companies knew each other well. Better still, no one at SmithKline could deny that Wyeth's star product was well worth having a share of. It's Premarin, a female hormone replacement treatment that has for many years been the top-selling prescription drug in the USA.

But the idea of an AHP–SmithKline link made a lot of people at Glaxo very nervous.

Zeneca was now in bed with Astra, meaning that, to all

intents and purposes, there were only two British pharmaceutical companies left. And even if one of them was really an American company, a SmithKline merger with AHP would leave Glaxo vulnerable to a foreign takeover.

So the Chairman of Glaxo, Sir Richard Sykes, jumped into the fray, to queer the AHP pitch and open his own discussions with Leschly. Some analysts saw it as a good but risky offensive play. However, as a conservative business strategy, it was more like a strong defensive manoeuvre. Glaxo didn't stand to gain a great deal of market share – the two were running about equal in the USA – although, combined, they would become the world's largest research-based pharmaceutical company. Yet having SmithKline as a partner would make Glaxo safe from predators.

The only problem was Sykes and Leschly.

Jan Leschly knew the score.

He found himself in the rather envious position of having two companies interested in his company. But before he'd agree to anything, he wanted to know who'd be doing what to whom.

Sykes had already worked that one out, and it wasn't necessarily going to please Leschly.

The two chairmen started talking in 1997, broke it off when personalities got in the way, swallowed some pride and came back together again in January 1998. What followed was twenty-three days of give and take – later, each side would accuse the other of more take than give – until, finally, there was nothing left except everyone else's inflexibility. SmithKline blamed Glaxo for failing to abide by earlier agreements and called their differences insurmountable. Glaxo agreed that the differences were insurmountable, putting the blame squarely on SmithKline.

'It was over that period,' Sykes explained subsequently, 'not at day number 23 but over that period of 23 days, it became clear that there were different approaches, different issues, that would not allow that vision to be realized.'

In less cryptic terms, the merger talks had disintegrated into a personal dispute about the pecking order of the five top directors.

Admitted one man present at the top-level discussions, 'Ego may have played some role.'

According to another man present, Sykes was never going to sit in London as Chairman of the combined company and allow Leschly, as CEO, to run the business out of Philadelphia. There was no way Sykes was going to see Glaxo turned into the junior partner. But that was hardly the only problem. Money played a very significant role, too. Not only was Leschly the highest-paid man in the pharmaceutical industry, he was one of the highest-compensated executives in any industry. Combining his pay, perks and shares, he stood to make £92 million ($140 million). What's more, SmithKline had a system that required its 350 top executives to own shares in proportion to their salary and rewarded them handsomely with perks and share incentive schemes. It dwarfed anything that anyone was making at Glaxo.

Says that former employee, 'Leschly set some astronomical precedents. It would have been very hard for Sykes not to have allowed the rest of his board to go to the pig's trough for similar sized portions. It messed up everything at the time. The total compensation package for the SmithKline boards was way out of whack, a huge multiple of the Glaxo's board's total package.'

SmithKline Beecham's press spokesperson proclaimed at the time, 'Despite considerable effort on the part of SmithKline Beecham, Glaxo Wellcome has been unwilling to proceed on the agreed basis.'

Glaxo Wellcome's press spokesperson said at the time, 'SmithKline were the ones that broke off negotiations, not Glaxo Wellcome.'

Twice bitten, no one could have blamed either CEO from staying well clear of the other.

Had they, there might still be a British pharmaceutical industry.

It was only towards the end of 1999 that the boards of SmithKline and Glaxo decided they might pick up where they'd left off because Leschly had agreed to retire. His stepping aside removed the major hurdle to the merger. Hardly by coincidence, he was still in a position reportedly to gain – through stock options and other interests – an estimated £80 million.

In January 2000, the boards of the two companies agreed terms. It was to be a marriage of equals, forming Glaxo SmithKline, with a combined R&D budget of £2.4 billion. The publicly stated purpose of the link-up was the usual soundbite double-talk – to sustain investment and leadership in R&D, to cut costs, to add shareholder value and to create a world-leading R&D organization.

Leschly himself had been critical of the much-vaunted savings aspect of the merger, noting that 70–80 per cent of all these mergers failed to deliver the cost savings and value that were predicted when the shareholders were being courted.

In scuppering the alliance of 1998 he remarked, 'If you look at the value generation we will do as an independent company, the success we will have, the support we will give to the science base in the UK will not be diminished through that I believe. If you look at those two compared with a merger that fails, we are much better off as two independent strong companies.'

Now with Leschly out of the way, Sykes and Leschly's successor, Jean Pierre Garnier, defined the management structure. Everyone knew who had responsibility for what. Sykes and Garnier seemed to get on well, perhaps because there was never any question of Garnier outranking Sykes. The two also agreed that the new company desperately needed to extract more out of the one market where there is more – the USA.

But before they could do anything, they needed to get the merger approved in Britain. And, in order to accomplish that, the new company had to appear to be British.

SmithKline and Glaxo had always both bragged about having a substantial research base in the UK where they conduct a disproportionate amount of their R&D. For SmithKline, that has been running at around £330 million, or 36 per cent of its total R&D budget. This at a time when only about 5 per cent of its global sales have been in the UK. Glaxo's figures are slightly higher, spending over £500 million in Britain, or about 42 per cent of its total R&D. This at a time when only 7 per cent of its sales come from the UK.

Parliament investigated the Glaxo SmithKline merger plans, just as it had the previous failed attempts, because MPs needed to reassure themselves that this last bastion of the pharmaceutical industry would stay British – even when it was obvious that one company never was British and the other wouldn't be for much longer by virtue of the merger.

'Glaxo and SmithKline can be regarded as US drug companies which just happen to be domiciled in the UK,' says Duncan Moore, at Morgan Stanley Dean Witter, and one of the industry's foremost analysts. 'The US market is by far the most important for any drug company. It is the fastest growing of the major markets and accounts for about 40 per cent the global demand for prescription pharmaceuticals. But the most important thing about the US market is that it accounts for nearly 60 per cent of the profits that are made by the global drug industry.'

Taking the ten largest pharmaceutical markets in the world, the USA leads with sales of just over $130 billion (£84.5 billion). Japan is second with around $53.5 billion (£34.8 billion). The next eight markets, added together, barely total

$83 billion (£53.9 billion). The UK comes in sixth with $11 billion (£7 billion), behind Germany, France and Italy.

With twenty of the twenty-five best-selling drugs marketed by American-based companies, it is evident that European firms that have not somehow tied themselves to America's market might see their global influence fade away.

Most analysts agree that there is enormous pressure on all of these companies coming from Wall Street to increase profits, and that the most direct way to do that is by grabbing a greater presence in the American market. Sales in the States more than trebled in the 1990s. It's understandable, then, why drug companies all over the world are desperate to have a greater presence in the US market.

The business environment is healthier in the USA, insists the Pharmaceutical Research and Manufacturers Association (PhRMA), the industry's Washington lobby. The reason they give is that European-style price controls do not inhibit innovation. PhRMA claims the US market supports its contention that, where the industry is allowed to grow and prosper, R&D is the main beneficiary. But industry critics say that argument puts the cart before the horse, that Big Pharma isn't flourishing in the USA because it is a healthier market, it's hiding in the USA because the Europeans have not bought into the argument that drug prices should be allowed to run wild.

Drug prices in the States, the world's only totally free pharmaceutical market, are much higher than anywhere else – averaging more than double prices in Britain – making the US market the most profitable.

It is, therefore, the key to a global presence.

Still, appearing British was essential to Glaxo SmithKline. It would ease the political process to get the merger approved in Europe, appease the Stock Exchange and protect funding in the UK. So executives from both companies paraded through Parliament telling MPs what they wanted to hear:

both companies maintain a huge shareholder base in the UK, and a united Glaxo SmithKline would not change that; around three out of every four shares would still be held in Britain; there would be a corporate headquarters presence in Britain.

Maintaining a headquarters in the UK was the obvious way that Glaxo SmithKline could appear to be British. But, if the economic advantages that kept the headquarters in the UK suddenly shifted, Glaxo SmithKline – like the former British chemical giants and the former British insurance giants – would pack up sooner rather than later, to become whatever it needed to be for the sake of a richer economic environment.

Richard Sykes even hinted as much when he told Parliament that, although it didn't make sense at the moment, 'if the shareholder base moved somewhere else, so everybody in the UK sold their stocks and everybody in the United States bought our stocks and 80 per cent of our shares were held in the United States, then you might think that it would be reasonable to have the corporate headquarters in the United States.'

But then Sykes, along with other executives from the two companies, reminded a House of Commons committee that the companies played a major role in British science. They hired top scientists. They collaborated extensively with universities and the research institutes. They spent money training and developing scientists whom they could employ. And so much of their research money was ploughed into the National Health Service.

Glaxo Wellcome and SmithKline Beecham had for years been running clinical trials on drugs at NHS facilities, paying huge sums to the health service for the privilege. This was money that the beleaguered NHS could hardly afford to lose and the hint that Big Pharma might one day find more fertile ground was enough for most MPs to put on their kid gloves.

Sykes wanted the members to understand that this had to remain a two-way street. 'Government has to invest. The Government has to make sure that the universities remain competitive in a highly competitive environment and that they continue to fund the universities in a way that the universities can really stay competitive and breed excellence within our top institutions.'

Garnier had already reminded them that the company would stay in the UK, 'as long as the environment in the UK is favourable to the pharmaceutical industry, and to research in particular'.

In a joint memorandum, submitted before the merger by the two companies to the Select Committee on Science and Technology Minutes of Evidence, the tone was very deliberate. 'These opportunities, however, can only be fully exploited with adequate Government support for public sector scientific and technological endeavour and research infrastructure. The Government must continue to invest in the science base, and must build on that investment, if companies are to continue to conduct their R&D operations in the UK or, indeed, are to be attracted here from elsewhere. This is essential to the competitiveness of UK industry.'

In other words, we'll do our R&D wherever it makes the most commercial sense to do it, i.e. where taxpayers help foot the bill.

The same goes for their headquarters. They'll live wherever it makes the most economic sense to live. Pharmacia & Upjohn abandoned London for New Jersey because its board agreed that the United States was the best market for new products, the best market for innovation and, simply put, the locomotive of growth for the entire industry.

Parliament gave the Glaxo–SmithKline merger its blessing, accepting the line that, as a British-headquartered pharmaceutical company, the country was getting a winner. As one of the parliamentary committees that looked into the merger decided, 'An annual R&D budget of some £2.4 billion, of which roughly half is expected to be spent in the UK, is potentially a huge asset for the science base and for the UK economy as a whole.'

The question must be asked, did the two companies ever plan to leave the command and control function of Glaxo SmithKline in the UK? The day-to-day global operational management would be in the USA. It had to be that way because the merged company could not possibly survive without the US market. R&D can be conducted anywhere on the planet, as long as the science is top-flight and the government subsidies flow. However, the commercial necessities of the industry are firmly anchored in North America. The real power base is where the real money is – in the States, where 55 per cent of the new company's revenue is, where there is nine times more money than in Britain.

If Parliament wanted to believe that Glaxo SmithKline would be forever British, that suited Glaxo SmithKline just fine.

Much like NATO, the headquarters are in Europe because it makes the Europeans feel better about themselves, but the triggers are pulled only in America.

CHAPTER THREE

Getting Down to Basics

Could you patent the sun?

(Dr Jonas Salk)

A drug manufacturer in Bombay, India, felt the suffering of the people of Ghana – where nearly one-third of the population is HIV positive – and decided to do something to help. So, in mid-2000, Cipla Ltd shipped to the Ministry of Health in Accra a drug called Duovir, which Cipla legally manufactures under Indian law.

For its effort, Cipla received this letter from Glaxo Wellcome:

'It has come to our attention that you have imported your product Duovir, which contains lamivudine and zidovudine, into Ghana. Glaxo Group Limited has exclusive rights under the following patents that cover lamivudine and zidovudine formulations in Ghana: AP11, AP136, AP162, AP3000. Importation of Duovir into Ghana by Cipla or any of its affiliates represents an infringement of our Company's exclusive patent rights.'

G. G. Brereton, Head of Patents in the Global Intellectual Property Department at Glaxo, understood that the shipment was characterized as a donation and therefore Glaxo would not on this occasion be seeking immediate redress. Still, G. G. Brereton made it perfectly clear that the company took patents and intellectual property very seriously – disregarding those people who could not possibly afford to pay Glaxo for the drugs they needed to stay alive – and that the company categorically reserved the right 'to enforce our patent rights against any further acts of infringement'.

As a grain of sand is to a beach, so a patent is to the pharmaceutical industry.

It is the basic component, the single most important ingredient, because, without patents, there is no innovation and, without innovation, there is no industry.

The *Oxford English Dictionary* defines a patent as 'an open letter or document, usually from a sovereign or person in authority, issued for various purposes, e.g. to put on record some agreement or contract, to authorize or command something to be done, to confer some right, privilege, title, or office; now especially, to grant for a statutory term to a person or persons the sole right to make, use or sell some invention'.

Historians trace the origins of modern patents back to the Venetians who, around 1470 or so, found themselves losing trade to Florence and the other city-states. They needed to stimulate local industry with new products. At the same time, they recognized two important facts of medieval business life: inventing a new product or a process to make a new product was expensive and risky; and no inventor could be expected to take such risks unless he had a reasonable chance to recoup his costs and possibly even make a profit.

Needing some sort of mechanism to shorten the odds for the inventor, the Venetians came up with a pact: if an inventor could prove that the 'fruits of his genius' were novel (a product or process the world had never seen before); and if his invention accomplished a task (basically, it solved some sort of problem); and if his invention worked (he had to build it or demonstrate it); and if a committee appointed by the state could understand how it worked (so that, eventually, other people could duplicate the product or process); then the state would award, guarantee and protect a time-limited monopoly during which the innovator was free to exploit the process or product for commercial gain.

The idea quickly spread from Venice through the rest of Europe, encouraged by trade guilds seeking protection of the manufacture and design of their products. More than half a millennium later, almost all nations maintain comparable deals with inventors.

Interestingly enough, patent law – along with the English language – is one of the more substantial vestiges of the British colonization of North America. First established in the Massachusetts colony in 1641, patents were set in stone in the United States – alongside copyright – by including them in the Constitution. Aiming to promote public welfare through private property rights, the founding fathers assigned Congress the power 'to promote the progress of science and useful arts, by securing for limited times to authors and inventors the exclusive right to their respective writings and discoveries.'

Arguably, the pharmaceutical industry's global might derives directly from those twenty-seven words in the Constitution.

The two industries most dependent on patent protection in the modern world are the chemical and pharmaceutical sectors. Pharmaceutical and related biotech industries file more patents each year than any other sector. Chemical companies, many of which have pharmaceutical interests – including Bayer, Hoechst, BASF, ICI and Roche – rank second.

There's no set time to file for a patent, nor any connection between the development stage of a drug and the patent filing. It can happen at any time during the process, but typically it comes as soon as possible after the invention is discovered. The philosophy is, file now and worry if it works later.

'As soon as they identify a compound family that they think will be valuable to them in their research,' says Dr Michael Ryan, who directs the 'Study on Innovation, Expression and Development' at Georgetown University in Washington and is the author of *Knowledge Diplomacy: Global Competition and the Politics of Intellectual Property*, 'they file for the patent right away.'

That gets into what he calls 'the appropriability problem' – how does a company appropriate its investment in a new product? As an example, he looks at an auto manufacturer such as BMW.

'They are known to have extraordinary engineering capabilities, and they produce this awesome sports sedan that nobody can quite copy. Is it because BMW has patents? Yes. But that's not the source of their competitive advantage. It's much more disperse than that. They have new technologies, the way they manufacture the car, their brand, their trademark, it's hard to actually appropriate what BMW puts into that car.'

Comparing BMW with a pharmaceutical company, it's easy to see that the investment is the patent. 'BMW's product is very difficult to copy. The product that a pharmaceutical company makes is very easy to copy. At the end of the day it's just a little chemical compound. It may take them ten years to innovate it but it doesn't take very long to copy. What then is the source of the competitive advantage of a pharmaceutical company? Manufacturing is important but manufacturing is easy. So, it's their marketing ability and the patent on the compound.'

Drug companies always equate returns on R&D with patent length, although there are arguments to suggest that, in fact, extended patent length can inhibit innovation.

Take the case of a drug well established in the marketplace.

Unseating it from a prominent position can be excessively costly. Included in those costs are the risks of patent infringement. Instead of competing, many companies simply choose to take a different direction and invest their R&D budgets in areas where they can win a prominent position, or they elect to extend the line of their own blockbuster drugs or they invest in me-toos.

Ironically, it is probably not the lure of a patent monopoly on just any drug, as much as it is a pending patent expiration of a blockbuster that drives real ingenuity. The impending loss of patent rights to Prozac has moved Eli Lilly & Company to new heights in its quest to replace it. The company even acknowledged in its 1998 annual report that 'the Prozac patent expiration is serving as a catalyst to bring greater intensity to everything we do'.

Similarly, AstraZeneca is racing to replace the ulcer drug Prilosec, Schering-Plough is looking to replace Claritin, and Merck needs to find a high-cholesterol medication to replace Zocor.

Back in the 1950s, US Senator Estes Kefauver set out to examine the prescription drugs industry. His staff studied innovative, widely used drugs, looking at such areas as price and also patents. What they found was that a large number of countries did not have patent protection. Either it wasn't written into law or, if it was, it wasn't enforced. In other countries, there was compulsory licensing. That's a system that permits a government to override a patent, legally permitting a company to produce under licence a product – in this case a drug – in which a valid patent is held by another company.

It's not a system Big Pharma likes at all.

'The issue Kefauver looked at was what happens without patents,' says Larry Sasich at Public Citizen. 'Our drug industry's argument has always been that without patents innovation is stifled and nobody would bother developing new drugs. But Kefauver's argument, based on what had been developed and was widely used, suggests that may not be true. Certainly patent protection and exclusivity is a driving force for some companies who go to extraordinary lengths to protect the exclusivity of their products.'

Some companies are less subtle than others when it comes to patents, and Schering-Plough ranks among the least abstruse.

Under US law, a drug company may be entitled to a six-month patent extension for every year the drug has spent in the regulatory approval process. Ever since the mid-1990s, Schering-Plough has been trying to convince Congress that, because unnecessary delays and ineptitude by the Food and Drug Administration (FDA) slowed the agency's approval of Claritin, the government really owes them an extra three years' protection.

Since the 1996 Congressional elections, Schering-Plough is said to have spent nearly $20 million (£13 million) lobbying Congress and donating money to campaigns. Public Citizen, which has been charting Schering-Plough's course through the political waters, estimates that for their investment, if they succeed, the company can expect an added return of $7 billion (£4.5 billion) over the next ten years. This is on top of their usual $2.7 billion (£1.75 billion) in annual sales. In the meantime, Schering-Plough swung an additional six months from the FDA under a law which grants extra patent protection for drugs that have been tested on children. That alone is worth another $1.35 billion (£877 million).

Actually, they almost succeeded in getting their three-year increase during the summer of 2000 when nobody was looking. The company's extension legislation was sneaked onto the bottom of a military construction appropriations bill. At the last minute someone spotted it, leaked the story to the press, and it was removed.

There's no disputing that FDA approval for Claritin took longer than most drugs. A Government Audit Office (GAO) report issued in mid-2000 explains that the FDA studied Claritin for six years and five months, which is nearly three years longer than the average for a similar drug. Six years in the process could, indeed, qualify the company for that extra three years. Schering-Plough's version is that one of the reasons for the delay was an FDA reorganization. But a closer reading shows that the FDA reorganization played no part at all in the Claritin approval process. Instead, the GAO found, the company had supplied inadequate studies supporting the tablet form of the drug and the FDA was concerned about the potential significance of animal carcinogenicity data for humans. Schering-Plough had also submitted thirty-seven major amendments during the agency's consideration of the drug, almost four times more than most companies and most applications.

When Jonas Salk invented the polio vaccine, back in the 1950s, researchers and pharmaceutical companies didn't rush head first to the Patent Office. Salk was even asked one day who owned the patent on his vaccine. He answered, 'No one,' then asked, 'Why? Could you patent the sun?'

The world is not the same place today.

Pharmaceutical patents fall into four basic categories. First, there are patents that protect the chemical compound. Second, there are patents that protect the compositional use of the compound as a drug. Third, there are patents that protect the specific way that the drug is to be used. And fourth, there are patents that protect the process the company uses to manufacture the drug.

By the time a drug reaches a pharmacist's shelf, there may be dozens of patents protecting the company's rights to it. That way, even though a drug may have only ten to twelve years of market protection under the first patent, it can still enjoy many more years under subsequent patents.

According to Steve Schondelmeyer at the Prime Institute,

a classic example of that was SmithKline's Tagamet. At one point it boasted twenty-six different patents. 'But that's not unusual. You can get a patent on the chemical entity itself and on every process by which you can make that chemical entity. That way, when the entity's patent expires, you still have a patent on all the processes by which you make it, so you're not going to have any competition. Then, you can have a patent on the dosage form that the product is placed in, such as a sustained release tablet or a patch or whatever fancy delivery system can be developed for it. You can patent use, that is, a patent on the drug for arrythmias, and another patent on the drug for AIDS. No, it's not unusual to have twenty–thirty patents on any given drug product because it keeps away the competition that much longer.'

The haste to patent every possible aspect of a drug has reached such proportions that multinational corporations are claiming patents on human genes. That's the result of a 1980 US Supreme Court decision. The court felt that, by allowing scientists to patent more than just a process, it would open up a unique American industry. In that sense, it was right. What it didn't anticipate were the conflicts in intellectual property it was creating and the impact that this would have on the rest of the world.

This colonization of the genome is similar to what happened when Europeans sailed to the New World. They carved up whatever they found and marked their rights to it by sticking flags in the sand. That's essentially what's happening with the genome. Pharmaceutical companies feel they should be able to patent indigenous plants found in countries where the pharmaceutical company is not even necessarily open for business. It's happening, for example, all over Asia, where Asians don't have the sequencing technology and can't just declare these things their property. Big Pharma and an army of biotech firms are claiming patents on these genes, ostensibly so that they can develop drugs which will help mankind, but, in practice, simply because some day they may be profitable. Anyway, it's only Big Pharma and western biotech that have the technology that allows them to say, we can patent it.

'Big Pharma is too politicized and too politically powerful,' says Dr Sheldon Krimsky, of Tufts University in Boston, one of the leading US authorities on urban and environmental policy. 'This is increasingly so, especially with the consolidations that are going on throughout the industry. Just look at the amount of capital now invested in these pharmaceutical companies. A lot of this happened because genetic engineering created even greater expectations on the industry. The tower of genetic engineering gave them that much more incentive to invest.'

During the first part of the Reagan era, in the early 1980s, it had become increasingly evident to Big Pharma that patent protection had weakened since the General Agreement on Tariffs and Trade (GATT) was established in 1947. The biggest risk it faced was to its return on investment in the developing countries where patent protection was either non-existent or otherwise totally disregarded. And while Big Pharma was hardly alone – the film and music industries had a stake in seeing their own intellectual property protections reinforced – Big Pharma took it upon itself to call Washington to arms, via its political lobby.

Helping to marshal the forces was the new Vice President, George Bush, an old friend whom Big Pharma knew it could count on.

After losing his job as Director of the Central Intelligence Agency when Gerald Ford lost the White House to Jimmy Carter in 1976, Bush made himself available for corporate directorships. Soon invited onto the board of Eli Lilly in Indianapolis, Bush remained active there for two years, until launching his own presidential bid. When he was beaten in the primaries by Ronald Reagan, Bush accepted the number two spot on the Republican ticket. At the time, the largest single holding in Bush's personal portfolio was $145,000 (£94,250) worth of Lilly stock. Once he took office, he was legally obliged to place his shares in a blind trust. But he had the right, which he exercised, to appoint one of his oldest and closest friends to maintain the trust. In theory, Bush should have had no way of knowing whether or not, at any point during his tenure in office, the trust continued to hold those shares.

In March 1982, the Vice President took the unprecedented step of intervening in a rule change then making its way through the Treasury Department. At issue were substantial tax breaks afforded to pharmaceutical companies operating in Puerto Rico. Treasury Secretary Donald Regan appeared to be ready to tighten the rules, which would result in America's pharmaceutical industry – including Lilly – paying higher taxes. Bush urged Regan to look at the rule changes with an eye to making them more favourable to Big Pharma. When someone at the Treasury leaked the story, Bush wrote to Regan asking that his original request be withdrawn, because he felt 'uncomfortable about the appearance of my active personal involvement in the details of a tax matter directly affecting a company with which I once had a close association'.

Nothing quite so nakedly transparent was attempted for the rest of Bush's Vice Presidency. At least not until the 1988 Republican Convention, once Bush had secured his party's nomination for president. He chose as his running mate Indiana's Senator Dan Quayle, a member of the Pulliam family, who were among Lilly's biggest and most influential shareholders. In fact, it had been Quayle's father who'd brought Bush onto the Lilly board eleven years before.

Giving a helping hand to Big Pharma would be easier if everything could be hidden inside the general theme of intellectual property. That set the stage for what would take more than a decade to pull off.

Until 2000, the length of patent protection varied from

country to country, the average being around seventeen years, usually starting from the date the patent was issued. But the World Trade Organization had been gearing up to take care of several global industries – including Big Pharma – by standardizing terms. There are exceptions, but for the most part these days, thanks almost entirely to political influence in the United States and American influence over the World Trade Organization, patents protect intellectual property for a twenty-year term. However, the United States could not have it all its own way, and was forced to concede that the clock would start ticking from the date of the patent filing.

Still, had Big Pharma been given its way, the WTO might have agreed to twenty-five or thirty years or, even better, for ever. After all, for a drug such as Eli Lilly's Prozac, at the time selling $7 million (£4.5 million) worth per day, whatever extra days you can arrange adds up fast.

Research and development is an obstacle course.

It begins with the synthesis and extraction of a new molecule which the scientists hope might produce a desired change in a biological system. They may be looking to arouse or to repress an enzyme, to somehow alter a metabolic pathway, or to create a physical change in a cellular structure.

Once those chemical compounds are identified, they are subjected to biological screening and pharmacological testing in the hopes of pinpointing any therapeutic potential. This goes from test tubes and isolated cell cultures to computer models and animals. As long as the compound continues to meet the therapeutic potential test, then structural modifications are made and every related compound is tested as well. The idea is to see which version of the molecule produces the most therapeutic promise and, at the same time, is the least potentially harmful.

Next, decisions must be made about dosage and stability. This is when the active compound is converted into a liquid, a tablet, a capsule, or any other delivery system. This is when strength dictates dosage: 50 mg twice a day, 100 mg before sleep, 500 mg once a week, etc. This is also when additional substances, called excipients, are added to the active ingredient – flavours to improve the taste, chemicals that bond the active ingredient into stable tablets, and chemicals that determine the drug's absorption in the body.

Further tests are now done on tissue cultures and animals to determine just how safe this new drug will be when it is finally administered to humans.

Drug trials are divided into three obligatory and well-defined stages.

Phase I is to determine how well the human body tolerates the drug at various doses, and studies the drug's rate of absorption, distribution, metabolism and excretion. The testing is normally done on a small sample of healthy volunteers.

Phase II uses a group of a few hundred patients suffering from the condition the drug is intended to treat. The idea is to look for efficacy and short-term side-effects.

Phase III is the big study. The drug is administered to the largest sample group – which can range from hundreds to several thousands of patients – to determine how it performs over an extended period of time. This is also the most expensive aspect of testing and can cost tens of thousands of dollars per patient.

More and more these days there is also a Phase IV. This is after-approval testing, which can look for adverse events associated with the drug – most of them don't appear anyway for the first year, and they must, by law, be reported to the regulatory agency – or can be turned into a cleverly disguised marketing device to interest doctors in the drug.

It can also be used by the marketing department to find the elusive USP – unique selling point.

Merck had been heavily promoting Mevacor and seizing a very large niche in the cholesterol-lowering market. It also had Zocor in the pipeline, a second anti-cholesterol drug which would one day replace Mevacor. Making the market even more crowded was Warner-Lambert's Lipitor.

So Bristol-Myers Squibb decided to come at the competition from the blind-side. Having spent nearly $150 million (£97 million) in clinical tests to win FDA approval for its cholesterol-lowering Pravachol, the company committed another $50 million (£32 million) to a Phase IV trial to prove that the drug didn't just lower cholesterol but could also reduce the risk of heart attacks in otherwise healthy people with high cholesterol.

A sample group of nearly 7,000 people received either the drug or a placebo for six years. When the results were in, four years after Pravachol was already being marketed, the group taking the drug had 31 per cent fewer heart attacks and deaths than the group taking the placebo. It was an investment worth the time and money. Having proved that to the FDA's satisfaction, Bristol-Myers was then legally permitted to advertise Pravachol as a heart-attack prevention drug. Sales skyrocketed.

From synthesis and extraction of the molecule through to the end of Phase III can be a decade's work. To ensure that the end result is a safe and efficient drug, the industry is, at least in theory, very tightly regulated. But the regulations governing pharmaceutical products come from two distinct reservoirs of interest – public despair and corporate expediency.

There was once something called the 1906 Food and Drug Act in the United States, which did little more than require manufacturers to believe that their drug worked. Companies could promise that their latest miracle drug would grow hair, cure cancer and alter the tides, but, as long as they mainly told the truth on the labels about what was inside the bottle, there was little the government could do about it.

In 1937 the S. E. Massengill Pharmaceutical Company of Bristol, Tennessee, changed that.

They'd developed a liquid form of Sulfanilamide, which was a popular concoction in those days to treat children's sore throats. Basically, what the company did was to take the powdered form of the drug and mix it with diethylene glycol to form a drink. The company was not required to do any testing or otherwise prove that the drug was safe.

As anyone who drives a car in winter knows, diethylene glycol is antifreeze. Children started getting very sick, and the fledgling FDA – only created six years before – issued warnings to physicians that this drug was not to be used. Then children started dying. Massengill denied any responsibility. But after its chief chemist committed suicide and more than 100 deaths were attributed to the drug, the government acted in the only way the law then allowed – S. E. Massengill Pharmaceutical Company was fined $26,000 (£16,900) for mislabelling.

A year later, Congress made certain that any company repeating an incident like that would be criminally responsible for producing an unsafe pharmaceutical. The Federal Food, Drug, and Cosmetics Act required drug companies to prove to the FDA that their product was safe and to include on labels such information as ingredients, recommended dosage and side-effects.

In Britain, at the time, the industry was also self-regulated. Drug manufacturers could say that their product was safe, but they didn't have to prove it. Here, too, the law was changed dramatically after a major tragedy, although Parliament was much slower off the mark than Congress. Still, whenever the need for primary regulation of the pharmaceutical is questioned, the thalidomide story is dragged out.

Developed as a sedative by Chemie Grünenthal in Germany

in 1957, the brand name was Contergan and it was billed as 'completely non-poisonous'.

Thalidomide was licensed in Britain to a firm called Distillers Company (Biochemicals) Ltd, which began selling it in April 1958. But, within a year or so, reports started coming in that patients who had taken it in tablet form were showing symptoms of peripheral neuritis – an illness that can cause severe muscular cramps and a lack of coordination in the limbs. The damage is often irreversible. Because the company was about to move the patient population away from a tablet to a liquid, nothing was done. Years later it would be reported that the company's pharmacologists had discovered, sometime in 1959, that liquid thalidomide could be fatal under certain conditions. That report, if it ever existed, doesn't now, and all these years later there's no way of being sure what the company knew.

The drug was extremely popular, sold in nearly fifty countries – at one point it was the third-best-selling drug in Europe – and, at least in some of those countries, was considered so safe that it was retailed as an over-the-counter remedy for morning sickness.

But not everybody was convinced that thalidomide was quite so harmless. Dr Frances Kelsey was the medical officer at the FDA who was handling the thalidomide approval dossier. Sometime in 1960, she'd heard of the peripheral neuritis side-effect and was basically dissatisfied with the way Chemie Grünenthal had handled some routine pharmacological tests. Kelsey's misgivings delayed the drug's approval for over a year.

By that time, stories of horrific birth defects were sweeping across Europe, Australia and Canada.

In the autumn of 1961, an Australian physician writing in *The Lancet* suggested there was a connection between thalidomide and this sudden wave of babies being born with malformed arms and legs. A few months later, a physician in

Hamburg published a study that directly linked those birth defects to thalidomide. He was roundly accused of incompetence by Chemie Grünenthal and vilified by drug company experts who insisted he didn't have any scientific basis for his wild accusations. Two days later, Chemie Grünenthal conceded defeat and withdrew the drug.

It stayed on the market in several countries for up to a year afterwards – Canada didn't take it off the market until March 1962 – but was removed from the shelves in Britain right away, albeit 450 birth defects too late. For some odd reason, sales to British hospitals were not ended for another year.

No one knows for certain, but it has been estimated that 8,000–12,000 thalidomide babies were born in Europe, Canada, Australia and Japan. Fewer than thirty were reported in the States. In those cases, the drug had either been obtained in Canada or was dispensed in Europe to the wives of US servicemen.

Frances Kelsey received a medal from President John Kennedy for having saved the nation from this catastrophe and, largely as a result of thalidomide, Congress passed the Food, Drug and Cosmetics Act of 1962, increasing the FDA's powers. Until thalidomide, drugs were approved for safety only. Senator Kefauver had been trying for years to include the concept of 'efficacy' in drug licensing, and that's what was done. Post-thalidomide drug approval in the States – the Kefauver–Harris Amendments to the Food, Drug and Cosmetics Act – now required that drugs had to be proven both safe and efficient.

But that wasn't the case in the UK.

There was no public inquiry into thalidomide, and much of the story remained buried in the same kind of dangerous official secrecy that still permeates Britain's relationship with the pharmaceutical industry.

In the face of public demand for action, Richard Crossman – Labour's opposition spokesman on health in 1963 – summed up what was then a reality of the British pharmaceutical industry: 'Any drug manufacturer would market any drug product, however inadequately tested, without having to satisfy any independent body as to its efficacy or safety.'

It took five years before the Medicines Act of 1968 was introduced. And three more before it was passed. A full decade after the thalidomide calamity, Britain finally came to terms with the idea that the pharmaceutical industry could not be trusted to regulate itself. It created the Committee on Safety of Medicines, which was charged with ensuring that pharmaceuticals were both safe and efficient.

The process of approving a new drug in the UK is straightforward. However, new drug applications are complicated and bulky – 80–100 removal cartons, each containing 8–12 documents roughly the size of a big city telephone directory. Making matters clumsier, when the cartons arrive in the office, it's the reviewer who has to unpack them and stack the volumes, a process that can take a full day of manual labour. Then, because the cartons are not in any specific order, after unpacking them, the reviewer has to sort all the documents out.

Those reviewers are physicians who, usually, review drugs only in their specialized field of medicine. The relationship between a reviewer and a drug company is neither cooperative nor adversarial. Both sides are looking for the same ultimate good. They're just looking from a different perspective.

Today, the industry is overseen in Britain by several agencies.

The Medicines Control Agency (MCA), created in July 1991 as an executive agency under the Department of Health, is advised by the Committee on Safety of Medicines and, like the FDA, licenses drugs for the British market. If you're a drug company looking to bring out a new product in the UK, the MCA has to say yes. Since 1995, thanks to the

European Commission in Brussels, there is mutual recognition throughout the European Union. Approval from the MCA can be rubber-stamped in each of the other member states. So if you're a drug company with MCA approval and you decide to bring your new drug out in France and Germany too, the assessment report from the MCA is accepted by the other agencies. In turn, approval by the French or German regulatory agencies can be rubber-stamped by the MCA. Of course, there are exceptions, mutual recognition is not always automatic and can get complicated – after all, this is a system designed by politicians – but that's more or less how it works.

Also, since 1995, there is the European Agency for the Evaluation of Medicinal Products. Based at Canary Wharf in east London, it is a one-stop operation that grants drug approvals for the entire fifteen-member European Union, plus a few extra countries that have signed on as junior partners in this endeavour. Those include Iceland and Norway and, soon, Liechtenstein.

Another difference between the two agencies is that the European Agency has been designed to handle drugs coming out of genetic, biotech and other high-tech research. Brussels also intended that it should be used for drugs in areas such as cancer, where speed in getting to market can save lives. By statute, the Agency is required to say yeah or nay within 210 days.

Bizarrely, at a time when there are reports that second-generation thalidomide victims have been born in Germany, Japan, Bolivia and Britain – the deformed children of the original thalidomide babies – the drug is seeing something of a resurgence. An Israeli doctor, having prescribed it as a sedative for leprosy patients, had noticed that it healed some of their sores. He reported his findings and serious testing began in the early 1990s. The FDA approved the use of thalidomide in 1998. It is being used today as a treatment in certain cancers, and also for the mouth and throat ulcers that accompany AIDS. Needless to say, at the same time the FDA imposed unprecedented restrictions on its distribution.

Neither the MCA nor the European Agency will say whether or not approval for thalidomide has been sought in Europe. But, then, secrecy is a part of the process Big Pharma counts on.

Larry Sasich at Public Citizen again: 'It starts with clinical trials that are designed and conducted and contracted for to get drugs approved. And we're seeing fewer and fewer published articles before a new drug is approved. What we think is happening is, because the companies control the publication of these trials, they are selectively only publishing the most favourable trials. You can influence a clinician's interpretation of the therapeutic value of a drug that way.'

One example he cites is of a drug widely available around the world. There were three trials submitted to the FDA. Only one of them was published. That was done in the southern hemisphere. It was small and came out positive and the researcher said there's more research that needs to be done. The largest of the three trials, which was almost as large as the other two combined, conducted in the United States and Canada, found no statistical difference between the drug in question and the placebo. That one was never published.

Another drug he points to is Celebrex, a type of drug that is known as a Cox-2 inhibitor. 'That drug sold $1 billion (£650 million) before a single trial was published. Now, the public doesn't often see the FDA's evaluations of these trials. In the past, they could be obtained through the Freedom of Information Act (FOIA) after the drug was approved. But now, because of a lawsuit we filed at Public Citizen and won, if a drug goes before an Advisory Committee, then the public has access to the FDA reviews of those drugs at the time, or even before the Advisory Committee meeting is held. So we opened up a smaller window and created a little more transparency in the process.'

Apparently, both Britain and the EU have bought into the Big Pharma argument that, until a drug is approved, regardless of safety concerns, the public either doesn't need to know or otherwise has no right to know anything about it.

To protect its markets around the world, Big Pharma has turned to Big Brother, somehow persuading the US government that its trade negotiators must protect branded products from all violations under the treaties of GATT or the North American Free Trade Agreement (NAFTA) or both.

As described in the *Journal of Commerce*, 'pharmaceutical companies worry that, absent strict controls and regulations, their investment in research and development will be chipped away by the creation of a generics market'. So trade representatives at embassies around the world – including the US Embassy in Grosvenor Square in London – maintain especially close relationships with the major pharmaceutical companies in those countries.

Patents work only when governments enforce the laws. Not all governments recognize all patents as valid and, when they choose for their own convenience to override a patent, there is often very little the patent holder can do except get tough. In those instances when muscle needs to be applied, US trade representatives do the business. For example, they cautioned the government of Argentina that it was in violation of the Agreement on Trade-Related Aspects of Intellectual Property (TRIPS) and threatened sanctions if it allowed generic Taxol to be used.

When enforcing TRIPS doesn't work, trade representatives preach a gimmick cooked up by Big Pharma called TRIPS-PLUS. They tell governments and health ministries that it is illegal for generic manufacturers to develop drugs in a country when a valid patent is still in force (which is practised in some countries, including Britain, but is not true everywhere); that compulsory licensing is completely illegal (they pitch this in the developing world, when in fact it is explicitly untrue); and that no national health system is permitted to use only the generic product when the brand is in the market (again, absolutely untrue).

A few years ago the Thais had only one drug available to treat cryptococcal meningitis, which is a fatal disease associated with AIDS. The drug, fluconazole, was manufactured locally by Pfizer under the name Triflucan. A month's treatment cost 15,000 bahts – over $400 (£260) – which pretty much put it out of the reach of the average citizen. So two Thai companies came along and manufactured a bio-equivalent version for less than a third of Pfizer's price. It was still too expensive for the bulk of the population, but it opened up the market to a lot of people.

Pfizer complained. And US trade representatives threatened the Thai authorities that, under TRIPS-PLUS, if the two copycat patent violators weren't shut down, Washington had the right to tax Thai exports to the United States. In less than six months, Pfizer's monopoly had been suitably restored.

It's referred to as TRIPS-PLUS because it's what Big Pharma would like to add to TRIPS. However, TRIPS-PLUS is nothing more than a figment of Big Pharma's imagination and does not exist in law or in treaty.

But, then, sleight of hand is something they're pretty good at. When it came time for the US Congress to ratify the Uruguay Round Agreements Act as part of GATT, the bill was put to a vote late one night when there was only just a quorum in the Senate. Big Pharma, whose strategy is simple – seek to extend patents wherever possible – had somehow lobbied an extra few lines into the bill which would grant an additional three-year patent extension to a number of top-selling drugs.

No one noticed it was there, or understood the ramifications of it, until the treaty had long been ratified.

The 'Phen' part came from the compound phentermine, another appetite suppressant, which had been around since 1959 and wasn't exactly setting the world on fire.

In separate approvals of the two drugs, the FDA stipulated that they be used alone and for only a few weeks at a time. The FDA had also listed some side-effects, most notably that fenfluramine induced fatigue. But, in 1988, the National Institutes of Health (NIH) sponsored a study at the University of Rochester in New York that combined the two drugs. Four years later, the data showed that patients taking this combination over a six-month period rapidly lost weight, sustained their weight loss for several years and did not suffer the drowsiness that had been seen with fenfluramine.

The combination was not approved by the FDA and therefore was considered an 'off-label' use. Yet doctors prescribed it to the point of a major sales boom, so much so that, for three years, just about all fenfluramine sales went into the mixture. Weight clinics proclaimed Fen-Phen the fastest and easiest way to lose weight.

Then, in June 1996, Redux arrived.

This newer, supposedly better variation on fenfluramine, a compound called dexfenfluramine, was also not recommended for use in combination with any other drug. Originally patented in 1980 by a professor at the Massachusetts Institute of Technology, Redux was first licensed to a French pharmaceutical company, Laboratoires Servier, which sold the drug under various brand names throughout Europe, including Isomeride and Adifax. It was approved in more than seventy countries and one estimate has it that more than 10 million people have used it.

A small drug development company called Interneuron obtained the US rights from Servier in 1990 and ran all the necessary trials to take it to the FDA. The first time the drug came up for approval, the agency's Advisory Committee voted no. They were concerned about side-effects. When the group met a second time to discuss Redux in April 1996, the meeting was unusually hot-tempered. The FDA chain of command recommended against approval. That was signalled first by the medical officer with the dossier, then by his immediate boss, who is called team leader, and then by the division director, the third person in the chain. The drug was approved over their recommendation by the next man up, the office director, Dr James Bilstad.

It's been said that his thinking at the time was, obesity in the United States had reached epidemic levels and the benefits of Redux outweighed the risks.

Towards the end of July 1996, the Warner-Lambert company submitted to the FDA a new drug application for a compound generically known as troglitazone, but which it intended to call Rezulin.

Just six months before, the company had admitted to fraudulently withholding information from the FDA about manufacturing problems with Dilantin, a drug generically called phenytoin and used for treating seizure disorders. It cost the company $10 million (£6.5 million) in fines. A Warner-Lambert vice president was charged with conspiracy and causing the shipment of adulterated phenytoin. The FDA has since ruled that the sloppy manufacturing practices have been solved.

Rezulin, the first of a brand-new class of type II diabetes drugs, controlled the blood sugar of people who'd become immune to insulin and other therapies. When blood sugar is not controlled, the results can include blindness, strokes, heart disease and kidney failure. The market for Rezulin was huge, matched only by its potential benefits.

The company was, of course, outwardly optimistic. But getting onto the market first was paramount to their strategy. Other companies had similar therapies in their pipelines – SmithKline was working on Avandia and Lilly was working on Actos – but it's the first drug that gets the lion's share of the business. The others are forced to play catch-up, usually at great expense and diminished reward.

Rezulin was granted a priority review, which means the FDA took action in six months instead of ten months. Later there would be questions about this, suggesting that Warner-Lambert had pulled political strings. But all drug companies ask for priority review – it's unusual when they don't – and, although most are turned down, Warner-Lambert wasn't. For a new chemical entity, the FDA says, it would not be unreasonable to review the drug in that time.

The FDA medical officer assigned to the Rezulin dossier was Dr John Gueriguian, an eighteen-year veteran of the agency who says he works in a very systematic way, staying in constant touch with the company before the approval application is made so that he knows what's happening, knows how the drug is being developed, knows how the safety issues are being assessed.

'I did that for three years with Warner-Lambert. But after three years of asking them about the development of Rezulin and urging them to do the development in a proper fashion, and after three years of them playing games with me and not responding, I got to the end of my review.'

There seems to have been a lot he didn't like. Most studies for efficacy are 'two-tailed', meaning that they will show either effectiveness or ineffectiveness. He claims that the company did what is called a 'one-tailed protocol', simply to show effectiveness, and then stacked the deck by using definitions that suited them, as opposed to definitions from unbiased experts. He was also uneasy about some of the things the company was telling him and how the company kept changing its story. Finally, he claims to have told the company that he wanted it to delay its application for three months, to wait for the results of a larger study, because he didn't like the toxicity numbers he was seeing.

Warner-Lambert refused.

'So they asked me, well what do you think of this drug? By that time they knew I was saying that the drug showed very low efficacy and a very high probability of toxicity to both the liver and the cardio-pulmonary system. They knew I was going to recommend non-approval. But they asked anyway and so I told them, the drug is shit. That's the word I used. And they attacked me on that. They said it was intemperate language.'

The company complained to the FDA – 'They went behind my back, directly to the higher-ups who conducted a kangaroo court without confronting me with the evidence' – which removed Gueriguian from the case. 'That shows how powerful these companies can be.'

The next man up the chain of command, Gueriguian's team leader Dr Alexander Fleming, wrote the primary review for Rezulin, recommending approval. From him, the review was signed off by the division director and then went to the office director for final approval.

The same Dr James Bilstad who'd approved Redux.

In January 1997, a doctor named Robert Misbin was assigned the Rezulin dossier. As medical officer, his job was to look at adverse reactions and deal with supplemental applications. Rezulin had been approved initially for patients with diabetes that could not be controlled by insulin. Subsequent submissions were for more general use in diabetes.

Some people inside the agency still contend that the approval of Rezulin was correct. Despite the manufacturer having been extremely aggressive in promoting this to the FDA – so much so that the diabetes community was led to believe Rezulin was a miracle drug and added its political weight to the concerted campaign to get it approved – liver failures hadn't been seen yet.

Misbin explains, 'The benefits of the drug were available to hundreds of thousands if not millions of people, whereas the adverse effect reports were usually limited to a few dozen. That's not to understate the problem. And one patient dying of liver failure unnecessarily is a tragedy. But one should not think that necessarily offsets all the benefit of what a drug can do.'

Several doctors at the FDA now claim they had doubts about the drug from the beginning. But their doubts weren't about the liver problems, they were related to cardiac matters. They now say there were reasons to believe that early clinical tests in animals had revealed difficulties related to fluid retention. But those were obviously not enough to keep the drug from being marketed.

Within two months, Warner-Lambert was promoting Rezulin at full steam. In its first year, it was one of the top-ten fastest-selling drugs on the market, hitting the $545 million (£354 million) mark. The following year, sales climbed to $748 million (£486 million).

However, by the autumn of 1997, the first cases of liver failure were being reported. Then there were deaths. It turned out three people had already died during the clinical trials.

On 28 October 1997, at the behest of the FDA, Warner-Lambert issued a 'Dear Healthcare Professional' letter to explain changes in prescribing information and some side-effects. A week later, the FDA issued a 'Talk Paper' on those prescribing changes.

Rezulin had already been approved by the Medicines Control Agency in Britain – the only agency in Europe to approve it at all – where Glaxo had been selling it since July under the name Romozin. But the MCA saw the adverse events reports too, and 122 days after allowing the drug to be sold in Britain, after reports of four deaths and 147 cases of liver damage associated with the drug, the MCA yanked it off the UK market.

That alarmed a lot of people at the FDA.

The Americans and the British had the exact same data.

Some people at the FDA had convinced themselves that the label change and the letter were the appropriate response to the problem. Now, there was a sense of panic.

Petitions poured into the FDA from concerned citizens and watchdog groups, urging that the agency act for the same safety reasons the British had. The FDA would not do that. As far as some people at the FDA were concerned, the British made their determination and the FDA would make its own determination. It was hard for some people in Washington to understand why, just because the British did something, the FDA should have to act as well.

Yet the agency did act again. It issued a second 'Talk Paper', this one warning doctors that they needed to increase patient monitoring to look for signs of liver toxicity. That same day, Warner-Lambert issued a 'Dear Healthcare Professional' letter that detailed the additional liver monitoring and was supposed to have mentioned three newly reported deaths associated with Rezulin.

The exact words in the company's letter were: 'You will be reassured to know that the additional reports received since early November do not indicate a greater frequency of liver injury or potential for serious harm than had been previously estimated.'

Some people at the agency argued that this was being downright deceitful, so the agency asked the company to send yet another letter. This time Warner-Lambert showed the FDA a draft, the Agency approved it and the letter was sent on 15 December 1997. Enclosed with it was a copy of the revised labelling and the FDA's previous 'Talk Paper'.

And more adverse events were reported.

In January 1998, with certain elements inside the FDA still reluctant to pull the drug – could a drug company's influence have made some people so blind? – the agency demanded that a bold warning be put on the label noting that the drug was dangerous. Four months later the *Los*

Angeles Times revealed that Rezulin had been used in a $150 million (£97.5 million) NIH-sponsored diabetes prevention programme since 1996 – before the drug had been approved by the FDA – and that a 55-year-old high school teacher from East St Louis, Illinois, had just died of liver failure after taking it as a volunteer patient. Rezulin was eventually removed from that study. The newspaper then revealed that the government physician with overall responsibility for that study, Dr Richard Eastman, head of the NIH's division of diabetes, endocrinology and metabolic diseases, had been a contracted consultant to Warner-Lambert since 1995.

As adverse events and deaths mounted, the official FDA stance, as revealed in a letter to Congressman Henry Waxman, was, '[a]t this time, after careful re-evaluation, we believe that the benefits of the drug outweigh the risks.'

Waxman wrote back, asking two questions: 'Why was Dr Gueriguian removed from the review of Rezulin?' and 'Did Dr Gueriguian recommend against the approval of Rezulin?'

The answer he received was from Diane Thompson, the FDA's Associate Commissioner for Legislative Affairs: 'FDA is unable to provide responses to these questions based on the confidential nature of the information which is not releasable under the Freedom of Information Act (FOIA) (5 U.S.C. S552) and FDA's implementing regulations. The issues also involve personnel matters which are not subject to disclosure under the same Act and regulations.'

Waxman followed up with two more questions. He wanted to know, what had been the response of Dr Gueriguian's superiors to his recommendations, and about a September 1996 meeting between FDA staff and representatives of Warner-Lambert, at which Dr Gueriguian voiced reservations regarding Rezulin.

This answer came back from the FDA: 'Although the Agency is not able to provide specific responses to these questions for the reasons noted in the above response, we would like to provide general information concerning the review of Rezulin. Dr Gueriguian did not complete his review of Rezulin and thus such review materials are not included in the new drug application file that is releasable to the public.'

Interneuron sold an exclusive licence for Redux to American Cyanamid and AHP purchased American Cyanamid. It signed a Co-Promotion Agreement with Interneuron and brought Redux to market on the Wyeth product list. Shortly thereafter, the FDA revised the labelling of Redux, requiring Wyeth to say that the drug brought with it a high expectancy of pulmonary hypertension.

Because Pondimin and Redux were so chemically similar, Interneuron and Wyeth had jointly accepted that any adverse medical experiences associated with one could affect the ongoing safety analysis of the other. Because monthly safety meetings were being held at Wyeth's offices to discuss Pondimin anyway, once Redux came to market Interneuron officials were invited to those same monthly meetings.

But the cosy relationship wasn't destined to last.

Dr Heidi Connolly, a cardiologist at the Mayo Clinic, had seen a young female patient with a heart valve problem, which was fairly rare, but not rare enough to think a lot about it. That is, not until a year or so later when the young woman returned to the Mayo Clinic with a second damaged heart valve.

A few months after that, Connolly saw another female patient with the same problem, and then learned of a physician out west who'd also seen several women with damaged heart valves. Before long, Connolly had put together a file on two dozen women with this problem.

The only thing that she could find these women had in common was Fen-Phen.

Now, in early March 1997, Connolly began writing an article that would find its way into the *New England Journal of Medicine*. As she was doing that, on 5 March, she contacted American Home Products and voiced her concerns to them.

The call was an upsetting one for the company.

Under the laws of the US Securities and Exchange Commission (SEC), information as significant as the problems Connolly was talking about – adverse medical events which could influence share prices and dealing – had to be disclosed. Wyeth's Pondimin-label fenfluramine was far more successful than Redux, selling around 140,000 new prescriptions per week. It would be reasonable, then, that it'd choose to protect the better-selling product. But telling the SEC also meant telling Interneuron. And that company, which had no involvement at all with Fen-Phen, could be reasonably expected to do whatever it had to do to save Redux from any collateral damage. A team from Wyeth agreed to meet Connolly at the Clinic.

At Wyeth's regular monthly meeting with Interneuron on 11 March, there was no discussion about Fen-Phen and heart valve problems.

A day or so after the meeting, executives from Wyeth and American Home flew to Minnesota. Connolly told them what she was seeing. And when the drug company executives left, their line was that more study was needed.

The following month, the company split the monthly meetings with Interneuron into two. It claimed it was 'due to operational requirements'. It meant that Interneuron would now be invited to discuss only Redux's safety. Later, Interneuron would come to believe that this was done specifically to conceal the Mayo Clinic data and prevent – or, at best, postpone – disclosures that could derail Pondimin's substantial sales.

At that April meeting, a circulated 'highlights' of the 11 March meeting was handed out, but made no mention of Pondimin, despite the fact that Interneuron officials present in March insist that the drug was discussed. It was titled 'Redux AE Overview Meeting'. A separate highlight, 'Pondimin AE

Overview Meeting', later appeared, making no mention of the Mayo Clinic data.

This, Interneuron insists, proves Wyeth knew about the problems with Pondimin and Fen-Phen and was deliberately keeping that information from becoming known outside the company. Given the similarity with Redux, Interneuron saw a threat to Pondimin and Fen-Phen as a threat to Redux. The company's lawyers would later claim: 'To avoid any risk of commercial disadvantage from disclosure of the Mayo Clinic data, and to maximize sales of Pondimin, AHP and Wyeth-Ayerst withheld that data from Interneuron.'

Dr Connolly's findings had originally been scheduled to run in the *NEJM* on 28 August. But she managed to convince the editors that the matter was urgent, and they agreed, exceptionally, to allow her to release her data before publication.

On 1 July, an official at the FDA phoned Dr Richard Gammans, Vice President for Clinical Research at Interneuron, to invite him to an emergency meeting the next day in Washington to discuss Fen-Phen and related cardiac problems. The FDA official explained that, because of that chemical similarity between Redux and Pondimin and because the Mayo Clinic data assessed safety issues for Fen-Phen and also for Redux, he wanted both Interneuron and Wyeth to attend.

That was a real bombshell. Interneuron insists that this was the first time it had heard about this.

The FDA announced at the meeting that the Mayo Clinic would hold a press conference on 8 July to say that twenty-four patients who'd used Fen-Phen had been diagnosed with cardiac valvular disease and that this would be discussed in detail in a forthcoming issue of the *NEJM*.

Interneuron CEO Dr Glenn Cooper confronted Dr Marc Deitch, then Wyeth Senior Vice President for Medical Affairs, and asked why his company hadn't been advised of the Fen-Phen problem. Deitch allegedly answered that there was no legal obligation to have mentioned it. So now Cooper wrote to AHP's Chairman and CEO, John Stafford, criticizing Wyeth for not keeping Interneuron informed. While Deitch is alleged to have claimed that he did in fact inform an Interneuron official of the Fen-Phen problem in a phone call, Interneuron insists that Stafford never bothered to respond to Cooper's letter.

Later, testifying under oath, Wyeth official Dr Ian Ballard would claim that the order to separate the meetings came from Dr Deitch. 'He felt it was a matter of corporate intelligence,' Ballard said. When asked if Deitch split the meetings so that Interneuron wouldn't find out what was happening with Pondimin, Ballard answered, 'That's correct.'

In her press conference from the Mayo Clinic on 8 July, Heidi Connolly told the world that there was a possible relationship between heart valve disease and Fen-Phen. That same afternoon, the FDA notified 700,000 physicians of the potential dangers of Fen-Phen and Redux.

At Wyeth, they were still maintaining that Connolly's study was inconclusive and that more work needed to be done before these alleged dangers could be verified.

The *NEJM* article was published in August.

Two weeks later, the FDA announced that it had compiled information on 291 patients, most of whom had been taking Fen-Phen for up to 24 months and many of whom were suffering abnormal echocardiogram findings.

On 15 September, Interneuron and Wyeth withdrew Redux from the market. The same day, Wyeth withdrew Pondimin.

But that was only the beginning.

There is something nauseatingly cruel and soulless when the deaths of innocent people, who have put their trust in pharmaceutical companies and regulatory agencies, are considered 'statistically acceptable'.

And yet, as more deaths were linked to Rezulin in the

press, Warner-Lambert announced it was 'disappointed with the mischaracterization of its actions and intentions regarding the development and marketing of Rezulin'.

Particular rage was levelled at the media for 'coverage of the drug that seems to focus primarily on risks, but largely ignores the significant patient benefits that this medication provides'.

For good measure, a corporate director of media relations added, 'I am clueless as to why there has been so much focus on Rezulin.'

Later, a senior executive in Warner-Lambert's pharmaceutical division would chastise the press because Rezulin sales had been hurt 'by uninformed commentary in the media'.

The FDA required one label change, which the company made, and then required a second label change, which the company complied with. Both were to warn patients that they needed to have their liver enzymes measured very regularly.

By July 1998, when it was reported that twenty-one people were dead after taking Rezulin, consumer watchdog Public Citizen petitioned the FDA to remove it from the market.

The agency said no.

Public Citizen would later allege that Warner-Lambert withheld evidence of liver toxicity from the FDA in twenty-one patients who'd contracted the abnormalities while the drug was in clinical trials.

In fact, sentiment was slowly building at the ground level around the FDA that something needed to be done about Rezulin. If it was to happen, the decision would have to be made all the way up the chain of command, and then the FDA could only ask nicely that Warner-Lambert comply. Despite the fact that the FDA is one of the very rare regulatory agencies in the world that actually has its own investigative force, it is, oddly, one of the few that doesn't have the authority to summarily order a drug off the market.

This is very different from Britain where the MCA does have that power. For the FDA to manage anything like it, there is a long-winded process that invariably winds up in court and takes years. The point of getting a drug off the market is that when the decision is made – because the drug presents a health risk – it must come off immediately. So the FDA 'persuades' companies to remove the drug voluntarily. And, in a society as litigious as the United States, the FDA doesn't have to exert much pressure to be persuasive. The moment the agency asks a company to remove a drug, the company is suddenly under a terrible liability risk. Once the FDA determines the drug should go, any adverse events that occur after that will have to be defended by the company in court, often facing class action suits of mega proportions.

In the span of twenty-five years, from 1972 to 1997, only fourteen drugs had ever been the object of the FDA's wrath and taken off the market. Yet from September 1997 to June 1998, the FDA had persuaded companies to yank four more, raising serious concerns about both the testing and the approval process of pharmaceutical products.

But by March 1999 the FDA had not spoken up about Rezulin.

Dr Misbin, still holding the Rezulin file, was coming around to the view that it was time to act. While he favoured waiting a few more months, at least until Avandia and Actos came on to the market safely to replace Rezulin, it wasn't his call. Anyway, Misbin was hardly the Agency's flavour of the month. He'd recently written a letter to the *Washington Post* complaining about how things were done at the FDA. He griped that the agency did not take ethical issues seriously, that patients were not being protected and, as far as he could see after more than four years there, the higher-ups at the FDA didn't seem to care.

When the agency held an Advisory Committee meeting

about Rezulin in March, Misbin wasn't asked to speak. However, it would take more than that to silence him. He heard the FDA saying, we don't have enough data yet, when he knew they had plenty of data all along. He found bureaucratic foot-dragging unacceptable. So, having failed to make his views understood by going up the chain of command, he decided to go to a higher authority.

He wrote a personal letter to several members of Congress, spelled out the problem for them – 'I have been frustrated in my efforts to convince my superiors that the time has come to remove Rezulin from the market' – and enclosed documents that would make the case. He asked them to intervene. No one at the agency knew he'd taken this step until Senator John Ashcroft, a Republican from Missouri, wrote to FDA Commissioner Dr Jane Henney voicing his concerns.

The FDA responded immediately, not by asking Warner-Lambert to take the drug off the market but by opening an Internal Affairs investigation into Misbin for 'the possible inappropriate release of information'.

The press got wind of that by mid-March.

A meeting took place a week later, at which time the director of the FDA's Center for Drug Evaluation and Research (CDER), Dr Janet Woodcock, personally made the decision to invite Warner-Lambert to remove the drug. The company complied immediately.

CBS News now reported that sixty-three liver deaths had been linked to Rezulin. Warner-Lambert's own press release claimed it was repeated media reports that had sensationalized the risks to the point that patients and physicians were unable to make well-informed decisions.

In that regard, the company was half right. The final blow to Rezulin was not liver toxicity but the publicity surrounding the FDA investigation of Robert Misbin.

It took lawyers acting for Rezulin patients under four weeks from the day the drug was pulled to file the first federal class action lawsuit against Warner-Lambert. It took lawyers representing the victims of Fen-Phen less than three to go after American Home Products.

Since then, suits have rained down on those companies like Noah's deluge. And to the utmost exasperation of the entire pharmaceutical industry, when these cases happen the advantage is with the plaintiff.

'Spreading the cases out widely, forcing the company to defend itself in multiple forums, makes it harder for them to hide documents,' affirms Mike Williams, an attorney in Portland, Oregon, who regularly represents plaintiffs in personal and class action lawsuits against big corporations. 'When you've got thirty or forty different lawyers with thirty to forty different judges all issuing orders for the company to answer questions and produce documents, it's a lot easier to get to the truth with these things.'

It's easier, too, he says, to find smoking guns. 'As soon as one judge orders some document to be produced, it's available everywhere. So when you suspect that a document exists, you really only have to get one judge to order it produced. This is especially effective when you've got a document that the defendant claims is covered by attorney client privilege. When executives in a company start getting into trouble, they send copies of everything to their in-house lawyers who then claim they don't have to produce the documents because they're privileged. Well, different states have different interpretations to that, so all you need to do is find one judge who'll let it out, and it's out.'

Among the smoking guns to emerge this way in the Fen-Phen case was a little yellow Post-it Note. Written in the handwriting of medical director Deitch, all it said was, 'I need to discuss implications re dexfenfluramine before proceeding.'

In the context of the case, Williams contends, it was very

damaging. 'What he was saying was, let's hold up making this warning change.'

Without that kind of evidence, the plaintiffs have to work their way through the maze of games that companies have become very good at playing. 'One of their tricks,' he points out, 'is to rely on a committee, especially when something needs to be signed off by different departments before it's communicated to the regulators. If all the department representatives say okay, then they tell. If one says maybe we shouldn't, then it doesn't get told. It's rare to see argument within the company. But then, they're very crafty about the way they couch things in their own internal memos.'

Another well-worn strategy is for a company to get a drug approved on the narrowest possible application where it has solid evidence of efficacy and safety. 'Once they've got it approved, they encourage doctors to use it for any damn thing they want, including in combinations, including in higher doses, including for other indications. The industry recently got Congress to relax the rules so they can better promote off-label uses. It's made the business much more of a free-for-all than it ever used to be.'

At the start of any big corporate lawsuit, Williams is willing to concede, it's likely that the company's own lawyers don't know the truth. 'They're so busy looking for defences, or legal technicalities so they can get the company off the hook, that it's hard for them to appreciate the truth. A lot of the time the company succeeds in hiding the truth from their own lawyers, at least for a while.'

But they're confronted with the truth eventually. 'In Fen-Phen, the company produced, maybe, a million pages of documents. Now, no single attorney on the defence team could read all of them. They're given to lower-level attorneys who have the time to read those documents. But because they're not very experienced, they miss stuff. It's only when you get the experienced plaintiffs' lawyers digging through this thing and you start to put the pieces together that the liability picture begins to emerge. By the time you're well into the litigation and you've hired experts on both sides, either to defend or condemn the company's conduct, that's when the lawyers know everything.'

The bigger the company, Williams says, 'the harder it is for them to hide any major trail of perfidy. You'll eventually come across it by just sorting through the multiple copies of documents and figuring out who reported to who when, and what the critical days were when they were making bad decisions.'

Williams had run up against American Home and Wyeth before. Some years previously, they'd been warned by the Canadians that their drug Cordarone could cause blindness, and the Canadians required the company to label that as a possible side-effect in Canada. In the USA, the FDA warned the company to add that side-effect. But the Canadian wording must have lost something in the translation heading south because the US label warned of inflammation of the optic nerve, noting that it occurred in less than 1 per cent of the patient population. There was no mention of sight loss.

That same year, 1994, a 56-year-old man named Douglas Axen was diagnosed with life-threatening cardiac arrhythmia and prescribed the heart drug Cordarone. What Axen didn't know was that, in 1988, the year after the FDA licensed Cordarone, studies had begun to show a link between the drug and optic neuropathy, which causes blindness. Within a month or so, Axen began complaining about vision problems and his doctor immediately took him off the drug. But it was too late; Axen's vision deteriorated and he eventually ruled legally blind.

In his suit against AHP, Axen claimed that the company had intentionally failed to warn that Cordarone could cause permanent blindness. A jury awarded him $207,000 (£135,000) in 'economic damages', $1.5 million (£975,000) in 'non-economic damages' and $20 million (£13 million) in punitive damages.

American Home called the award 'irrational, ill-considered and excessive', and appealed on those grounds.

It turned out that the FDA had in fact been highly critical in 1989 of the way the company had promoted Cordarone. What's more, the Oregon appeal court ruled there was clear and convincing evidence that AHP 'had acted with extraordinary disregard of, or indifference to, known or highly probable risks to others'.

Williams notes, 'We won that case. They appealed. And only after they exhausted every possible appeal did they pay up. My guess is they made more than $20 million while they appealed.'

He's been left to conclude that some companies do this sort of stuff all the time. 'There is a spectrum of evil. Some companies are not as good as others at being honest. Often, the employees don't conceive that what they're doing is evil. It's the culture in some companies to conceal, to interpret the regulations in such a way as to require the minimum possible disclosure and to look at everything as a bottom-line rate of return issue. What I saw in the Cordarone case was a pattern.'

Like Williams, Dan Sigelman is a lawyer who saw the Fen-Phen case up close. Then out of Atlanta, now out of Washington, he took the deposition of a medical officer accused of being responsible for the Fen-Phen cover-up. 'What never ceases to amaze me about the pharmaceutical industry is how people accept responsibility when something goes wrong, but then deny they're responsible. When I probed him, he was willing to take responsibility for his decisions but wrote them off by saying that these decisions didn't matter. He acknowledged that responsibility but then wanted us to believe that he was only responsible for doing what he was supposed to do and that the fuck-up was somewhere else. In other words, I'm responsible but we really didn't do anything wrong.'

This sort of thing is nothing new to Sigelman, who served in the 1980s as the principal investigator on a congressional committee with oversight of the FDA. 'I became very jaundiced about the drug industry. And I don't believe they've gotten any better. Frankly, I think it's worse. There's no oversight of this industry any more. You have to wonder what's going on. Obviously Big Pharma has a lot of clout.'

That clout, he says, was clearly demonstrated in the case of Rezulin. 'The drug was pulled in the UK in 1997. It's disgraceful that the FDA allowed it to remain on the market in the United States. An absolute disgrace.'

The day after Rezulin was yanked off the US market, and for the next several weeks, full-page ads appeared in newspapers, barking headlines like 'Attention Rezulin Users'. SmithKline wanted Rezulin-users to switch to Avandia. Eli Lilly wanted Rezulin-users to switch to Actos.

Largely ignored, that same week, Johnson & Johnson pulled their billion dollar seller, Propulsid, off the market over FDA concerns about irregular heartbeats and death in some users. And SmithKline won an appeal at the European Agency for the Evaluation of Medicinal Products for approval of Avandia, originally rejected by the agency. This was the first time the Agency had ever reversed one of its own decisions.

At the last count, there were more than 9,000 suits filed in the Fen-Phen case.

A federal grand jury was convened in New York in May 2000 to investigate the way American Home reported to the FDA – or failed to report to the FDA – adverse events in relation to Fen-Phen.

Another federal grand jury has been looking into Rezulin.

In June 1999 Interneuron set aside $70 million (£45.5 million) to pay for all Redux-related claims against the company. In August 2000, a federal judge in Philadelphia cleared the way for American Home to settle claims made against it in the Fen-Phen matter for $3.75 billion (£2.44 billion). Included in the suits against American Home Products and Wyeth are 45,000 people who have refused the settlement, and 266,000 others in class actions.

In one of those lawsuits, a plaintiff in Texas outlined the way the company hired a media consultancy to write ten articles that were to be submitted to various medical journals, which just so happened to be owned by the media consultant's parent company, Reed Elsevier Plc.

Only two of the articles were published before the company pulled the drugs. According to editors at the journals, both articles were scrutinized for fairness by independent editorial boards. Whatever plans there were to publish the remaining eight articles were abandoned.

Despite the fact that the researchers who signed the articles now claim to have been unaware of Wyeth's financial or editorial interest in the articles, a spokesman at Wyeth defended his company to the Associated Press. 'This is a common practice in the industry. It's not particular to us. The companies have some input, it seems, in the initial development of the piece, but the proposed author has the last say.'

The FDA attracted its share of criticism. In response, Commissioner Jane Henney wrote in the newspaper *USA Today* that the FDA had revised its policies towards clinical testing by establishing safeguards to protect participants in drug trials and rules that require fully informed written consent.

Misbin believed that wasn't the case. If there had been a revision of the FDA's rules, the changes had never filtered down to him. So he further endeared himself to his superiors by writing a letter to *USA Today* refuting Henney. He explained how, when he'd complained that written informed consent had not been properly obtained from approximately 300 patients in SmithKline's Avandia trials, he was instructed to keep quiet. He suggested, 'The FDA could have sent a message to the pharmaceutical industry that it took informed consent seriously.'

To that he added, 'Although Henney states that her obligation to protect patients' rights is "deeply felt", her method of implementing that obligation seems designed to be ineffective. Why did she write to *USA Today*, but not to her own staff?'

CHAPTER FIVE

Taking Care of Business

Technically, they shouldn't get any tax deductions for worthless products.

(Richard Walden, Operation USA)

They say, *it's all about research and development.*

They contend, *everyone agrees that the innovative work of our scientists has been extraordinarily successful.*

The spiel never changes. *Our dedicated scientists are devoted to their work and want to continue developing new treatments for Alzheimer's, cancer, heart disease, Parkinson's and many other diseases.*

They even make promises. *We're closer than ever to finding new medicines, and perhaps cures, and want to go full speed ahead.*

What they mean by that is, be grateful for all the wonderful things we do and don't be so rude as to ask why we charge so much for it.

*   *   *

Prescription drugs rarely compete on price because they don't have to. For most patients, priority number one is getting well. Price comes into the equation only when it is so high that they cannot afford to pay for the drug – or a health service refuses to pay for it – and therefore treatment is hindered.

One of the rare instances where price reductions come into play is when a drug company wants to get its products listed on a hospital formulary. They treat it like a loss-leader. Ever since hospitals turned themselves into businesses and have begun applying cost-containment measures to supply purchases, drug companies make some of their more expensive drugs so cheap to hospital buyers that the hospitals can afford to put patients on them. Then, because we all feel more comfortable with continuity, when the patient leaves the hospital, the company can charge real money for the renewal prescriptions.

The price of branded drugs has nothing to do with supply and demand. Well, at least not supply. The cost of supply includes the investment in research, an allotment to cover the costs when R&D fails to deliver a drug, the costs of meeting all of the various regulatory requirements and the marketing of the product to doctors, hospitals and patients.

Since 1985, Big Pharma claims, development costs have more than doubled. And that's when it throws around the $500 million (£325 million) figure. But if you press drug companies about this, they shuffle about and mostly ask you to take it on faith. When you look at that number closely – and Big Pharma doesn't make it easy because it won't release the real numbers – you find it's based on drugs developed entirely in-house by American-owned companies and does not factor in pharmaceuticals developed outside the USA that are licensed in, which account for around 40 per cent of drugs introduced by Big Pharma in the States.

It's the same in Britain. It's much cheaper when it brings a drug in from the States, but the cost is always the highest price it has to pay in-country. Nor does the arithmetic factor in drugs researched and developed in government labs, universities or hospitals. It neglects to consider me-toos, line extensions and tax write-offs for research.

As for the demand side of the equation, that's much less complex. As long as the marketing department can convince doctors that the drug is the best in the field – and that it's safe – they will prescribe it for their patients, without considering cost.

Therefore, drugs can be priced pretty much at whatever the company chooses. The risk of pricing too low is the wrath of the shareholders when dividends are announced. The risk of pricing too high is the wrath of some legislative body complaining that the company is swindling the public. Only rarely does mispricing affect sales. Accordingly, companies err on the side of shareholders and price higher rather than lower.

According to Steve Schondelmeyer at the Prime Institute, the best indicator of what it really costs to make a drug is what happens to prices of the branded product when a generic version enters the market. 'As soon as the first generic comes in, they set the price at 75–80 per cent of the brand name. As other generics enter the market, the price comes down until it's somewhere around 25–30 per cent of what the original brand name was. So the actual cost of production and distribution of the drug, with a reasonable level of profit to keep a firm in business, is about 25–30 per cent of what the selling price actually is. Promotion costs get added on to that, ranging from 25 to 40 per cent.'

Granted, R&D must be factored in on top of that. But Schondelmeyer raises another point. 'Are the companies who spend the most on R&D finding the most new drugs? That's not always the case. A number of years ago, one of the Wall Street firms did a comparison of the amount spent on R&D with the number of innovative products that companies brought to the market. They found clear differences in efficiency. Some produced a lot more for the money than others. And yet the market doesn't discipline this. In other industries, if one company is more innovative than another, they will grow and develop and prosper more than others. But in pharmaceuticals, even the ones who aren't particularly productive with their R&D expenditures seem to continue and prosper. That's because they can simply raise their prices to cover their expenditures.'

He concludes, 'People in the pharmaceutical industry must live in a kind of a fairy world. They isolate themselves, talk to people who think like they do, and lose their sense of reality. They justify their prices by arguing that the rest of us don't know what the real world of business is like. I argue, they're so isolated doing business they don't know what the rest of the world is like. They make policy based on their own experience with healthcare, and with a $100,000 a year job, and with a health insurance policy that covers everything. They say, I don't have trouble with my drug costs, so why is everybody else complaining?'

Politicians such as US Congressman Bernard Sanders, an independent from Vermont, is complaining because he finds the pharmaceutical industry's pricing methods disgraceful. 'Taxpayers get hit twice. Once when their tax dollars go to develop these drugs at government labs and again when they have to buy the medication.'

The example he frequently cites is a drug called Levamisole. Originally marketed by Johnson & Johnson as an anti-worm treatment for sheep, the company was charging veterinarians a mere 6 cents a pill. Then it learned that Levamisole could be used to treat colon cancer. The price shot up to around $6 (£4).

It's not the only example. A one-month supply of Medrol cost $3.90 (£2.54) as an anti-inflammatory for dogs, but when it was priced as a treatment for human asthma, it cost $20.10 (£13.06).

'I represent one of the poorest districts in the United States,' declares Congressman Marion Berry from Arkansas, and the only pharmacist currently in the House. 'I come from a rural part of the state where there are about 800 people. Now, we don't lock our doors. And I can tell you that if someone came into our homes and started stealing from us, we'd have our own way of dealing with those folks. But that's exactly what the pharmaceutical companies are doing. They're coming into our homes with their outrageous prices and they're literally stealing money, especially from people who can't afford it.'

They get away with that in America, he goes on, because the United States is the only free pharmaceutical market in the world. 'They get away with it in the United States because the drug companies reckon that Americans have more money than anyone else and can afford to pay the highest prices.'

In other words, drug prices really boil down to purchasing power.

For instance, a month's supply of aerosol Pentamidine, a powerful drug that effectively prevents a type of pneumonia that is the leading cause of AIDS-related death, costs £16.75 in Britain and £97.50 in the United States.

Bruce Downey, Chairman and CEO of the generic manufacturer Barr Pharmaceuticals, emphatically agrees that Big Pharma's pricing policy has nothing to do with cost. 'Absolutely nothing. They're not related at all. They price on what is called the marginal revenue curve. As long as they're obtaining marginal revenue, which they do because their markups are so great, they continue to increase the price. Prices go as high as they can until the product becomes so prohibitively expensive that they start losing revenues.'

Rationalizing all of this, claims Barry Sherman, Chairman and CEO of the generic manufacturer Apotex in Toronto, is Big Pharma's assertion that, because its product is 20 per cent more effective than some other product, it should be allowed to charge 20 per cent more. 'It's absurd. It means that progress drives prices up. It's like saying that our airplane can get you somewhere in an hour while a horse and buggy will take a week, so the airfare should be 168 times more than the cost of the horse and buggy. The salvation of the economy in a competitive market is that, if someone charges too much, someone else will come along and undercut that price. But with pharmaceuticals, where there is no real competition, the natural desire of the brand name drug company is to get whatever it can, regardless of cost.'

It makes the pharmaceutical industry unique, Sherman continues, despite the fact that it's not the only business relying on patents. 'Compare the drug industry to the computer industry. They have patents. What do you see? The rate of progress is phenomenal and prices come down. Computer memory doubles every so many months and the prices halve. That's with patents. What happens with drugs? They don't get cheaper. Every time there's a new drug it's more expensive than the last one. And that's not to say it's necessarily better. The rate of real progress has slowed because no one is in any hurry to increase the rate of replacement. They've got twenty years of monopoly to exploit this one. In other industries, patents don't stop progress. In other industries, if you don't want to pay for something, you buy something else. But here you can't do that. The patient has to buy what the doctor prescribes, and the doctor doesn't care about the price.'

Dr Krimsky at Tufts agrees that prices depend on a company's view of market conditions and what it can get. But he suggests there are exceptions, and they're usually political. 'They have to have people working inside the company who understand the politics of disease. Some diseases are politically more important than other diseases, therefore governments will pay for those diseases even if the costs are very high.'

In September 1999, Congressman Sherrod Brown – as ranking member of the Commerce Health and Environment Subcommittee – introduced the 'Affordable Prescription Drugs Act', declaring at the time that Big Pharma had finally outdone itself. 'When a majority of Americans believe Congress should establish a prescription drug benefit for Medicare beneficiaries and buy your products,' he wrote, 'you protest because you're afraid you wouldn't be paid enough. When some members of Congress propose that senior citizens get the same price discounts that large, profitable HMOs enjoy, you buy very expensive television advertisements and accuse government of meddling in your medicine cabinet. And when a few members of Congress suggest we bring some good old-fashioned American competition into the monopoly drug pricing system, you spend millions lobbying Congress and threatening to stifle the development of new drugs if we take that step.'

Troubled that Americans pay significantly higher prices for drugs than anyone else in the world, he couldn't understand any longer how the companies got away with it. 'Taxpayers fund much of the basic research that produces new drugs. You are granted generous tax subsidies for your own research. You charge outrageous prices to taxpayers to buy your drugs. You tell taxpayers you can't do any more research if your prices drop to the same levels as citizens in every other country in the world pay. You devote huge amounts to promote lifestyle drugs. And you earn windfall profits.'

He also went after the CEOs' salaries. 'A woman in Elyria, Ohio, told me she spends $350 on prescription drugs every month out of her social security check of $808. It takes 5,134 senior citizens like her to pay your typical CEO salary every year.'

It was becoming increasingly difficult, he believed, for Big Pharma to convince anyone that prices can't come down to more reasonable levels without bankrupting the industry.

'Despite your well-oiled lobbying machine, despite your scare tactics, something will be done to bring down the cost of prescription drugs. It's just a matter of what.'

His bill called for the compulsory licensing of patented medicines deemed to be unreasonably priced. It would, he promised, finally open the market to real competition. Under the Act, other companies would be given the right to manufacture and sell patent-protected drugs by paying a royalty to the patent holder. Drug companies would also be required to disclose audited financial information justifying the prices they charged.

'If drug prices are where they need to be, prove it.' He wanted Big Pharma to explain why royalties would not be enough to fund the percentage of R&D that the companies themselves actually paid for. To explain why direct-to-consumer advertising for a product that consumers didn't choose was more important than research and development. To explain why prescription drug prices in the United States were one-third higher than in Canada and 60 per cent higher than in Britain.

An average dosage of Zocor for high cholesterol was priced at £65.80 in the United States, £28.38 in Canada and £31.09 in the UK. One month's supply of Tamoxifen for breast cancer sells for £100 in the United States, £7.74 in Canada and £6.69 in Britain.

He conceded to Big Pharma, 'You're not going to like it,' and was dead right about that. They didn't. They used their heavyweight lobbying muscle to make certain Brown's bill never became law.

With many drugs it would perhaps be unfair to compare prices in different parts of the world. But some drugs are so out of line that they make the point. The price of 100 units of Nevirapine, a medication that prevents transmission of the AIDS virus from mother to child, costs £277.42 in Norway, where the market for the drug is small, and £563.87

in Kenya, where AIDS has reached epidemic levels and where the healthcare system is, to all intents and purposes, broke. Glaxo sells Betnesol, a drug used in ophthalmology to help prevent blindness, especially among the elderly, for 12.3 pence in India and £1.52 in Sri Lanka.

In Britain, the actual price of a drug is hidden from the public. Prescription charges may be a nuisance, but most people agree that the £6 flat charge hardly, if ever, covers the real cost of the treatment. How prices are actually set in Britain is an enormously complicated affair.

It was 1957 when the government of the day decided that the easiest thing would be to implement straightforward price controls. But Big Pharma took that as a direct threat to its profits and consequently spent the next twelve years lobbying to make the politicians understand price controls weren't such a good idea. In 1969, the system was changed to the one in force today.

The price of branded drugs sold to the NHS is negotiated between the Department of Health and the drug companies, using a series of calculations worked out by politicians and bureaucrats gone wild with a slide rule. The Pharmaceutical Price Regulation Scheme (PPRS) does not control prices but rather aims to control the branded company's return on capital. And the oddest thing about such an eccentric system is that it mostly works, at least in comparison with drug prices in the rest of the industrialized world, as Britain is usually ranked towards the bottom half of the price table.

The price of generic drugs is established in another way. They're regulated by the Drug Tariff, a type of commodities market pricing scheme, determined monthly by the Department of Health by weighting average market prices and then figuring in various discounts. Taking the total NHS drugs bill, which is something approaching £7 billion, around 10 per cent – or £700 million – is for generic drugs. The rest, £6.3 billion, is for branded drugs. But generic drugs account for about 55 per cent of the prescriptions, which means there's a huge discrepancy in terms of value for money. Whether that's the result of a deliberate philosophy for 'headroom' – the difference between branded drugs and generics – or it just happened that way and someone came up with the philosophy to explain it is not clear. The way they tell it at the Department of Health is that 'headroom' allows the NHS to keep its drug bills down enough to pay for those more expensive branded drugs. But it can come as a nasty shock to some people who need treatment when they find out that, in Britain too, drug prices can still be too high and that the NHS can't always afford them.

At the end of August 2000, Roche announced it was bringing to market a brand new drug to fight breast cancer. Herceptin was approved by the European Agency for the Evaluation of Medicinal Products, received approval from the European Commission and had been shown to increase survival by 40 per cent in women suffering from a specific type of aggressive cancer. But Roche set the price of the drug at £407 per dose and the treatment course is said to last thirty-four weeks. The total cost per patient could exceed £13,000. So it's not certain that every health district will be able to afford it.

A few years before, the Health Secretary had already decided Britain couldn't afford any extra erections – or, in some cases, any erections at all – and put limits on doctors prescribing Viagra. The pill had come in at £6 a tablet and the much-hyped demand was expected to reach £1 billion. Rules were put into place which limited prescribing.

The National Institute for Clinical Excellence (NICE) opened its doors in April 1999 with a brief to assess new medicines. It looks for both clinical effectiveness and cost effectiveness. The first drug it looked at was Glaxo's flu treatment Relenza, a powder that needs to be inhaled at the start of the illness. NICE decided it wasn't very effective and should not be supported. Glaxo's protest was heard all the way to Downing

Street. 'The consequences of such a decision', wrote Richard Sykes, 'could wipe out at a stroke a key element of the UK's competitive advantage in the global Pharmaceutical Industry.'

There was the threat again.

Keep fooling around with our market and we'll find greener pastures.

Sykes might have had a better argument if he'd pointed out that, no matter what the government's intentions were in creating NICE, the result is rationing – postcode prescribing.

When NICE reviewed Beta-feron, a Schering drug to treat multiple sclerosis – and heralded as the only drug effective against the disease – the decision was based entirely on price. At £9,600 per patient, NICE decided 'the benefit gained from use of the drug is too modest to warrant its cost to the NHS'. Patients already on the drug should be allowed to stay on it, NICE acknowledged, but did not want it prescribed more widely because resources could be better used elsewhere.

It is estimated that as many as 10,000 MS sufferers in the UK could benefit from Beta-feron. It hardly matters to them if the villain is NICE for moving the drug beyond their reach or Schering for pricing it beyond the NHS's reach.

In May 2000, NICE ruled on Taxol. Whereas 30,000 women in the UK are diagnosed with breast cancer every year and approximately 14,000 die of it, Taxol might be appropriate for only 5,000 of those women. Until the NICE ruling, price alone determined whether or not a patient who needed the drug received it on the NHS. Four out of ten local health authorities did not fund it. Others included Taxol in the chemotherapy mix only when single-drug chemo failed. As a result, British women who received the treatment were chosen by where they lived instead of by what they needed.

After the NICE ruling, that is still the case.

The judgment was made that Taxol should be available on the NHS but limited to the treatment of advanced ovarian cancer and also advanced breast cancer when other treatments failed. That would add another 4,000 women who might benefit from the drug, but at an additional expense to the NHS of £16 million a year. Again, some health authorities can and will pay for it, others can't or won't.

The British public is not alone in being denied certain drugs because the government finds the price too high. Almost all of black Africa is in the same boat.

But there, Big Pharma has worked itself into an embarrassing little corner. The public derides, do something about people in Africa dying because they can't afford your prices. Big Pharma answers, we have to help or we'll look totally heartless, but we can't just give our drugs away in Africa, because then people who are dying because they can't afford our drugs in South America or the Orient will demand that we give them away there too, and we can't just cut our prices in Africa, because we're overcharging Americans so much that they'll demand we cut our prices there too.

It's a recurring dilemma that the industry deals with clumsily.

In July 2000, the 13th International AIDS Conference met in Durban, South Africa, and shook at the very base of Big Pharma's foundations. This was when Pretoria waved the dreaded stick of compulsory licensing and parallel imports if drug companies didn't come to the rescue voluntarily.

Three years before, Nelson Mandela's government had passed the Medicines Act, a law granting the authority for compulsory licensing. Big Pharma had gone screaming all the way to Washington, where Congress and the US trade representatives promised to help. At the same time, a pharmaceutical industry lobby went to court in South Africa and won an injunction blocking the law.

One year later, a New Jersey Republican, Congressman Rodney Frelinghuysen, managed to stick a clause into the 1998 federal budget which obliged the State Department to tell Congress what it was doing to keep compulsory licensing from being enforced in South Africa. The effect of Frelinghuysen's handiwork meant that no US foreign aid could be sent to South Africa until Congress was satisfied that Big Pharma's interests were protected.

In February 1999, the State Department reported to Congress that it was 'making use of the full panoply of leverage in our arsenal' to take on the South Africans. That included, the report said, the Vice President's office, with Al Gore himself putting the problem at the top of his agenda in his meeting with the man who would become South Africa's president, Thabo Mbeki.

At that point, the industry lobby, PhRMA, admitted it was pushing the administration to label South Africa a 'priority foreign country' in order to establish a deadline, after which trade sanctions would come into effect.

Towards the end of 1999, having decided to become a full-fledged candidate for the Presidency, Gore was softening his stance. He wanted a solution in South Africa that would help those people who needed medicine, and promised to get affordable drugs to developing countries. He said he opposed legislation to extend the patent life of Claritin, labelling Schering-Plough's efforts a typical example of a drug company protecting profits at the expense of consumers. And he commented that some drug companies 'are trying to pull the wool over the eyes of Congress and tag the American people with more of these absurdly high pharmaceutical prices'.

But, by then, Bill Clinton had already shifted US policy by ordering the trade representatives to stop trying to bully South Africa on the Medicines Act. The White House exempted South Africa from US trade laws on the compulsory licensing and parallel important of AIDS drugs. South Africa softened its stance just enough to appear as if there had been a real agreement and the drug companies there suspended their court action, leaving the Medicines Act in limbo.

The crisis didn't go away.

Pressure continued to mount on Big Pharma. In Spring 2000, United Nations' Secretary General, Kofi Annan, made a personal appeal to the drug companies. Their first response was to fend it off by discussing patents and intellectual property rights and how prices equated to innovation.

The South Africans, in particular, didn't give a damn.

Next the drug companies tried blaming the Africans for their own plight. They said that these countries needed to educate the population better and needed to create an infrastructure through which drug donations would be efficiently distributed.

No one bought that one.

President Clinton then issued an executive order exempting the rest of Africa from those provisions of US trade law – just as he'd already done with South Africa – and saying that the United States would not interfere with African countries that happened to violate American patent law in obtaining cheaper AIDS drugs.

Opening the door to both parallel imports and compulsory licensing would be a help to Africa. And it wouldn't really hurt Big Pharma all that much. The companies feared that it might inadvertently create a black market, that corruption in many of these countries would see drugs sent abroad instead of given to the people, which would in turn undermine Big Pharma's own pricing structures in the rest of the world. Eastern Europe, for example, is becoming a very lucrative market for western pharmaceuticals. But it is still a fragile market. Flooding it with drugs that had been destined for Africa could easily ruin it. Compulsory licensing and parallel imports lessened the chances of that happening. So now, having held out as long as they dared, five pharmaceutical companies – Boehringer, Bristol-Myers Squibb, Merck, Glaxo and Hoffmann–La Roche – claimed they'd always been anxious to help and agreed to negotiate steep price cuts for AIDS drugs. This was when Glaxo offered Combivir, a blend of AZT and 3TC that normally sells at £10.75, for £1.30.

The other four spoke only vaguely of cuts up to 80 per cent off US retail prices. That would take the price of a common triple-therapy cocktail of AIDS drugs costing an American $15,000 (£9,750) a year, down to $3,000 (£1,950). In countries where the healthcare spending was as little as $10 (£6) per year per person, that would help fewer than one in 300. And the others would have to go without any healthcare that year.

PhRMA came up with its expected criticism, saying that, by encouraging compulsory licensing and parallel imports, the White House was setting 'an undesirable and inappropriate precedent, adopting a discriminatory approach to intellectual property laws, and focusing exclusively on pharmaceuticals'.

Trust PhRMA to miss the point – that all those people in Africa who are still dying are also focused exclusively on pharmaceuticals.

Sometime after Glaxo announced it would cut the price of Combivir – but didn't say how long it would keep the price way down or how much Combivir it would sell at that price – Pfizer took a different approach. It announced that it would donate a supply of its anti-fungal drug Diflucan to South Africa.

It's better than nothing, but the problem with donations is that they're never a long-term solution.

Nobody knows that better than Richard Walden. A health lawyer by training, he is also the son of a pharmacist. 'In the fifty-five years that my dad was a pharmacist, the shelf life of pharmaceuticals, including antibiotics, never significantly increased. With all of the fancy new coatings for capsules, time-release capsules, it's amazing to me that they're so short.

What they won't do for profit. The drug companies don't want to change the dates.'

He'd specialized in what he describes as 'civil rights kinds of cases in the health field', and wound up annoying California's Governor Jerry Brown so much that in 1979 Brown challenged Walden to put his talents where his mouth was. Brown appointed him Commissioner of Hospitals for California.

It was at about that time when Walden and a friend dreamt up a one-time-only relief flight to help Vietnamese boat people washed up in a refugee camp in Malaysia.

They got a plane from McDonnell Douglas for free – 'We told the head of McDonnell Douglas that we were calling from the Governor's office, which was almost true' – and, because they knew a lot of people in the pharmaceutical industry, and knew that the industry often donated outdated drugs, they started making the rounds with a begging bowl. However, Walden also knew that a lot of charities often supplied needy areas with drugs that weren't of any use. So he asked the drug companies what they were prepared to give him. He then drew up a list of what he could get and sent it off to Malaysia to see where it matched what was needed.

'We did it all without any money and twenty-nine days later we were airborne with a load of stuff.'

They got a ton of publicity, which gave them a ton of access to other drug companies with pharmaceuticals to give away. Walden got so into it that he literally gave up his law practice, gave up his appointment as Commissioner of Hospitals and went into this charity business full time. He called the charity Operation California, but changed it in the mid-1980s to Operation USA, although he admits that sometimes sounds a little too governmental and when it turns people off in foreign countries he reverts to Operation California.

Anyway, he quickly realized that the problem with donating drugs to the Third World was that not just any drugs work, that the people receiving the drugs need to understand the contraindications and read the labels, that it takes a lot of coordination – '300 airplanes landed in Armenia filled with broken kidney dialysis machines but no chemical agents or manuals to operate them, good stuff, bad stuff and silly stuff, which the Armenian government, then still part of the USSR, sold to the ministries of health of other Soviet republics for hard currency' – and that, even with half-decent coordination, things can still go wrong. 'Some well-minded people sent Bosnia 17,000 tons of useless medical supplies.'

When he visited a UN refugee camp in Split, he says, 'drug supplies were coming in from England and Germany. Half-empty bottles, seven years out of date from someone's medicine chest. And wildly out-of-date stuff in bulk from Germany. I told the UN camp director he had to shut that down because people were going to get killed with these medicines. This camp barely had any English or German language capability. How were they supposed to read the labels? A lot of the stuff should never have been accepted in the first place.'

What makes Operation USA different is that Walden always matches what he gets with what people in the field tell him they need, and then makes certain that it goes out quickly and properly, so that those people in the field can have what they need in time to make the most use out of it. He's worked in eighty countries and always matches in-kind donations – drugs from the pharmaceutical industry – with needs.

But he turns out to be the exception. 'Some of the high-visibility groups are really awful. Big Pharma supports them for all sorts of reasons, mainly because they get the press that makes Big Pharma look good. In one case, a group shipped 10,000 cases of oral rehydration medication to Zaire for the Rwanda refugees which turned out to be the sports drink, Gatorade. They also sent $2 million (£1.3 million) worth of medical aid to St Petersburg which was really just 2 million candy bars. These groups are shills for the pharmaceutical industry. They don't smell like a charity. They may be non-profit, but they're not a charity.'

The reason they get away with it is because the pharmaceutical industry doesn't discriminate enough when it comes to who it deals with. 'There are some complete wackos out there, bogus groups who seduce drug company executives with evaluations of what they were giving away, moving outdated stuff that couldn't be sold, and sending these drugs to the Third World by sea, in hot container ships so that the gelatin capsules melt. The groups don't care and the companies got their tax write-offs.'

What Big Pharma used to do, back in the days when nobody was looking, was send its surplus production to some country, wildly exaggerating its value. Or it'd send goods that had passed their sell-by date. It was cheaper to give drugs away than go through the expense of properly destroying them. But the charity business has grown up and the old tricks are harder to pull off. Walden says he recently looked at the top seven pharmaceutical companies that supply surplus to charities, and then looked at the top five non-governmental organizations (NGOs) that take donations from pharmaceutical companies, and saw that the drug companies were honestly valuing what they gave away – it totalled something like $50 million (£32.5 million) – but that the NGOs had valued those exact same donations at over $1 billion (£6.5 million).

Walden tells drug companies that, because Operation USA needs to ship these drugs to far-away places in a timely manner, they need a minimum of a year's dating left on the drugs and prefer it when there's more. He admits to saying to some of his contacts, if you want to seduce us with some very expensive, vitally needed antibiotics that have only six months left on the sell-by date, we'll take them and fly them out to where they're going to be used. But he doesn't want too great a quantity because he knows it's only going to sit somewhere and rot.

'The problem is, other groups don't give a shit about that sort of thing.'

He says companies either underproduce or wildly over-produce, especially in analgesics. 'They spend a ton of money on advertising and the product falls flat, so they wind up with 10 million extra doses with two years of shelf life. They give that away. That's great. One year we sent Tylenol, aspirin and Dristan in 8 million doses to the Ministry of Health in the Philippines, which allowed them to divert $1.2 million (£780,000) they would have spent on those medicines to buy more expensive stuff for malaria and to buy antibiotics.'

But it doesn't always work so well.

At the end of 1998, during the Hurricane Mitch disaster in Nicaragua, he went to the health department down there to ask what they needed. He was told they were seeing an outbreak of leptosporosis, a horrible rat-borne fever. They said they needed doxycycline, so Walden's people went to a Nicaraguan pharmaceutical wholesaler who gets his stuff from Panama or Costa Rica and tried to buy some. A bottle of 1,000 normally costs $20 (£13) in the States. The wholesaler in Nicaragua said he wanted $95 (£61.75). Walden found it in Amsterdam for $12 (£7.80).

'We could have gone directly to the drug companies to ask for it, and we did that in the old days when there were only two or three charities asking. Now there are thousands of groups asking and it's just caused so much confusion.'

With so many groups begging for just anything, there's no telling what the pharmaceutical companies might be willing to unload. That's when you hear about planes landing in some disaster area and dumping stuff on tarmacs. 'Some companies are better than others. I have to say that, as a class, the cancer companies are the stingiest. One of the reasons is, and they say it with some justification, that every cancer case is a compassionate case. So if you call them for Little Joe in Vietnam who's got some sort of cancer, they're getting 150 requests from all over the place and prefer to sell the drugs. They don't have a ton of surplus.'

But, with the rest of Big Pharma, there's a great deal of confusion about who's giving what and how. 'For the most part, the pharmaceutical companies give everything away for free. We get a fax from, say, Glaxo saying here's what we've got, do you want it? We'll say, sure, send it to us and then we'll see it gets sent to some place that needs that drug and distribute it for free, just like the drug company intended. But some charities resell the stuff they get for free, supposedly to cover their own costs. And that sometimes looks as though the drug companies themselves are selling it.'

Tax law is supposed to limit drug companies on the amount they can deduct of any donation. Theoretically, there is a tax advantage. But, then, the pharmaceutical industry pays some of the lowest taxes. They take R&D expenses. They take unsold inventory expenses. They move money around the world to declare profits in the low-taxed jurisdictions.

A study done by Professor Michael Reich of Harvard's School of Public Health, called 'The Global Drug Gap', looked at 16,566 charitable drug shipments between 1994 and 1997, going to 129 countries. He found that drug companies combine their donations programme with inventory management. It makes sense because disposal of unwanted, unusable, expired or otherwise unsuitable drugs can be an expensive process. Drugs must be destroyed in specific ways.

Technically, Walden says, the companies should not get any tax deductions for worthless products. 'If it expires on the shelf, it gets written off and that's all. But I can tell you that in twenty-one years of being an in-kind distributor, we've never been asked by the IRS (Internal Revenue Service) whether we've received a product from any company, or what it was worth or what it was valued at or what we thought it should be valued at. They can write off whatever they want. There seems to be no oversight by the IRS.'

Further confusing the issue, some charities that take drugs from companies fool around with the valuations they assign to those drugs. 'There really should be some initiative by the pharmaceutical companies', Walden continues, 'to keep abreast of what's happening with the drugs they donate. If I have any gripe with the pharmaceutical companies it's that they should be better educated about the groups they're giving stuff to. They should know enough to tell these groups, you're putting us in a bad light by taking ten times the value of what we give you. Maybe the pill we give you costs us 5 cents and maybe we sell it for 5 bucks, but you should only declare the donation at 5 cents.'

Walden says that one company got in touch with him one day to announce that it had 20,000 vials of A influenza vaccine they wanted to donate. This was good stuff, with a long enough sell-by date, and would be enough medication for 200,000 injections. Walden was interested but asked if there were any restrictions. Sometimes there are because drug companies have offices all over the world and they don't want these free drugs going into a market where they've got an active sales force. In this case, there weren't.

At the time, Walden was putting together a shipment for the Philippines. He mentioned this to the drug company executive offering the vaccine. The executive said it was okay, and Walden agreed to include the vaccine in the shipment and the drug company's name on his press release. He then asked for a faxed copy of the specs on the vaccine. That arrived in a few hours and he re-faxed it to the World Health Organization. The next morning, WHO came back to Walden to say, don't bother, it's the wrong strain for the Philippines.

So he put in a call to the drug company, got that executive on the line, said thanks but no thanks and please keep us in mind.

'The next I heard was that another charity took the vaccine and sent it through a partner agency to . . . guess where . . . the Philippines. The drug company never bothered to tell them what we'd told them about it being the wrong strain. So it wound up in the Philippines getting injected into the arms of all these people to absolutely no effect. The drug company didn't care who got the drug, or what happened to it.'

It is, he says sadly, a typical story.

CHAPTER SIX

A Tale of Two More Drugs

I saw no problem with that. It was the right thing to do.
(Roy Vagelos, former CEO of Merck)

It was 1949.

Clement Attlee was living at Number 10, Chiang Kai-shek fled China leaving it to Mao, Gussie Moran shocked Wimbledon with her lace panties and Carol Reed directed *The Third Man*.

Richard Strauss died, Israel was admitted to the United Nations and the United States Department of Agriculture (USDA) embarked on the first large-scale collection of plants ever undertaken specifically for scientific study. Over the next ten years, USDA botanists would collect some 7,000 samples. When the initial research showed that certain plants could produce anti-tumour activity, a small but determined group of scientists at the National Cancer Institute petitioned the USDA to send more teams out to look for even more plants.

Arthur Miller won the Pulitzer Prize for *Death of a Salesman*, William Faulkner won the Nobel Prize for Literature and the British government was forced to admit that the NHS was costing 2s 6d a head per week, which was 1s 4d more than first thought.

The Berlin blockade was lifted, Britain devalued the pound and a young, first-generation Greek-American was a senior at the University of Pennsylvania. That campus in west Philadelphia was a wonderful place to be young, and fifty years later he'd recall those days with enormous fondness when he returned to dedicate a research laboratory which would bear his name. But now, in the winter of 1949, it was time to plan his future.

I want to be a doctor, Roy Vagelos told his family, *to understand the nature of human disease and to make a difference.*

He was accepted at Columbia University's Medical School in New York, earned his MD there in 1954 and did his internship and residency at Massachusetts General Hospital in Boston. Years later, one of his supervisors at Mass General would recall, 'Roy was probably the most brilliant and impressive young doctor any of us had ever seen.'

After Boston, he moved to Washington, giving up patients for a research post at the National Institutes of Health. For Vagelos, who would spend the next ten years of his life immersed in cellular physiology and biochemistry, the plains of West Africa were very, very far away.

Flash forward to 1963.

A botanist and three college students spent that summer traipsing through northern California and up into Oregon, gathering bark and leaves. It seems someone at the USDA had actually listened to the researchers at the National Cancer Institute (NCI) and, even though it took fourteen years, funding did come through to send more teams out looking for more plants. By the time that summer was over, the botanist and the three college students had collected samples from 450 species.

Back in Washington, the samples were sorted and catalogued and then sent to various contract laboratories around the country for analysis. One of those labs was the Research Triangle Institute in North Carolina where two scientists –

Dr Monroe Wall and his associate Dr M. D. Wani – set out on what would become an eight-year quest.

Included in their batch of samples was the bark of the *Taxus brevifolia,* otherwise known as the Pacific yew tree. Although they didn't yet know it, Native American tribes had ascribed healing powers to the tree and ethno-botanical records dating back several centuries referred to its medicinal properties. But, until the bark arrived in North Carolina, no western scientist had ever done any serious work on it.

'Our job was to do a bio-assay,' says Wall, now in his eighties and officially retired, but still working in his lab every day. 'We were to take extracts from these plant samples and look for biological activity. When there was none, we abandoned it and moved on to the next extract. When there was some, we continued to purify the extract until we could isolate the molecule that killed the (cancer) cells. Then we determined the structure.'

Which is what happened with the bark of the Pacific yew tree. The two researchers found that it killed *in vitro* cancer cells. But purifying it down and establishing the structure of the compound – which is called paclitaxel – was a very laborious process.

Wall explains, 'To begin with, the compound had an extremely complicated structure. In addition, the purification instrumentation that we were using then was very primitive compared with what we have nowadays. I think we finally had the compound isolated and the structure of it by 1970. It took that long. We published our paper on it in 1971. I decided to name it Taxol.'

After ten years at the National Institutes of Health – some of which were spent working at the National Cancer Institute – Vagelos moved to St Louis, Missouri, to join the medical school faculty at Washington University, where he eventually became Chairman of the Department of Biological

Chemistry. 'I was doing there what I had always been doing, basic biochemical research. And I was very happy to keep doing that.'

But in 1975 an offer came that he simply couldn't refuse. One of the premier pharmaceutical companies in the world invited him to head their research group. 'I accepted going to work for a pharmaceutical company because I wanted to use what I thought was a new way to discover drugs. That was the challenge.'

The company was Merck & Co. in Whitehouse Station, New Jersey, and it had been suffering a decade-long dry spell. Drug development had slowed to a critical point. Vagelos' reputation as a scientist was indisputably established. So was his reputation as an original thinker. These days, that new way of discovering drugs is known as 'rational drug development'. But, in those days, his philosophy was considered radical.

Instead of randomly screening compounds in the hopes that a molecule might someday develop into a drug – the way the NCI was doing with Taxol – Vagelos had come to believe the process should start from the other end of the equation. He wanted to prioritize diseases he was familiar with and for which no effective therapies were available, and create specific molecules to attack those specific targets.

'In the life of each drug-development project,' goes his often quoted remark from those days, 'there is always a crisis, a moment when it looks like years of research will go down the drain and the drug will never come to market. There are a million ways to fail in this business.'

The backwards approach sounded like one of them to the marketing people at Merck, especially since no other drug company ran its R&D this way. Today, they all do.

Because he was personally interested in finding treatments for glaucoma and high levels of cholesterol in blood, he committed company resources to the development of Timoptic for glaucoma and Mevacor and Zocor for high cholesterol. All three became blockbusters and are among the most successful products in the history of the company.

He also encouraged the marketing people to take risks that they were not used to taking. Merck broke the mould for advertising with Mevacor – including TV spots to warn the public about the dangers of high cholesterol – and it was for a time the most-promoted drug in the world. Mevacor captured a one-third market share for cholesterol-reducing drugs and racked up the highest sales ever of any prescription medicine.

While other companies grew through mergers and acquisitions, Merck stayed ahead of them by growing organically, by developing new and important drugs through formidable research strength. Still, the victories did not come easily. Vagelos stressed science, but the corporate marketing people did not share his enthusiasm for some of the diseases he was targeting. In fact, he says, they found many of his targets unimportant.

'Marketing people have marketing backgrounds. They work on surveys. They went into the market to see what important drugs were used for the control of high blood cholesterol and because the drugs out there then weren't very effective and had a lot of side-effects, because at the time there were no good drugs for the control of high blood cholesterol, they decided there wasn't much of a market for that. Unless there's an obvious leader out there, marketing people don't recognize what's important. They don't have the scientific background to realize it. Of course, you try to educate them, but in the end you go about doing what's important. You follow your own instincts.'

His instincts told him to make certain that the marketing people stayed out of his hair. 'I never paid a lot of attention to marketing people. Early on, they opposed some of the things I wanted to work on, but they couldn't stop me because I was head of research. I reported to the CEO who had great confidence in me for whatever reason. So I was left alone.'

Besides coming up with a whole series of blockbuster drugs for the western world where patients and healthcare services had the money to afford them, Vagelos helped to develop a vaccine for the control of hepatitis B. A serious enough problem in the developed world, it is an even greater problem in Asia where money for drugs is not always available. The infection is carried in about 13 per cent of the Chinese population, can lead to liver cancer and is one of the leading causes of death in China. Merck, under Vagelos, developed a vaccine to prevent the infection. But Beijing complained that China couldn't afford it. The marketing people haggled with the Chinese government for a couple of years trying to come up with a fair price and, when it didn't happen, there was a real risk that Merck would walk away.

Without Vagelos, it might have.

Certainly Big Pharma has never been shy about doing that. But Vagelos saw another way. He committed the company to help the Chinese build two manufacturing plants so they could make their own vaccine. Beijing paid a very low price for the licence, which Merck then spent on the technology transfer.

'It took over a year to get them ready. We had Chinese people working with us to learn how to do it. We built the process in one of our manufacturing plants, took it apart, shipped it to China and rebuilt it there. Today those two plants in China have the capacity to immunize 20 million infants per year, which is essentially the birth cohort there. Eventually that disease will disappear in China.'

Vagelos also swam against the tide on drug pricing. In 1985, the year he became Chairman and CEO of Merck, the industry was in the midst of steeply rising prices, trying to catch up with steeply rising inflation rates. 'I don't like to see people not getting drugs or feeling that pharmaceutical prices are too high, so I asked the financial people to show me how much we had lost to inflation and what we'd made back by the increases in our prices. When we extrapolated, we found a point where we'd have caught up. I said, once we've done that and once we've established a fair price for our products, we should not raise our prices faster than the increase in the consumer price index for the inflation rate. We made that Merck policy. And it had a remarkable effect on the industry. Although, I must confess, there was a fair amount of grumbling because we were the market leaders and we clearly enunciated our policy.'

The rest of the industry was slow to follow – annual hikes were in the 10–12 per cent range – and for a while it looked as if government might step in with price controls. By 1991 Vagelos was openly criticizing his competitors. 'I detest regulation,' he said at the time, 'but it may be brought about by my colleagues. Drug prices are such an obvious target.'

The Clinton administration took aim at drug prices, and even questioned Merck's figures. Whereas aggregate price rises had been low, the price increases of certain popular drugs were much steeper. In response, Vagelos instituted even more stringent voluntary controls.

His plan was to limit increases on any single product to 1 per cent above the inflation rate, to allow independent auditors to monitor this, and to impose penalties for violations. The fines would go into a government fund to improve healthcare. He calculated that, if every company in the industry signed up to the programme, consumers would save $7–9 billion (£4.5–5.8 billion) over a three-year period.

Big Pharma responded publicly with every reason under the sun why this should never happen, and privately called for Vagelos' scalp. It was only under pressure from the Clinton administration that other companies reluctantly, but eventually, agreed to join.

Unfortunately, albeit to the great relief of most other Big Pharma CEOs, the Merck plan fizzled out. These days the industry is back to the usual excuses – how research and production costs must be factored into the price of a drug, along with how much money the drug saves by keeping patients alive and out of the hospital and, also, what price the market will bear. It all brings Vagelos to the admission that 'prices have gotten out of hand again'.

But then, the independence he brought to his job at Merck and all the battles he won there pale by comparison with what happened in 1981, when a physician walked into his office and told him about the blackfly.

Neither Wall nor Wani understood how Taxol worked – at the time, no one did – but it was obvious to them that this was something very special and needed to be studied further. Unfortunately, several problems got in the way, not the least of which was the scarcity of the substance. It was so scarce that, years later when the major pharmaceutical companies considered using it to make a drug, they found out that it required an entire tree simply to supply one patient with one dose.

But Wall was determined. Having seen the structure of it and being so firmly convinced of its promise, he spent the next four years trying to convince the NCI to make a large-scale collection.

'I desperately wanted them to do more work in the lab and then go into clinical testing. But they chose not to do so at the time. They gave me every excuse in the book. They said it was expensive. They said the yield would be low. No matter what I said, they had more excuses. I tried desperately hard to get them to move faster but I was unsuccessful.'

At least it looked that way, until 1978.

The government had, by then, spent $270,000 (£175,500) on Taxol, for which it had the structure of the molecule but little else. Whether it was to protect that initial investment, which is not usually the way the government thinks, or because the people who believed in Wall were now senior enough to do something about it – and that is the more likely of the possibilities – the NCI picked up the project again, and funded it for the next step.

Dr Susan Horwitz is a biochemist at Albert Einstein College of Medicine in New York. Her expert work on small molecules had attracted the NCI's attention and they now wondered if she would be interested in taking a look at this one. After seeing the structure of the molecule as Wall had described it, she agreed to do a detailed study. Horwitz was the one who discovered the particular mechanism in Taxol that prevents a cell from dividing.

What happens is that microtubules, which are fibrelike structures, sort of like cables inside the cells, pull the cell apart when it divides. As the process begins, these microtubules build up. At the end of the process, they normally break down. What the mechanism does is prevent the microtubules from breaking down, in turn clogging those cells with microtubules, stopping them from growing and, in turn, preventing them from dividing.

This was something never before seen in any other anti-tumour drug, which meant that science suddenly had a new class of chemotherapeutic agent to work with.

Based on Horwitz's results, the NCI's interest was sufficiently renewed to ask for a larger sample and to begin the tests that Wall had always hoped for. Phase I clinical testing with Taxol began in 1983. Some of the initial results showed promise, but not all of them did and the picture became confused. Then allergic reactions to the solvent in the formula stopped some trials and delayed others. Questions were now raised about the rationale for further funding. But the doubters were in the minority and more money was put into the project.

The NIH contracted with a company called Hauser Chemicals to collect yew tree bark and manufacture Taxol so that there would be enough for Phase II trials.

In November 1988, with Taxol now being used in experiments on refractory ovarian cancers, the head of the Cancer Therapy Evaluation Program at the National Cancer Institute left the government to become Senior Vice President for Cancer Research at Bristol-Myers.

Three months later, encouraging clinical results were reported and published by Johns Hopkins University. They claimed Taxol had produced a 30 per cent response rate in patients with advanced ovarian cancer.

Encouraged by that, in August 1989 – with the US taxpayer having funded over $9 million (£5.8 million) worth of research in Taxol – the NIH decided to shop around for a company that could take this drug to market. A notice was published in the US Federal Register giving any interested concern a month to respond.

Mohammad Aziz was a Pakistan-born infectious disease specialist who, before he came to Merck, had been with the World Health Organization (WHO) stationed in West Africa. At the time, Merck had a drug which was very potent in the control of certain parasites, but unfortunately it didn't work on the two most important human parasitic diseases, which happen to be tapeworm and hookworm. Instead, the drug was marketed to treat parasites in animals, especially heart worm in dogs.

It was popular with veterinarians, worked well and Vagelos had never given it a second thought. At least not until the day Aziz came to see him and mentioned the blackfly.

'Mohammad told me it was possible that this drug could work for river blindness. And I had to say to him, what's river blindness?'

Medically known as onchocerciasis, it's a disease caused

by a parasitic worm which can live and reproduce for up to fourteen years in the human body. Victims suffer constant itching, loss of skin colour, skin sores, premature ageing and eventual blindness.

The worm is transmitted to humans by the bite of the blackfly, which breeds in fast-flowing rivers. Very prevalent in West Africa, especially along the basin of the Volta River, blackflies spread the disease as much as 250–300 miles from where they breed, threatening around 80 million Africans a year.

Vagelos admits that when you're running the research department of a major pharmaceutical company in New Jersey – whose paramount market is the developed world – river blindness is not the sort of disease that most Big Pharma executives would spend a lot of time worrying about.

But, then, Vagelos was never like most Big Pharma executives.

'Mohammad told me about the disease and the parasite. He explained what had been done to try to eradicate the blackfly and told me how many people were at risk. He asked if he could take some of this drug we had and go to Africa. I said sure. Well, he went and he tried the drug on a very small number of patients and, sure enough, it had a remarkable effect. Six months later, after a single initial dose, the worms were gone.'

Without any hesitation, Vagelos ordered more testing. 'I saw no problem with that. It was the right thing to do.' And in so doing, he committed the company to a multi-million dollar investment. Six years later, when the studies were complete, Merck had a drug called Mectizan that successfully treated the disease.

But Mectizan's success seemed only to create additional headaches for Vagelos.

The marketing folk and the corporate accountants wanted to know how much the company would charge for it. And they weren't exactly overjoyed when Vagelos reminded them that the people who so desperately needed this drug lived in mud hats and couldn't possibly ever pay for it.

The word 'donation' was not one that certain factions inside the company wanted to hear. Philanthropy might make for good short-term public relations but, as the adage says, no good deed goes unpunished.

Vagelos heard from the legal staff that they had apprehensions about corporate exposure to liability if the drug caused unexpected adverse reactions.

He heard from his people dealing with Wall Street and shareholders that this might upset the investment community, who expected the company to be in the business of profits not charity.

He heard from his finance people, who felt this could set a precedent that would make Merck look terrible if it didn't give away other drugs to people who needed them.

And he heard from other Big Pharma CEOs, who complained that, if Merck made a habit of this, they might be expected to follow suit – to give away for free the products of their research into diseases of the developing world – which they really didn't want to do. They warned that one alternative, if Merck continued to put them in such an awkward position, was simply to stop doing the research.

But by this time Vagelos was running Merck and, as Chairman and CEO, he was not going to be challenged on this. 'Everyone knew where the disease was and that there was no money. So, yeah, a lot of people worried about it. I knew going in that there was no way those people in Africa could ever pay for this drug. But this was something so incredibly important to do that there was no way Merck was not going to do it.'

Needing around $20 million (£13 million) to help cover costs and distribution of the drug for the first year, his initial plan was to convince the World Health Organization to join forces with Merck. But WHO didn't want to know – a bizarre attitude, considering that many people believed this project was exactly what WHO was supposed to be doing and, moreover, now does.

Vagelos then went to some of the African governments where the illness was rampant, but they couldn't raise the money.

Next stop was Washington. Hat in hand, Vagelos easily lined up plenty of Congressional support and found loads of people in the government who said they were behind the project all the way. But when those people said, all the way, it didn't mean what Vagelos hoped it meant, which was all the way to the bank.

'We weren't asking for a lot of money. Everyone kept telling me, this is good and we need to do it. I met with Don Regan at the White House, he was Ronald Reagan's chief of staff, who said this was something we ought to do and that he wanted to do it. But as soon as we walked out of his office, the fellow I'd been in there with from the Agency for International Development said we'd love to do it but we have no money. I also went to the State Department and had exactly the same experience. The Deputy Secretary of State said he wanted to do it but as soon as I stepped out of his office, his guy said, yes we'd love to do it but we're broke. Can you imagine that?'

All these years later, he still finds it pitiful. 'The trouble with these bureaucrats is that they have their own priorities, their own agendas, their own opinions of what's important. Parasites in Africa was simply not very high on their list. But here was a chance to affect lives in a positive way and to plant the American flag for very little money. I tried to put that idea into their heads. I tried very hard. But they just didn't get it.'

Government laboratories and publicly funded institutions

throughout the world are always turning out ideas that could qualify as being 'for the advancement of the public good'. Transcending all the various disciplines, they can be especially potent when they touch on new technologies. And Big Pharma is always keeping an ear to the ground, just in case one of these ideas can be exploited as a blockbuster drug.

Believing that ideas 'for the advancement of the public good' should indeed be exploited, Congress passed the 1986 Federal Technology Transfer Act, which created Cooperative Research and Development Agreements (CRADAs). The thinking behind the agreements was sound. Here's a product that taxpayer money has researched and helped to develop, and, because the government has decided it is for the advancement of the public good, the public will turn over its rights to the idea to some private company to market it so that, in return, the public will benefit.

No strings attached.

The company has to pay for the manufacturing and marketing of the idea, and there may well be some additional development costs. But the bulk of the research and development has been paid for by the taxpayer and handed to the company as a gift. The only clause in the agreements that protects the public from monopolistic pricing is the company's promise to 'price it reasonably'.

No one in Congress seemed to think at the time that the taxpayer might be entitled to a royalty on sales of the item – some reasonable percentage that could be funnelled back through the government's coffers to fund future research – or that any company exploiting an idea could somehow confuse 'price it reasonably' for a licence to swindle the public.

Dr Sheldon Krimsky, an expert on corporate ethics at Tufts University in Boston, labels the process 'reverse capitalism'. 'The pharmaceutical companies justify themselves by saying that the public good is served by the very expensive product they produce. We say, what is your public value? We say, you not only used the research that is publicly funded, but you also get all kinds of benefits from government subsidies, etc. What do we get in return? They say, you get a very expensive drug. The way capitalism is supposed to work is that private risks generate private profits or private losses, and public risks should generate public profits, or public losses. In this case we have public risks generating private profits. That is, we take risks with public funds by putting money into research, and when the scientists get results, the company gets the intellectual property rights.'

The pharmaceutical industry often reminds critics that it funds 60 per cent of all healthcare R&D. What it doesn't appreciate is when that statistic is turned around the other way – to wit, the government funds 40 per cent of all healthcare R&D. At the same time, when it comes to government largess, every drug company on the planet sings off the same hymn sheet – public money is vitally important and must be encouraged. It is, they say, the essential groundwork on which the development of new drugs is built. Anything at all that might somehow discourage government from maintaining this partnership with Big Pharma, is incontestably detrimental to science.

Funny how they want to have it both ways.

Leading the chorus is the Pharmaceutical Research and Manufacturers Association, which never hesitates to take aim at anyone daring to suggest that drug prices are too high – 'We are a research-based industry and the costs of developing new drugs are very great' – or daring to suggest that Big Pharma might somehow be made more accountable when taxpayers' money is used – 'It would be harmful to erect deterrents to this public/private collaboration.'

Reading between the lines, what they really mean is – government funding is money in the bank for the industry, but just don't ask us to pay any of it back because, once the government stops writing cheques for research, we have to foot the rest of the bill, which makes us entitled to whatever profits we can reap on these drugs.

That taxpayers' money ought to earn money and that companies with successful products should reimburse the government is not what they want to hear.

A team of investigative reporters from the *Boston Globe* found that forty-five out of the fifty top-selling drugs in the world were discovered, developed and/or tested with the taxpayers' money.

One example they cited was $46 million (£29.9 million) spent by the taxpayer on the cancer drug Proleukin. Treatments with the drug reportedly cost up to $20,000 (£13,000). Another example is Abbott Laboratories' use of $3.2 million (£2 million) of government monies in the design and development of Norvir, a protease inhibitor which is used to slow the progression of AIDS. In the first six months of 1997, Abbott's Norvir sales topped $41 million (£26.65 million).

It has always been a sad reality of economic life that certain diseases afflict so few people that there's simply no money to be made by investing in a cure. Which is why, most of the time, Big Pharma doesn't bother. It is not, however, for the lack of trying. In 1983 Congress passed the Orphan Drug Act thanks to a big helping hand from actor Jack Klugman.

In 1980, at the behest of Congressman Henry Waxman, the House was holding a hearing on a young child with a rare disease who couldn't get treated because there was no treatment. A reporter covering the hearing wrote an article that Klugman's brother happened to read. It moved him enough to show it to Jack, who created an episode around it for his hit series *Quincy*. Viewers responded by writing to Klugman to ask how they could help. Klugman passed the letters on to Waxman. More hearings were held – Klugman's testimony at those hearings got the media's attention – and a second *Quincy* episode was done. This one was about a congressman trying to pass a bill to help rare disease sufferers.

By the time that show was broadcast, the Orphan Drug Act was in the works.

Most recently, an Orphan Drug Act has been passed in Europe.

What these acts do is create a series of incentives to encourage companies to develop drugs for rare conditions. Rare is defined as an illness that affects fewer than 200,000 persons, of which there are more than 5,000 such diseases. For their efforts, the government grants companies a seven-year exclusive marketing contract and lucrative tax incentives which, among other things, allow 50 per cent of the clinical trial costs to be taken as a credit against taxes owed.

The multiple sclerosis drug Copaxone had been developed by researchers in Israel who, with the help of collaborators in the USA, had received a grant of around $5 million (£3.25 million) from the NIH. When they licensed the drug to Teva Pharmaceutical Industries, an Israeli company, Teva turned to the FDA and, under the Orphan Drug Program – which further subsidizes the development of treatments for rare diseases – it picked up $300,000 (£195,000) in grants, the usual tax breaks plus that seven-year marketing monopoly. But Teva priced a year's treatment at around $10,000 (£6,500) and the company's first-year returns in the USA alone were reported to be $50 million (£32.5 million). It's not quite the way government philanthropy and the Orphan Drug Act are supposed to work. A Teva executive has been quoted as saying that the company might be willing to reimburse the government for grants in the future, but this time the money had no strings attached.

In some of these deals there are royalty schedules attached to government funding, but they are not aggressively administered. It's almost as if no one really wants to upset the industry by asking for the rent because the industry has got everyone believing that, metaphorically, if you press it for the rent it'll pack up and move.

The *Boston Globe*'s reporters estimated that, for every $1 billion (£650 million) spent by the government, royalty returns had amounted to a paltry $27 million (£17.5 million). However, the government really surpassed itself – and set a precedent – with the very first CRADA, which was the marketing agreement for Taxol.

When the NCI invited pharmaceutical companies to develop the drug, twenty firms were interested enough to look into the possibility. But only four applied. And when three of the four dropped out – a common complaint was that the minuscule supply of the compound severely hindered development of the drug – the winner was Bristol-Myers Squibb (BMS).

In subsequent statements, BMS has claimed that it was really taking a huge gamble to join the CRADA, insisting that success was never guaranteed and that the supply and purity problems could prove to be insurmountable. Yet, within two years of signing the agreement, BMS had solved those problems, obtained initial marketing clearance from the FDA and was producing enough Taxol to supply patients in the States.

It got around the supply problem by discovering that some of the compound could be isolated from the leaves. When it found the same tree growing in India, this further assured supply. While this was going on, the NIH had been funding a project at Florida State University (FSU) to reproduce the molecule semi-synthetically. Over a twelve-year period, Dr Robert Holton, a professor of organic chemistry, received a total of $2.3 million (£1.49 million) for the work. The university licensed the method to the BMS, which pays FSU every year. Royalties have now surpassed $125 million (£81.2 million). Holton personally receives a 40 per cent share.

Once the FDA approval came through in 1992, BMS announced that the wholesale price of Taxol would be $4.87 (£3.16) per milligram, which was more than ten times the price the NIH was paying Hauser Chemicals for Taxol, and twenty times the amount that BMS was paying Hauser for bulk Taxol. Today, the price of bulk Taxol is half what it was then – about $0.125 (8p) per milligram – while the cost of packaging and final preparation for distribution to doctors is about $0.15 (9.7p) per milligram. That leaves an unexplainably large margin, considering that the cost to the patient is around $8.61 (£5.60) per milligram.

When a Dutch firm began conducting its own Taxol trials in the European Union, BMS decided that litigation would cost too much to keep it out of the market, so it bought the company.

When Congress wouldn't accede to a BMS request to block generic competition in 1997 by extending the company's exclusive rights to the taxpayer-funded data on Taxol from five to ten years – despite offering to pay the government a 3 per cent royalty for the privilege – BMS first claimed that generic competition would infringe one of the patents taken out to protect the methods of administering the drug, and then returned to the public feedbox and got Taxol declared an Orphan Drug for the treatment of AIDS-related Kaposi's sarcoma. That special status gave BMS extra funding, tax breaks and the additional exclusivity it had asked for. This, despite an apparent earlier promise not to use Orphan Drug status for Taxol.

Since then, BMS has used what political pull it has in Washington to fight generic Taxol coming onto markets in the EU, Canada, Australia, New Zealand, Indonesia, Pakistan, Taiwan, China, Thailand, South Africa, Argentina and Turkey. The basis of its objections is the World Trade Organization provisions on intellectual property, which protect undisclosed information – the same taxpayer-funded data that BMS claims is exclusively theirs.

It is true that, early on, BMS supplied the NIH with 17 tons of Taxol – bought from Hauser for around $5 million (£3.25 million) – and eventually negotiated a deal with the government to extend the monopoly on the drug in exchange for a $3.4 million (£2.2 million) payment to the NIH. But the company continues to defend its pricing of Taxol by asserting that it has had to commit huge sums to secure future supplies of the drug. On closer inspection, a watchdog agency in Washington revealed that this commitment consists primarily of long-term contracts with companies such as Hauser and has nothing at all to do with the research and development of the drug.

To give the company its due, it now offers the drug for free to women who can't afford it or are uninsured. But 'free Taxol' isn't listed in the Yellow Pages. And many people who can't afford it, and don't know how to get it from BMS for free, wind up going without.

Faced with the predicament that, if Merck didn't donate Mectizan to the people of Africa, it wasn't going to be used, Vagelos took the decision that Merck would make the drug available to anyone who needed it and for as long as it was needed.

As far as Vagelos can see, Merck is still dedicated to doing that. 'Once the decision was made, we did what we had to do. A year later, 100,000 people were treated.'

Just before he retired, Vagelos went to see how the drug was working. In early 1994 he and his wife visited Africa with former President Jimmy Carter and his wife, Rosalynn.

'We went in by big plane, then further in by little plane, then further in still by Land-Rover and finally we walked until we got to a village. These people are dirt poor, they live in mud huts, they have barely enough to eat. And in a population like that, 20 per cent of the adults might be blind. It's devastating. I saw young people, 17, 18 years old, completely blind.'

Although Mectizan hasn't yet eradicated the disease, he thinks it will. 'If you go into a region and give one tablet to all the population, then the blackflies no longer have a source of the infectious parasite, so that whole area becomes free until flies come in from elsewhere. Once the whole population in the endemic area is treated by drugs, the flies will have no source and the disease will disappear. That's on track, but it might take another ten years of treatment.'

The key to that is the partners who, as it became more and more obvious that it was going to be a success, happily jumped on the bandwagon. The World Health Organization came along to deliver the drug to the bush and to administer it, and the World Bank came along to commit over $100 million (£65 million) in funding. Merck's success even shamed a few other companies into programmes of their own. Dupont developed a small piece of fabric that's used in Africa and Latin America to filter water to stop guinea worm; SmithKline Beecham contributed a drug, albeit on a small scale, to control elephantiasis; Glaxo is providing some parts of the Third World with a new anti-malaria drug; and Pfizer put together a programme to control trachoma, another eye disease.

'They've all referenced Merck's programme,' Vagelos says with unabashed pride. 'But they'd never say that they patterned their actions on ours. They wouldn't want to admit that. When, in fact, they did.'

It was 1999.

Depending on whose accounting you use, American taxpayers had shelled out somewhere between $12 million and $35 million (£7.8–22.7 million) funding biological cell screening, chemical purification, isolation and identification of the molecule, dosage formulation, toxicology, filing the new drug application and sponsoring clinical studies, so that Bristol-Myers Squibb could commercially exploit Taxol 'for the advancement of the public good'.

At the University of Pennsylvania, the senior who dreamed of being a doctor fifty years earlier returned to dedicate the Roy and Diana Vagelos Laboratories of the Institute for Advanced Science and Technology.

The fair pricing clause in the CRADA that Bristol-Myers Squibb once signed still reads: 'NCI has a concern that there be a reasonable relationship between the pricing of Taxol, the public investment in Taxol research and development, and the health and safety needs of the public. Bristol-Myers Squibb acknowledges that concern, and agrees that these factors will be taken into account in establishing a fair market price for Taxol.'

In Africa, the total number of people who had received Mectizan from Merck, and been saved from river blindness, surpassed the 25 million.

In 1999, worldwide, Bristol-Myers Squibb sold $1.5 billion (£975 million) worth of Taxol.

CHAPTER SEVEN

Secret Science

You can talk about caveat emptor, buyer beware, but patients are emptors that can't caveat.

(Dr Drummond Rennie)

The woman, who happened to be in her late sixties, had gone to see her physician for an annual check-up and, in the course of what was normal routine for a patient her age, the doctor recommended she have a colonoscopy. She was sent to a specialist who, when the results were in, phoned asking to see her again. Believing that if everything was okay he would have said so, she nervously returned to his office. He assured her there was nothing to worry about, but added that he wanted to treat her with a new drug.

She instantly asked why.

He said he wasn't going to bring up the subject of colon cancer . . .

Now she panicked.

No, he said, colon cancer was not the problem.

But every time she asked what the problem was, it was as if he didn't want to tell her. All he'd say was that he wanted her to take a series of drugs and to return for another examination in a few months' time.

Instead, she raced back to her own GP and related the story to him. Her GP looked into the matter and, when he discovered what was happening, he ripped up her prescription, persuaded her that she did not have colon cancer or, in fact, any problem whatsoever, and swore he would never again refer a patient to that specialist.

It turned out that the specialist had been hired by a drug company to run trials on a new treatment and was being paid on a per patient basis for recruiting people to take part in that trial. His behaviour was totally unethical and his failure to inform his patient that he was working for a drug company was in direct violation of the drug company's own rules.

This is said to be the cardinal sin of medical research. But the patient has not reported him to any regulatory authority, nor has her GP. And the specialist is still recruiting patients for the drug company.

Conflicts of interest and secrets permeate Big Pharma's relationship with medical research. Some are less dangerous than others but, when patient health is involved, even those less dangerous conflicts and secrets can have serious ramifications.

Full disclosure is not the norm. Because drug companies are paying for the tests to exhibit the efficacy of their drug, they are hands-on when it comes to the design of the tests. Knowing the results that will suit them best, it's easy then for a clever designer to stack the deck.

Testing a drug in a young patient population may result in fewer side-effects. That's what a company developing a non-steroidal anti-inflammatory drug (NSAID) – to treat osteoarthritis – found when it tested a young patient population, despite the fact that the drug would be used most often by elderly patients.

Comparing the drug being tested with a placebo does not always produce better results, but it's sometimes a better bet than comparing it with a competing drug already on the market. Unless, of course, dosages are different. Again, the company testing the NSAID found that, when its drug at full dose was compared with a competitor at less than recommended dose, the results came in on the desired side of the equation.

Researchers can also stack the deck by mixing delivery systems. Orally administered drugs cannot usually be compared with drugs administered intravenously, except when the company sponsoring the drug needs to find a better result.

On those occasions when results haven't gone the drug company's way, results are buried. If there is any sort of confusion about what the tests have shown, it's easy to find people with serious credentials to interpret those results in a favourable way.

A few years ago, some academics looked at 151 published studies of NSAIDs. In 149 of them, they found that the drug being tested was compared with equally or more expensive NSAIDs. Only two studies bothered to compare their drug with a much less expensive, and otherwise risk-free analgesic, such as aspirin. That was done so that the drug being tested could be shown to be more effective than a competing NSAID, which would give the company a selling point. If it had turned out to be no better than aspirin, nobody would bother paying for it.

'I always talk about the gold standard and we're nowhere near it,' says Dr Sheldon Krimsky of Tufts University. 'For the pharmaceutical industry, it would be something like the following. A company wants to have a drug tested for efficacy and safety. They would be required to put a certain amount of money down to pay for these tests at some sort of National Institute of Drug Testing. The tests would be assigned a crew in the Institute and the results would be available to anyone in the scientific community. The company could use the results to get the drug through the FDA or to promote it, whatever they want. But there would be a distant relationship between the company paying for the test and the data. It would all be carried out independently. No one who works at this Institute could have any direct equity in any of these companies. That would be the gold standard. Anyone I've suggested this to says it's ridiculous, they don't want the government involved in this.'

Or, for that matter, any organization that would be totally independent.

A second study of clinical trials on NSAIDs looked at fifty-six tests in which the sponsoring company's drug was compared directly with a competing NSAID. In every single case, the sponsoring company's drug came out equal to or better than the drug used in the comparison.

'You can talk about caveat emptor, buyer beware,' wrote Dr Drummond Rennie, West Coast editor of the *Journal of the American Medical Association* and one of the most prestigiously vocal people in the profession when it comes to identifying and condemning conflicts of interest and secrecy, 'but patients are emptors that can't caveat because they don't know how. When you are a patient, it's not like buying a Toyota. Patients don't know how to choose their own anaesthetic.'

We all, therefore, depend on our doctors and other people with scientific degrees to protect us from what could easily turn into a personal disaster. After all, we put our health in their hands. And yet there is no shortage of people willing to take drug company money and, in some cases, to do so at the expense of our health.

In 1984, the *New England Journal of Medicine* (*NEJM*) became the first of the major professional publications to formulate a workable policy on conflicts of interest and secrecy between authors of original research and the private sector. Financial agreements were nothing new, but the *NEJM* felt they were becoming sufficiently widespread that readers needed to know who was paying whom. So it ruled that authors must disclose any arrangements they might have with the products or companies they were writing about. The journal next decided that anyone writing in an editorial capacity, such as a peer review, should have no direct financial ties with anyone, any product or any company named in the article.

It worked in theory, but in reality required everyone to be honest enough always to disclose interests that, in many cases, those same people wanted to keep secret. When the *Los Angeles Times* decided to put the policy to the test, it looked at thirty-six drug therapy articles published in the *NEJM* between 1997 and 1999 and found eight that had been written by researchers who had not disclosed their financial links to drug companies. Within a year, the *NEJM* was embarrassed again and forced to admit that it had violated its own conflict of interest policy by publishing nineteen drug reviews written by researchers who did not disclose financial links with the companies making those same drugs.

It was almost as if full disclosure never stood a chance, not just at the *NEJM* but throughout the scientific community. Industry links have grown more and more important to research, so much so that, by the time the *NEJM* published its May 2000 issue, the financial ties between the authors and the companies discussed in one article were so extensive the journal simply had to amend its own policy for the sake of space and merely summarize those connections. Full disclosure was available on its website, but you had to have access to the website, and then go to the trouble of sifting through it.

Without even suggesting that there is anything untoward or unethical about these authors and their associations, the sheer weight of the list is worth noting. Financial associations included support from Bristol-Myers Squibb, consultancy work, research grants and/or honorariums from Pfizer, Bristol-Myers Squibb, Forest Laboratories/Parke-Davis, Wyeth-Ayerst, Merck, Janssen, Eli Lilly, Pharmacia & Upjohn, SmithKline Beecham,

Glaxo Wellcome, Abbott, AstraZeneca, Neurocrine Biosciences, Organon, Otsuka, Lipha Pharmaceuticals, Johnson & Johnson, Mead Johnson, Hoechst Marion Roussel, Shire, Sanofi Research, Scios, Biovail, TAP Pharmaceuticals, Mitsubishi Pharmaceuticals, Scirex, Solvay and Quintiles. Some authors also held advisory board appointments with Wyeth-Ayerst, Pfizer, Bristol-Myers Squibb, Eli Lilly, Parke-Davis, Organon, SmithKline Beecham, Merck, Janssen, Mitsubishi Pharmaceuticals, Zeneca, Scirex and Otsuka. Others revealed shareholdings in Pfizer, Forest Laboratories, Warner-Lambert and Eli Lilly.

When Dr Allan Detsky of the University of Toronto tried to establish who'd been saying what about calcium-channel blockers – a class of drugs used by millions of people for angina and hypertension – he looked at seventy articles published between March 1995 and September 1996. He divided the judgements made on calcium-channel blockers into three categories: critical, neutral or supportive. He and his staff then sent a questionnaire to eighty authors listed on those papers asking what sort of financial support they might or might not have received from the drug industry. Detsky also asked forty drug companies what their support had been. It turned out that a startling 96 per cent of the authors who wrote favourably about calcium-channel blockers had some sort of financial relationship with the drug company manufacturing the specific calcium-channel blocker being discussed, and that in only two of the articles did the authors divulge their financial ties with drug companies.

Detsky was careful to say that the results of his study did not necessarily mean the views of those researchers had been in any way altered by their relationship with the industry. But he did add, 'That doesn't mean that there couldn't be an unconscious bias.'

When the *British Medical Journal* (*BMJ*) carried an article saying that anti-depressants such as Prozac are not addictive, it turned out that the doctors who'd written the article had once been flown to Arizona as the guests of Eli Lilly, the company manufacturing Prozac. This is not to say there was actual bias, but it is hardly the most suitable of relationships.

And when the UK Committee on Publication Ethics (COPE), a group funded by several medical journals, decided to look at medical research in Britain, it concluded that 'research fraud' was more prevalent than anyone had previously recognized. The reasons it listed were increased pressures on scientists to publish and financial incentives for research.

The *BMJ* too asks authors to declare any competing interests. It also asks authors to declare non-financial interests – personal, academic, religious, moral, political, whatever – but doesn't necessarily publish those interests.

'Our policy is that you cannot get rid of competing interests,' explains Dr Gavin Yamey, an editor at the *BMJ*. 'Every person in the world has competing interests and we on the staff have declared all of ours. That's on the website. We disclose the various charities we're involved with and our political affiliations, that sort of thing. We want to give the readers enough information to make up their own minds as to whether competing interests affect what we publish.'

The *BMJ* receives around 5,000 articles every year for possible publication but accepts only about 15 per cent of them. The basic criteria are: it must be original; it must be important; the methods must be sound; it must be relevant to its readers. If a paper meets those four requirements, it's considered. If it's accepted, it is then sent out for peer review – a detailed critique by a recognized expert. If the peer reviewer thinks it's important and correct, the article goes to another committee where further decisions are made.

At each step along the way, everyone involved is asked to reveal any interests that might somehow influence an opinion. 'But we don't believe in censorship,' Yamey continues. 'We don't believe that's in the interest of science, truth and democracy. If someone has done some research and that research is rigorous, important, sound and relevant, we believe readers should make up their own minds given the author's interests.'

In 1996, Sheldon Krimsky at Tufts wondered how many journal article authors had a personal financial interest in the outcome of the study they were writing about. It took him two years to sort through fourteen of the leading bio-medical journals, to choose nearly 800 articles and to query some 1,100 lead authors.

He discovered that in 34 per cent of the articles – 267 in total – the authors held a patent related to the inventions they were writing about, or were employees or stockholders of a biotech company exploiting the research, or were members of scientific advisory boards of a drug company involved with the research, or held some other financial interest in the outcome. And not one of those 267 papers mentioned authors' financial interests.

'You'd be surprised', Krimsky says, 'how many doctors don't know how to make a critical judgement when journal articles look respectable. You'd be amazed at how many of them don't even know the difference between a peer reviewed and non-peer reviewed journal. Or where to go to find the difference. There are tens of thousands of journals out there. We had one expert come in recently on a case, a leading expert in his field, and when we showed him citations from journals that claimed to be authorities in his field, he'd never heard of five of them. These things can be very easily masqueraded.'

Krimsky wrote *Hormonal Chaos*, a book about how a small group of scientists came to link some synthetic chemicals to over a dozen human and animal abnormalities and how, when public safety is involved, industry rushes to defend its turf. In his book, he quotes a scientist whom he describes as 'very credible' about an incident in which the Dow Chemical Company sent a toxicologist to the scientist's laboratory asking him not to publish a result, and hinting that, if he obliged, it might be mutually beneficial. True to industry form, Krimsky soon received a letter from Dow objecting to the story. Krimsky was appalled and fired a letter back to Dow standing by his version of the event. A few weeks later, he received a journal in the mail dedicated to the very chemical that the scientist in Krimsky's story had questioned.

'An industry group published it. It looks like a journal and has articles in it, abstracts, literature and nice drawings. But they invented it. They created their own science to talk about how safe this compound is.'

It's so very dangerous, Krimsky notes, because people fall for it, and the reason they fall for it is because the companies themselves purposely make it hard to tell what's real and what isn't.

'Non-peer reviewed journals and industry-supported journals are everywhere. You also find peer reviewed journals that are industry supported. That makes it even more complicated. The industry goes out and gets their own peers. The independence of science is at stake here. It's about, who do you trust. In pharmaceutical studies, that's increasingly a problem. We're looking at direct marketing people, at more and more industry conglomerates that have more and more money, and at academic departments that are more beholden to companies than ever before. We're looking at for-profit clinical trials, which change the whole nature of the game.'

Contract research organizations (CROs), which are commercial businesses set up specifically to handle clinical testing for drug companies, have sprung up everywhere. Many of them are well qualified to do whatever it is they're asked to do. But critics are fast to point out that some of them take on work they're not qualified to do – after all, these are commercial enterprises – while others are perhaps too willing to give the drug companies the results they're looking for because, in business, you keep customers by satisfying customers.

Here, the possibility of conflicts of interest aren't even couched in polite terms. What happens, critics ask, when one of these research companies for hire finds something wrong with the drug it's testing? Is it being paid by Big Pharma to tell the truth or is it being paid to get results? Big Pharma would say, right away, we need to be told the truth, but the anecdotal evidence suggests that they may not always get it or, for that matter, sincerely want it.

Doctors conducting research for profit and seeing an experimental drug failing may be tempted to take their patients off the drug and put them on something they know works, thus distorting the testing process. Or they may be tempted to leave their patients on the drug, regardless of the risk. Or they may think, we'll tell the drug company what's happening and then it's up to the drug company whether or not it's going to tell the regulators, meaning it's no longer the doctor's problem. Or they may do whatever they have to do to give the drug company the results it's hoping to get, which might ensure that the for-profit research company will get a contract to test the next drug.

Academic institutions generally have review boards which, at least in principle, operate at arm's length to ensure patient safety. Most CROs also have oversight procedures, but many do not have sufficient independence, and, according to a White House Advisory Commission on National Bioethics, 'significant revision' is called for.

Not that everything is perfect in the world of academic research, either. Pharmaceutical companies speak of universities as 'partners'. But not all partners are created equal. The partner with the chequebook gets to talk the loudest.

A researcher in the States writes a proposal and begins hunting for grant money. Let's say she goes to the government or some public body and, for the sake of argument, the grant is a small one, $100,000 (£65,000). The university where the researcher works has 'an institutional overhead rate', which can be as much as 50 per cent. That means, in this case, the university gets $50,000 (£32,500) for keeping the lights on, paying the janitor, that sort of thing.

Now take the same researcher who goes to Big Pharma and is paid on a per patient basis. Say that figure is $3,500 (£2,275), although the more important the study the higher the capitation fee. In this case, the researcher's costs may be $1,500, meaning that she's going to clear $2,000 per patient. Out of that, instead of an overhead rate, she pays the university a small piece of the fee, usually 15 per cent.

This is a typical example of how public funds can subsidize industry research.

Until 1988, British universities were not allowed to exploit the intellectual property they generated. Instead, money was funnelled into a central government agency called the British Technology Group (BTG). At least it was until BTG failed to patent the work of some Cambridge scientists, Cesar Milstein, Georges Köhler and Niels Jerne, who'd published a study in *Nature* magazine called 'Continuous Cultures of Fused Cells Secreting Antibody of Predefined Specificity'. Apparently, no one at BTG saw any commercial use for what the scientists described, which turned out to be the production of 'monoclonal antibodies', for which the three were awarded the Nobel Prize in 1984.

Margaret Thatcher privatized BTG and allowed universities to exploit their own intellectual property. As a result, research contracts, including those for drug trials, are almost always negotiated by the university looking to incorporate milestone payments, royalties downstream, overhead fees on direct costs – 50 per cent is a ball park figure – and, at times, capitation fees that are comparable to those in the States.

In almost all cases, if the university receives royalty income, inventors get a share, the department hosting the inventor gets a share and the university gets a share. Oxford, for example, has been particularly successful in taking technology developed there and spinning it off into companies in which the academics responsible often have a stake. It's slightly different at Cambridge where faculty can elect to do research privately or funnel it through the university. The 1977 Patents Act in Britain stipulates that the rights to an invention belong to an inventor unless he or she is employed, and then the rights belong to the employer. At Cambridge they have made provisions which, in certain circumstances, permit scientists employed there to own patents on their own intellectual property.

The picture becomes slightly more complicated when you factor in the NHS. Traditionally, the NHS focuses on healthcare provision and universities undertake research and teaching. But teaching hospitals are considered partnerships between the university and the NHS and there is an overlap of functions. There is also, where research is concerned, an overlap of staff. People can and do move back and forth between the two cultures. Just like the universities, the NHS operates research grant offices. For the most part, doctors working inside an NHS hospital are employees and, therefore, are not automatically entitled to payment for work on a drug trial. However, general practitioners – whether they're working in the NHS structure or practise private medicine – are technically considered self-employed and are permitted to contract with drug companies for research.

The UK General Medical Council (GMC) dictates strict rules. Among them, trials must not be contrary to patient benefit, each patient enrolled must give written consent, and there must be a properly established system of oversight in place to govern the trial. Where an NHS-affiliated doctor is involved, it's the NHS that provides oversight through research ethics committees. It is slightly more problematical when a private doctor is involved, simply because the oversight there is often provided by the pharmaceutical company's own research ethics committee.

It must be pointed out that, where drug trials are concerned, Big Pharma does not have a sense of humour as regards doctors who in any way provide fraudulent results.

Geoffrey Fairhurst practised general medicine in St Helens, Merseyside, where he was also a member of a local medical research ethics committee. Over the five-year period 1988–93, he conducted clinical trials on anti-hypertensives for three different manufacturers, who paid him up to £900 per patient. In at least one of the tests, he was also reportedly paid £15,000.

Following the death of one of his patients, unrelated to the trials, a doctor sharing the surgery with him found out that patients had been enrolled in these trials without informed consent. He reported this to the GMC. An investigation followed, accusing Fairhurst of forging patients' consent forms, prescribing drugs without their knowing it was part of a trial and falsifying reports. No suggestion was ever made that drug companies were in any way involved in Fairhurst's behaviour and, in fact, all three cooperated fully with the GMC's investigation. Fairhurst was struck off in 1996 for professional misconduct and is not permitted to practise medicine in the UK.

It was much the same with John Anderton, a former secretary of the Royal College of Physicians in Edinburgh. He was discovered running a sham drug trial and struck off in 1997. Again, the drug company which had contracted Anderton was not in any way involved with his behaviour.

'There are around 3,000 clinical trials being run in the UK at any given time,' says Dr Frank Wells, a former Director of Medical Affairs for the Association of the British Pharmaceutical Industry (ABPI). He and his partner, retired detective chief inspector Peter Jay of Scotland Yard, run MedicoLegal Investigations, a private agency that specializes in medical fraud. 'We have around thirty cases that we're investigating at any given time. So, although it's hard to tell how much medical fraud there is in clinical trials, we use the figure of 1 per cent.'

Almost all of the cases involve doctors who have misbehaved. 'There are very strict controls in place in this country for doctors in clinical trials. Research ethics boards approve protocols to the extent that they even approve the fees doctors receive. More and more, the boards are insisting, for example, that there is some mention on the consent forms that patients must sign that even says the doctor involved with the trial is being paid. It's much stricter here than it is, say, in the United States. It's also a smaller country and easier to investigate. But there is still fraud.'

He says the Fairhurst and Anderton cases are fairly typical of what happens. But he's very quick to add that none of the cases investigated by MedicoLegal has ever revealed a major pharmaceutical company involved with clinical fraud. 'There is an absolute commitment to integrity by the pharmaceutical industry in Britain.'

However, the extent to which industry can bias research is hotly debated. Many researchers with financial ties to industry are adamant that those associations could not and do not affect their work. They insist that, as scientists, they can and do remain objective. Undoubtedly, many try. How well they succeed over the course of time and in the face of constant attempts to influence them is another matter. If they do succeed, then what's the chance of landing the next industry contract? After all, it's Big Pharma that hires the researchers and there is a growing body of evidence to suggest that drug companies know what they're getting for their money.

Or, at least, what they can expect for their money.

Commercial research is a business. In a perfect world, academic research is not supposed to be. 'Researchers with ties to drug companies are indeed more likely to report results that are favourable to the products of those companies than researchers without such ties,' wrote *NEJM* editor Dr Marcia Angell. 'That does not conclusively prove that researchers are influenced by their financial ties to industry. Conceivably, drug companies seek out researchers who happen to be getting positive results. But I believe bias is the most likely explanation, and in either case, it is clear that the more enthusiastic researchers are, the more assured they can be of industry funding.'

At the same time, physicians are freelancing.

The American College of Physicians and the American Society of Internal Medicine jointly reported that the number of private doctors conducting clinical trials nearly tripled during the 1990s. Clinical research has become a multi-billion dollar industry and doctors have been lining up to get their share of it. With drug companies offering $1,000–5,000 for each patient enrolled in a trial, there's no shortage of physicians willing to enrol patients.

Problems arise, the two professional bodies agree, when these stipends perhaps entice physicians unduly to influence their patients to enlist. In some cases, patients agreeing with their doctor's request to sign on to a trial don't have the medical conditions being studied. Occasionally, the doctors aren't right either. One recently reported case was of psychiatrists asked by a drug company to participate in a study on hormone replacement and on diabetes and to do Pap smears. Another was of asthma specialists dispensing experimental psychiatric drugs.

According to the *New York Times*, doctors who know the ins and outs of recruiting patients can earn as much as $500,000– 1 million (£325,000–650,000) a year from drug companies for their efforts.

'Patients expect you to be a dispassionate advocate for them,' notes Dr David Shimm, a member of the ethics committee at Porter Adventist Hospital in Denver and someone who has not been afraid to speak out loudly about the conflicts doctors face doing clinical research. 'Patients assume that you're making decisions in their best interest. They have no idea that if a doctor puts them on a clinical trial he may be making money for doing that. They don't even know to ask the question. The problem that I've often seen is patients run through a series of clinical trials that really have very little chance of bringing them any benefit. One short-term study for anti-depressants that I saw at the University of Arizona had a capitation payment of $42,000 (£27,300) per patient.'

David Shimm is among those doctors who feel that some colleagues doing drug company research for hire can sometimes forget that their primary responsibility must always be to their patient.

'The most egregious problems I've seen in terms of patient care are people who came to me in terrible pain with metastatic cancer. I asked, how long have you been hurting this bad? They said, perhaps six months. I asked, why didn't you come in sooner? They told me they came in when the pain started and their doctor put them on a bunch of experimental drugs. In other words, these people were being used in clinical trials until they ran out of options and only at that point was their primary problem being addressed.'

It is a prime example of how drug company money can distort a doctor's loyalty. Schimm recalls an American College of Clinical Oncology study some years ago that looked at the probability of a patient obtaining a complete response during a Phase I trial for a cancer drug. He says it was in the region of 1 in 1,700. 'Typically, partial responses are four or five times as common, so you figure the probability of a complete or partial response is perhaps 1 in 300–400. It's fine to try drugs on patients but only if you level with them. If you have somebody in a lot of pain and say to that person, there's a chance this might help you, what they're probably hearing is that there's a 50 per cent chance. Or maybe even a 10 per cent chance. But unless you tell them, they're not going to know it's less than a 1 in 100 chance.'

Patients must be told that they're taking part in a trial, and they must sign consent forms. That's required. What patients are not generally told is who's paying for the study, if the doctor has an equity position in that company, if the doctor is on the board of directors or an advisory board of that company, if the doctor is a paid consultant, if the doctor is receiving a capitation payment and, if so, how much that capitation payment is. The reason for not giving patients that information, Big Pharma knows, is because a lot of them will then have second thoughts about signing the consent forms.

Of course, trials have to take place in order for a drug to get regulatory approval. But Shimm insists it is the indisputable responsibility of everybody involved with the trial – physician and drug company alike – to make certain that the patient knows everything that's happening.

'It's a hard circle to square, to make sure that physicians' loyalties aren't going to be torn between the drug company and the patient. If a doctor tells a patient, I'm putting you on a Phase I study, he may say, you'll be contributing something in developing a new drug, but he's also got to say, this is basically a toxicity study and your chances of benefit are minimal. Unfortunately, all too often patients hear what they want to hear. When you tell somebody who's in a lot of pain there's a chance you'll be helped, they say, that's great, there's a chance. Well, yeah, there's a chance if I flap my arms I can fly to the moon, but it's not a very big chance.'

The corporate sector is dishing out the funds and the academic sector is taking them. Researchers receive grants, serve as consultants, are brought onto advisory boards and are included in company-sponsored speakers' bureaus. Academics share patent and royalty arrangements with drug companies and are hired to put their names on articles ghostwritten by the companies. Academics are invited to promote products and receive fees for attending company-sponsored symposia.

Most academic institutions have rules about these things, but they are particularly difficult to enforce, especially when the schools themselves maintain financial relationships with industry and are, often, dependent on corporate funding for major projects. Colleges and universities regularly enter into partnerships of all kinds with drug companies and not only allow, but actively encourage, the private sector to establish research facilities and programmes.

That process was greatly distorted in 1980 when the United States Senate passed the Bayh–Dole Act, allowing American institutions supported by federal grants to patent and license products developed in their labs and to allow those researchers to share in royalty payments.

The ramifications for institutions outside the USA have been momentous. As a result of Bayh–Dole, the biotech sector was born. As a result of Bayh–Dole, drug companies have been able to turn academia into subsidiaries. Prior to the act, American universities were issued with around 250 patents a year. These days, more than 200 colleges and universities are at work developing products, with patent awards now averaging 1,500 a year. One estimate suggests this has become a $33.5 billion (£21.7 billion) industry.

There is so much money in the pot, it hardly matters that the act doesn't cover anyone working at Oxford in England or McGill in Canada or the Pasteur Institute in Paris. The lure of sharing the bounty is such a magnet to researchers all over the world that it forces everyone else to compete. In this regard, American universities are way ahead of their Canadian and European counterparts. They have tapped into a vein of funding and are exploiting it mercilessly. For example, the entire plant pathology department at one of America's most prestigious universities is now under contract to a biotech company. Everyone in that department has signed on.

The reason it's not happening in Europe yet is because, traditionally, there's more distance between corporations and researchers. But traditions change and, if universities outside the States expect to compete, their options will come down to a simple either–or – either they too seek closer corporate bonds or they risk losing big name researchers to much wealthier US campuses.

'Universities are eager to share in the profits,' comments Sheldon Krimsky. 'There's so much competition for corporate money, that they're forgetting the traditional values of the university. They're willing to give up on things like openness and the sharing of information. Institutional conflicts of interest are not being addressed.'

He refers to it as 'the colonization of academia' and feels it is getting close to the point where the next step is the outright sponsorship of a university.

'I think we have really crossed some very important boundaries and the next stage is for an American corporation, a large corporation, simply to buy a private university. Imagine a large American corporation that wants to have as one of its sub-units a university. Would that be an outrage? Well, we're getting close.'

No institution is immune, not even the often-praised, ethically backboned Harvard.

For years, Harvard has maintained the strictest of conflict-of-interest policies, so forbidding that it was usually described as the model other universities should aspire to. Faculty members must disclose their financial interests in any business which has a relationship with the university and their job there, they are barred from spending more than 20 per cent of their time on outside work, they are not permitted to hold more than $20,000 (£13,000) worth of stock in any company funding research that involves them or their lab, and they are restricted in the fees and royalties they are permitted to receive from corporate benefactors.

Over the past couple of years, however, some administrators at the university began to think that perhaps the rules were too strict and that, to compete for entrepreneurial researchers with other top universities, it might be prudent to allow staff and faculty a little more leeway in their financial dealings with the private sector.

A meeting was proposed to discuss changes to the rules. The instant this proposal became public, academic outrage ensued. 'It's unthinkable', commented one professor, 'that while university and industry ties are creating more and more conflicts of interests in the sciences, here's Harvard deciding rather than raise the bar to lower it.'

The cry of 'Harvard sells out' became so earsplitting and so shook the administrators that the meeting was cancelled and the plan has, at least for the time being, been abandoned.

At Oxford, there is a conflict-of-interest policy that is described as 'reasonably tight'. But one senior administrator reports an 'increasing unease' with those academics who have close collaborations with industry. It is possibly unfounded, he adds, but he worries that one day something will happen to blow the whole system apart. He admits the university is looking at how this is policed so that conflicts of interest do not arise.

'We haven't got to the Harvard stage yet,' explains Dr Richard Liwicki, who heads Oxford's Research Services office. 'This whole area is something we're keeping under view. We're watching what's happening in America quite closely. It is an area of concern.'

At Cambridge, they rely more heavily on the collegiate system to keep people honest.

'There is a high-trust environment at Cambridge,' says Richard Jennings, who runs the Wolfson Industrial Liaison Office at that university's equivalent of a research grant office. 'We take a very pragmatic view and allow academics to receive money for research in which they have a financial interest, but at the same time remain very concerned with conflicts of interest. We believe that everything must be done in the open and still within the rules, which puts Cambridge above personal gain. It's a system that we find works well for us.'

Universities such as Oxford and Cambridge hold the official status of 'exempt charity', which requires them to demonstrate a public benefit. 'One of the ways the university does that', Liwicki notes, 'is by ensuring the publication of results. When industry funds research here, we make absolutely certain that the legal terms of the agreement allow for free publication of the work we do. There are secrecy clauses to the extent that a delay can be imposed to allow for patenting. But that's it. There are no other secrecy clauses.'

'Nor are there at Cambridge,' Jennings adds. 'We would not sign any sort of agreement that prohibited publication or disclosure, with the exception of a delay for patenting.'

The delay for patenting is important because, in Europe, a patent is awarded to the first inventor to disclose, as opposed to the States where it's awarded to the first person to invent.

Therein lies a substantial safeguard to science. Big Pharma's ability to rewrite, delay or bury academic research would make it the ultimate arbiter of truth. It's a world, Sheldon Krimsky insists, that must never be allowed to happen. 'The whole reason we have ethics is not to allow profits to dictate everything. They should dictate some things, and maybe a lot of things, but they should not dictate everything. That's why we have ethics and try to define ethical behaviour and put restraints on conflicts of interest.'

While the desire to maintain secrecy in science is understandable, many academics agree that it is rarely, if ever, justifiable. Corporations defend secrecy in science by claiming that misuse or leaking of proprietary information presents a real financial danger. What those corporations really mean is that, where the choice is truth or profits, coming down on the side of truth is not a given.

Dr Andrew Millar, who made headlines as a whistleblower when he was head of clinical trials at British Biotech, has seen the problem from two different viewpoints.

'When you're a relatively junior manager in a country operation of a large pharmaceutical company, you're very isolated from the board of directors. You don't actually realize why they're trying to suppress what are clearly problematic factors. All you can see is what the company is doing. And you think to yourself, it's not all that clever long term to cover things up or to plaster things over, because these problems are real. These problems are there all the time that the drug is being administered to patients.'

The conflict is easier to see, he claims, in a biotech company. 'You're in the same building as the board of directors. You're much more on top of the different factors. You start off with the same sense of puzzlement about what the company appears to be doing and what you see as the best thing to do. Then you start realizing they're doing what they're doing because the guys making those decisions are thinking about the share price. They're worried about what the City thinks, and about their own stock options.'

British Biotech was once a darling of the London Stock Exchange. There had even been talk of the company one day becoming the next Glaxo. Although the shares had been slipping for nearly a year, there were a few drugs in the pipeline in the mid-1990s that seemed to hold out some hope. That is, until Millar told the truth about some of those drugs.

In a series of meetings with a pharmaceutical analyst at Goldman Sachs, Millar admitted that he did not believe in the prospects of two key pipeline – Marimastat, which was a cancer treatment, and Zacutex, which was a treatment for acute pancreatitis.

The reason he spoke up, he says, is because he had to. 'Share prices have nothing to do with doctors treating patients for their diseases. I felt we were in the business of treating diseases.'

At Goldman Sachs they're in the business of valuing expectations and, based on what Millar had told them, their assessment of British Biotech sent the shares into a free fall. Millar was fired and sued by British Biotech for what it considered gross imprudence. He fought back and eventually won. And, despite the trouble and stress that came from telling the truth, he says he did not see this as an ethical dilemma.

'If patients are going to be misled or harmed, it's not a dilemma at all. It's very clear-cut what your responsibility is. I was forever telling the board that we need to remember our product, that doctors use drugs to treat patients, and that's what our market is. All boards of directors, I think, finish up being at significant risk of viewing their main market as the City and the shareholders.'

As academia becomes more savvy about gagging clauses, and institutions vet contracts to make sure they don't contain any, Big Pharma gets smarter. Contracts are written to hide those clauses, clearly stating that the researcher indeed has the right to publish, but somewhere much further on noting that the company owns all the data in the study.

It means, you're welcome to publish, but it's not going to be this study.

Big Pharma has even become more creative about the reasons.

At a recent meeting of the American Association for the Advancement of Science's Committee on Scientific Freedom and Responsibility, one of the featured speakers was a representative of the research industry. When he was asked about secrecy in science, he said there were several reasons information had to be suppressed, and listed as his top answer 'to sabotage the competition'. After all, he explained, when a company is spending millions of dollars looking for a solution to a problem, and the solution it's researching turns out to be ineffective, it's important to make sure that competitors also waste money heading down the same dead-end.

CHAPTER EIGHT

Nancy O. Talks Fast

*Her responsibility is to her patients and not to the bloody
company.*

(Sir David Weatherall, Oxford University)

Nancy O. talks fast.

'I published the paper in the *New England Journal of Medicine*
on August 13, 1998, and this was when the hospital was
expecting a huge donation from Apotex to the tune of £5
million, and the university was expecting one to the tune
of £12.5 million from Apotex, so unknown to us when we
raised this, the hospital was nervous as a kitten.'

With a backpack instead of a handbag, jeans, trainers and
curly blond hair offsetting her college girl looks, it's still
not easy to mistake her for what she really is – a force of
nature.

'Apotex went after me like a ten foot pole and said you'll be
sued, which was very lucky, I've never been luckier because
if they had been subtle, I mean, they said, you're going to be
sued if you tell anyone, and it's tape recorded.'

It's a neat trick trying to keep up with her because she talks
at the same speed as she thinks.

'So Leslie Stahl at *60 Minutes* says, well, but there's a transcript, and there's Barry Sherman on camera, right, and then they showed it and everyone who's watching with us starts cheering. I mean, come on, it's hard to beat a tape recording.'

Pharmaceutical companies can be bullies.

Universities can be cowards.

And long before Dr Nancy Olivieri discovered the hard way what happens when you find yourself squeezed between the two, there were Dr David Kern and Dr Betty Dong.

Kern is the former head of Occupational Medicine at Brown University in Providence, Rhode Island, and of the Occupational and Environmental Health Service at Memorial Hospital in Pawtucket, Rhode Island.

In 1994, an employee of Microfibers Inc., a textile manufacturer in Pawtucket, came down with symptomatic interstitial lung disease (ILD), a condition considered rare in young men. It was brought to Kern's attention and he asked the company if he could take some students of occupational medicine on a tour of the factory. The company agreed, but insisted that everyone in his group sign a confidentiality agreement, ostensibly to protect the company from industrial espionage and to safeguard trade secrets. Everyone in the group agreed. After all, this was a one-time visit under the auspices of medical student education.

Two years later, and completely unrelated to that visit, another Microfibers' employee was referred to Kern as a patient at Memorial Hospital, also suffering from ILD. Kern was now brought in as a consultant by the company to investigate the cause of the problem. He quickly uncovered ILD at other Microfibers' plants. The hospital had provided a formal consulting contract, which Microfibers never signed, although the company paid the hospital over $100,000 (£65,000) for Kern's consultation.

Kern now decided to present his findings at the Spring 1997 conference of the American Thoracic Society. Microfibers heard that and threatened to sue him and Memorial Hospital if he did. The company claimed that Kern's publication would be a violation of the confidentiality agreement he'd signed in 1994. Insisting that he had never signed a non-disclosure agreement relevant to the study, Kern published. One week later, the hospital announced it would not renew his contract. Because his university appointment was contingent on the hospital, the university also announced his contract would not be renewed.

A claim that the family owning Microfibers is a substantial contributor to and maintains connections with the hospital corporation was met with the company's published response, 'This is insulting.'

Support for Kern poured in from around the world. In a half-hearted face-saving exercise, the Dean of Medicine at the university assembled a Committee of Inquiry. Their conclusion was, 'The company's attempt to have the abstract withdrawn is not considered by the Committee to be an attempt to compromise the health of its employees but rather an effort to avoid bad publicity and to protect its economic position.'

Kern noted that, when he was invited by the company to consult on the illnesses, he handed Microfibers a copy of the operating principles that would govern his consultancy. Included was a clause saying, if necessary, he reserved the right to report his findings to the appropriate scientific and public health communities. In other words, if he found something that was a matter of public health, he would take the necessary steps to protect public health. Since then, Kern has claimed that a dozen lawyers and legal scholars have checked the company's confidentiality agreement and unanimously concluded that it is irrelevant, unenforceable and contrary to the public good.

For Microfibers, the Kern affair has been a self-made public relations disaster. Brown University and Memorial Hospital have suffered greatly as well. But then, that's the nature of these disputes. They don't go away. They don't get better. They can't be whitewashed for very long. And, while everyone loses something, it is generally the institutions that not only have the most to lose but usually lose the most.

It was that way, as well, with Betty Dong.

A highly respected professor of clinical pharmacology at the University of California in San Francisco (UCSF), Dong had published a small study in 1988 suggesting that the leading thyroid medication in the USA – a drug called Synthroid – might prove more effective than its competitors in a randomized trial.

Some 8 million Americans were then taking the drug and the company making it, Flint Pharmaceuticals, was eager for yet another selling point to justify the high prices it was charging. Flint decided Dong was on to something and paid her $250,000 (£162,500) to compare Synthroid with its three leading generic competitors. Its own scientists designed the protocols.

By the time Dong finished the trial, in 1990, Flint had been acquired by Boots Pharmaceuticals. Unfortunately for Boots, the study it inherited concluded that Synthroid was no better than the three less expensive generic versions.

Dong's contract contained a clause that gave the company exclusive access to her data and the ultimate right to veto anything she wanted to publish. So Boots spent the next five years attacking Dong's study at every turn, discrediting her science and preventing her from publishing the damning results.

Believing that she had every right to publish her findings, Dong sent an article to the *Journal of the American Medical Association* in April 1994. It referred her manuscript for peer review to five independent experts, accepted it for publication in November and tentatively scheduled it for an issue ten weeks later. But, on 13 January 1995, Dong received an injunction prohibiting her from publishing and was forced to withdraw the article.

Two months later, Boots was taken over for $1.4 billion (£910 million) by Knoll Pharmaceuticals, a division of the German chemical group BASF. With it, Knoll acquired the rights to manufacture and sell Synthroid, and to continue the fight against Betty Dong.

Clearly, it had been in Boots' interest to keep the Synthroid story out of the papers, especially while the deal with Knoll was being put together. If consumers knew that there were three cheaper generics proven to be just as good, the Synthroid market might collapse and that would have a bearing on the deal. Accordingly, Knoll now needed to protect its investment. So, the medical services director of Knoll published a sixteen-page re-analysis of Dong's data in a new publication called the *American Journal of Therapeutics*. It just so happens that he was also one of the editors.

By this time, the FDA was on to the case. It queried the company's claim that Synthroid was both unique and superior to the competing products, decided the company was misleading the public and eventually accused Knoll of misbranding Synthroid. In the face of mounting criticism and particularly good investigative reporting by the *Wall Street Journal*, Knoll had little choice but to allow Dong to publish her work. The article appeared in *JAMA* in April 1997. Along with it was a letter from Knoll apologizing for having delayed publication for so long, a statement from Knoll challenging Dong's conclusions and a rebuttal from Dong defending her conclusion.

As soon as the report came out, an $8.5 billion (£5.5 billion) class action suit followed, alleging that Knoll had defrauded Synthroid users by overcharging them for the drug.

The attorneys general of thirty-seven states also stepped

in. Among other things, they didn't like the marketing of Synthroid and the company's communications with the FDA, particularly a 1990, unpublished, in-house study that showed Synthroid's potency to be more consistent than that of its competitors. Ignoring the Dong study, the company had claimed that this report was credible and objective and contained new information.

Boots and Knoll both insisted they'd really been saying all along that the Dong study was neither an adequate nor a well-controlled study. This despite the fact that their own scientists had designed it.

Facing lawsuits, Knoll now added that it'd been willing right from the beginning to publish Dong's work as long as the errors of fact and interpretation were corrected.

That might well have been the end of this episode, had Boots not systematically complained about Dong to her chancellor, all her vice chancellors and several department heads at UCSF. The university investigated the controversy twice but never uncovered anything that would significantly support Boots' accusations. The problem it saw was that the University of California specifically prohibits secrecy clauses and any contractual restrictions on the right to publish. Dong had signed the contract with the clause, mistakenly believing that it was routine. She'd even been assured by the university lawyers that such clauses had not in the past prevented anyone from publishing. But, by going to the university, Boots had inadvertently thrown the administration into a quandary. To the administrators, it looked as though Betty Dong and her Synthroid report might somehow become embroiled in the Knoll takeover of Boots. They worried that the university could find itself party to lawsuits stemming from the sale of Boots to Knoll.

There was also the sentiment by some at the university that Dong was at fault for signing the confidentiality clause and that the ensuing controversy somehow jeopardized their own research grants. Although the university had, at first, encouraged Dong to publish, it had quickly and firmly backed down. It had warned Dong that she and her fellow researchers might be putting themselves in personal danger by publishing because the university would not defend them. In other words, it had not only refused to stand up to a drug company, it'd also been willing to sacrifice Dong.

Knoll maintained its tough stance right up to the end. Yet the more it tried to defend the indefensible, the worse it got for the company. In August 1997, looking at years of litigation in the class action suit, the company announced that the prudent thing would be to settle. It paid $135 million (£87.8 million) to sixty Synthroid users who were claiming that, because the company had suppressed research relevant to their condition, they otherwise would have been unaware of effective, cheaper alternatives.

At the end of July 1999, Knoll and the attorneys general reached an agreement which included – as the company is quick to point out – no finding of wrongdoing. Knoll maintains it settled to avoid the burden and expense of lengthy litigation. Included in this agreement was a payment by Knoll to the states of $41.8 million (£27.2 million) and assurances that its marketing of Synthroid would be 'fair and accurate'.

The class action settlement and the agreement with the states may sound like a lot of money, but, at $400 million (£260 million) a year, seven years' worth of manoeuvring to suppress Dong's report earned back $2.45 billion (£1.59 billion).

Nancy O. didn't know what fate awaited David Kern or Betty Dong – or how her own life would abruptly change – as she read an article in 1987 in the *British Journal of Haematology*. The subject was a drug scientifically known as deferiprone but referred to as L1.

Born and raised in Hamilton, Ontario, where her father was a paediatrician, Olivieri was a straight-A high school student for whom med school seemed an obvious answer. She graduated from the University of Toronto in 1975, got her MD at McMaster and did postgraduate clinical and research training in haematology and oncology at Toronto and Harvard.

She was by all accounts, a brilliant and dedicated doctor. In less than ten years she worked her way up to a full professorship in paediatrics and medicine at Toronto, was awarded a Career Scientist prize from the Ontario Ministry of Health, and was directing the Hemoglobinopathies Program at both Toronto Hospital and the Hospital for Sick Children, affectionately known as Sick Kids.

In the meantime, she also established herself as an internationally recognized expert on thalassaemia. That's a rare group of blood disorders characterized by insufficient haemoglobin, the protein which carries oxygen through the body. It used to be called 'Mediterranean Anaemia' because there was a very significant patient population clustered around Cyprus, Turkey, Italy and what once was Macedonia – northern Greece, southern Yugoslavia and south-west Bulgaria. It is also prevalent on the Indian subcontinent and in Sri Lanka, in the Philippines, Indonesia, Thailand, Burma, Malaysia and China. Some variations of thalassaemia are relatively minor. A few, slightly more serious, resemble anaemia. The most brutal forms, however, show up in infancy, stunt growth and almost always bring about premature death.

Treatment of the severest variation is brutal. Regular blood transfusions must be given to keep iron levels from becoming dangerously low. The transfusions are given overnight and, especially when children are involved, are a horrible nightmare for both the child and the parents, who often administer it.

Understandably, for thalassaemia sufferers, for their families and for the medical staff who treat them, the Holy Grail is a simple pill that will do the same thing as the transfusion. That's what L1 appeared to be. And, at least for a while, Nancy Olivieri was its biggest champion.

The drug had been discovered in a research laboratory in London, had shown some early promise but turns out to have had a checkered history. Ciba-Geigy (now Novartis) thought enough of L1 after early tests to patent it. But, when Ciba did some testing in animals, its conclusion was that it was too toxic to develop further. Because the thalassaemia community was desperate for anything that would eliminate those harrowing transfusions, other researchers continued to look at the drug. Olivieri phoned the doctor in Britain who did the research for the article, but found him extremely dismissive. Unable to get the information she wanted from him, she decided, in typical Nancy O. fashion, 'I'll just do it myself.'

She easily obtained the structure of the molecule, showed that to Robert McClelland – a highly respected professor of chemistry at the University of Toronto – and asked if he could replicate it. He said it was easy, and he did. For the next four years, Olivieri ran trials with her consenting patients at Toronto and Sick Kids, funded by the Medical Research Council of Canada.

'It was an experimental drug in Britain,' she says. 'We needed an alternative to the standard infusion and this looked exactly like what we needed. An oral alternative would be a God-send. So we made the first pills at the University of Toronto and a huge Canadian generic drug company called Novapharm agreed to encapsulate them for us for free. The Health Protection Branch gave us approval and we started using it.'

Along with Dr Gary Brittenham – then at Case Western Reserve University in Cleveland and now at Columbia University in New York – the two decided that the next step should be to find out what they needed to get approval for this drug in the United States.

The FDA has a service that it provides to drug developers, one that other agencies around the world don't offer. The agency will actually sit down with an investigator or a company and go through the knowledge that's available about a drug, examine the proposed package of trials that are likely to be done in the future and tell the investigator or the company what the agency would likely find wanting if that development plan went forward. In essence, it helps you do your homework.

'The FDA told us we needed four things,' she goes on. 'We needed to continue the long-term trial. We needed a comparison trial between standard therapy and this experimental drug. We needed a large toxicity trial. And we needed a commercial source of the drug to make it under good laboratory practice.'

The long-term trial wasn't going to be a problem because she'd been following the same patients for four years. A comparison between therapies wasn't a problem either. There was plenty of data to relate L1 to the drug used in the transfusion, deferoxamine. The toxicity trial did, however, present a worry because the patient population in Canada is small. She and Brittenham decided they could get around that by going to Europe and the Far East where there were plenty of patients.

'In Sardinia where I've worked,' she interjects, 'there's an entire hospital where all three floors are just for thalassaemia.'

As for a commercial source of the drug, she didn't have to look far. Her connection was right down the hall at Sick Kids.

Gideon Koren was a physician from Tel Aviv who'd been on the Toronto and Sick Kids staffs since 1986. He too was a full professor in paediatrics and medicine but had added pharmacology to his studies and had established his own international reputation in clinical pharmacology and toxicology. He was highly successful at bringing in funding and was described by one university colleague as 'our poster boy'. He was head of the Pharmacology/Toxicology division and ran extensive programmes through the Research Institute at Sick Kids with support from, among other sources, the pharmaceutical industry.

Enter, here, Koren's friend and sometime benefactor, Dr Michael Spino. A former full-time member of the university's Faculty of Pharmacy, Spino had also held an appointment in the Department of Pediatrics. In 1979, he'd established a laboratory at Sick Kids where he conducted research and supervised graduate students. In 1992, he resigned from the university to take a job at Apotex, Canada's leading generic drug company, where he was now Vice President for Scientific Affairs. But, uniquely, he was awarded a full professor 'status-only' position by the university, allowing him to keep office space there and at Sick Kids, and also to maintain his lab at Sick Kids. Spino continued doing research at the hospital and supervising graduate students who were assigned to work with him and alongside Koren.

This relationship lies at the heart of the matter.

'There are many people who would say, this is unacceptable,' claims Dr Michele Brill-Edwards, a former senior physician responsible for prescription drug regulation at Canada's Health Protection Branch, who watched the drama unfold with growing disgust. 'It is unacceptable behaviour for Michael Spino to hold a post with a pharmaceutical firm and to retain his post in the clinical pharmacology division at the hospital. That clearly mixes the work of the pharmaceutical firm with the work of the clinical pharmacology division. Most people would say, wait a second, there is too much opportunity here for his role as the vice president of Apotex to colour his thinking about the products they make and then to colour the thinking of the unit at the hospital. It becomes homogeneous. In essence, with Michael Spino there, the clinical pharmacology unit becomes an outpost of Apotex.'

But that didn't particularly concern Nancy Olivieri. At least, not yet. Koren was a prestigious colleague and also the route to Spino. And Spino offered the possibility of money from Apotex.

The company had flown high for many years, driven by its Chairman, Bernard 'Barry' Sherman, one of Canada's twelve richest men. Sherman started Apotex in the 1960s, at a time when the generic drug business was a buccaneering exercise in free-wheeling capitalism. The market for copycat drugs was wide open, the government had been encouraging generic companies – in those days Ottawa believed it needed to keep drug prices down and this was the best way to do it – and, by selling Big Pharma's drugs cheaper than Big Pharma, fortunes could be made. But the politics of drugs in Canada had changed over the years and Sherman's business had slowed down considerably. Still, when he heard about L1, he insists he didn't hesitate to say that Apotex would get involved.

'The regime that thalassaemia patients have to go through is so terrible that many patients just refuse to do it and die as a result. Or they don't do it regularly and die. Or the reactions to it are so bad that they can't take it. What's needed is a tablet. That's deferiprone. Mike Spino came to me and said, we could take this over, we have the chemical plants and the know-how, we would have to fund all these studies to get it approved, it will cost us C\$20–30 million, and by the way, we won't make money on it, but we're going to save a lot of lives. He asked, will we do it. And I said, yes, we'll do it.'

So, in 1993, Olivieri joined forces with Gideon Koren, despite the fact that he was not an expert in thalassaemia and would not be an active participant in the trials, and both signed contracts with Apotex Research Inc. to evaluate the use of deferiprone in the treatment of iron overload in patients with thalassaemia major.

Apotex did not come up with C\$20–30 million (£10–15

million). At this point, the company's commitment was only around C$120,000 (£60,000). Still, in those days, Mike Spino and Barry Sherman liked Olivieri's credentials. And, in those days, she appreciated the money they were putting into the studies that she would design for 180 patients in Toronto, Montreal, Philadelphia and Italy. But included in her contract was a clause to protect trade secrets – just like the gag clauses that tried to shut up David Kern and tried to shut up Betty Dong – designed, the company said, to prevent any researcher from disclosing proprietary information. For Spino and Sherman, L1 was their first expedition into international clinical trials and this sort of drug development. For them, the gag clause was perfectly normal. For Olivieri, this was her first contract with a pharmaceutical company. She believed the gag clause was standard.

The same clause was written into Koren's contract. He'd been around the block often enough with pharmaceutical companies to have noticed it. But apparently he never said a word to Olivieri about it.

The trials finally began in January 1995.

In the meantime, Olivieri had been analysing all the data she'd collected to the middle of 1994. She liked what she was seeing, and wrote a paper saying as much. 'In case you're thinking that Apotex took a big chance with this drug,' she asserts, 'don't forget that I'd been doing this since 1989 without their support. This was not a huge, out on the diving board risk.'

She submitted her paper to the *New England Journal of Medicine* that autumn, the *NEJM* accepted it in December and published it in April 1995.

To thalassaemia sufferers, it looked as though the Holy Grail might be at hand.

Three months later, Nancy O.'s life started to come undone.

By Summer 1995, she was seeing a different picture.

Whereas the data she'd used for the *NEJM* article had demonstrated a steady decline in iron levels in her study group of twenty-one patients, liver biopsies in some of those same patients now indicated seriously increasing iron levels.

Shaken by this development, she spent a good part of the summer going over the data with Brittenham and trying to convince Spino and Apotex that they needed to change the protocols of the trials to find out what this problem was. She also told Apotex that the Research Ethics Board (REB) at Sick Kids would need to be informed about any change of protocols. In August, she sent Spino a draft of the report she intended to present to the REB, dealing with L1's 'loss of efficacy'.

Spino objected. He said Apotex needed more data and time to study her claims. He wrote to her that, unless the company was shown all the raw data and was able to carry out its own analysis, Apotex would not be able to form its own opinion and would, consequently, have to terminate her study.

The Olivieri–Apotex relationship deteriorated from there.

She was looking at data obtained through serial biopsies, liver samples taken over a long period of time, and was the only one doing them. It wasn't being done in any of the other trial centres. She'd also been doing them long enough to understand the changes she was seeing. 'We told Apotex what we were seeing and they, basically, said, we don't believe you.'

In the middle of September, Olivieri sent Spino a brand-new protocol for the trial, specifically designed to investigate the irregularities that concerned her. She desperately wanted to continue the trial and, if Apotex had agreed to these new studies, she feels everyone would have had a clear answer as to whether or not her concerns were justified. But Spino and Apotex refused. As far as the company was concerned, her findings were wrong.

To support the company's views, Spino and Apotex summoned a panel of twelve scientists who decided that Olivieri was mistaken. Many of those scientists had direct financial ties to Apotex.

Joining the bandwagon was Spino's chum Koren. Put on the spot, with no particular expertise in thalassaemia and possibly fearing that, if he turned his back on Apotex, his own funding would be jeopardized, Koren reinforced the company's line. He too didn't think the data revealed any danger.

Olivieri now produced her own list of supporters.

The line drawn in the sand got very deep.

And vitriol flew across it.

Spino contended, 'She's highly opinionated and if you don't see things the way she wants, then you're wrong.'

Olivieri was equally terse. 'I am not going to be bullied. Apotex thought, we'll just railroad this dumb-looking little blonde. Bloody hell.'

By February 1996, both sides had so firmly dug in their heels that the trials were now doomed.

Olivieri was characterizing Spino and Apotex as unwilling to recognize and respond appropriately to an evident decrease in the drug's efficacy. She urged the company to reconsider what she'd been telling it. Apotex responded that at no time had it denied that some patients showed a decreased response to deferiprone. And it even acknowledged that some patients were responding less than desirably. But it objected to her interpretation that there was a change in responsiveness beyond what could be expected. It said the decision to present her information to the REB rested with her, and urged her to do that if she felt it was warranted, but it wanted her to include its side of the story.

So she went to the REB and told them about the nineteen patients she'd been following in Toronto. She explained how twelve of them had shown increased liver iron, some to levels dangerous enough to risk iron-induced complications and even death. Spino submitted a rebuttal, explaining the Apotex view and basically saying that none of the other trial centres was seeing this and none of the various experts they'd consulted agreed with Dr Olivieri.

A second meeting was held, during which Olivieri rebutted the Apotex view. At the end of that, Dr Stanley Zlotkin, who chaired the REB, confirmed that Olivieri had to change the patient consent forms and further got her to report her findings to the Drug Directorate, which is the Canadian government's drug approval office.

Zlotkin's answer to Spino was, 'The Research Ethics Board does not act as an intermediary between the investigator and the sponsoring company when different opinions arise. Consequently your correspondence should be directed to Dr Olivieri for resolution.'

While this was going on, the hospital's contract to conduct the study for Apotex expired.

On 20 May 1996, Olivieri submitted her revised information and consent forms to the REB and to Apotex. Four days later, Apotex announced it was not renewing the research contract, not renewing Olivieri's contract, and in effect terminating her trial.

It meant she could never obtain enough data to prove her point.

Spino said the other three trials would be continued. Then he warned Olivieri that Apotex would take all possible steps to ensure that her obligations of confidentiality were met, and that the company would vigorously pursue all legal remedies in the event that there was any breach of those obligations.

The secrecy clause had come back to bite her.

She suggests, 'You could say, what an idiot I was for going off into a blind alley and signing that. On the contrary. The hospital doesn't want this out but the guy who co-signed it was the associate director of the Research Institute at the time. Koren. So let's not make out like I was trying to go through some back door here. Of course, they're very anxious not to let this out because they have only one avenue of blame. They can say, Nancy you signed a contract and we didn't know anything about it. Damn it all, your second in command knew everything about it.'

The usual excuse, the same one used against Kern and Dong, was brought out this time too – confidentiality is vital to keep trade secrets. But, she points out, 'the drug had already been written about at length in dozens of publications. The drug was there. It was being used in thalassaemia and the molecular structure was published. I mean, come on, I'd been making it for four years. What was Apotex trying to protect?'

Incensed, Olivieri consulted a lawyer, who recommended that she contact the Canadian Medical Protective Association because the matter had serious ethical implications for the safety of her patients. A letter to that effect was sent to Dr Arnold Aberman, Dean of the Faculty of Medicine of the university. At Olivieri's request, he met with Apotex, looking for a way to settle this so that the clinical trials could continue. He also told Apotex that he hoped it would not proceed with its threat of legal action against Olivieri.

Apotex agreed to continue the supply of L1 to the hospital, but would not reinstate the trials. Nor would it withdraw the threat of legal action.

In June 1996, Spino wrote to Brittenham, 'Since we do not concur with her assessment of the drug's effectiveness, we could not allow such information to be transmitted to patients, thus misinforming them. In addition we could not justify Nancy as the Principal Investigator in studies of a drug she does not believe works.'

The following month, Spino convened a panel of experts to reinforce his views of the data. Although their conclusion disagreed with Olivieri, the data they looked at were not hers, but rather an Apotex summary of her data. One of the experts

Apotex called on was Dr Beatrice Wonke of the Whittington and Royal Free Hospitals in London. Apotex says her opinion was that the drug was adequately effective for ensuring the safety of patients in the trials. But she too had a financial relationship with Apotex. The company was supporting some of her research, albeit in a minor way.

Ever defiant, Olivieri announced that she was intent on publishing her findings and planned to do so at the December 1996 meeting of the American Society of Hematology. Apotex again reminded her that, if she did so, she would be in breach of her contract with the company. Allegedly, Spino personally petitioned the chairman of that conference session to refuse her this forum.

She managed it anyway.

At this point she was beginning to say that the data demonstrated that L1 might itself cause liver fibrosis.

Apotex demanded to review her data but Olivieri's lawyers insisted it had no entitlement to them. Her intention was to present her data at the International Conference on HIV and Iron in Bruges in March 1997, a second time at the International Conference on Thalassemia and the Hemoglobinopathies in Malta a month later, and a third time at Biomedicine '97 in Washington DC a few weeks after Malta. Apotex successfully lobbied to get the presentations stopped, insisting that, before the data could be shown, it needed to evaluate them.

To head her off at the conference in Malta, Koren furnished an abstract apparently co-authored with Apotex, making unauthorized use of her data to refute her findings. This, in spite of the fact that he'd not actively participated in the research.

Olivieri wrote a second article about L1 for the *New England Journal of Medicine*, this time being very critical. The journal published it in August 1998. The editors acknowledged that there was disagreement about her results and that there were limitations to the study. But the editors determined, 'It is important to make a concentrated effort to ascertain the safety and efficacy of this agent.'

As the story gained momentum in the media, Olivieri became a lightning rod. 'A lot of people didn't want to publicly identify with me. I realized that no one wants to be on a whistleblower's side until the truth comes out. Even then, they won't agree with me, they'll just lean over and whisper, we were always with you. But nobody wants to be publicly identified with a controversial figure when the controversy is raging.'

Olivieri had turned both to the university and to Sick Kids looking for help, asking them to back her. The university washed its hands of her by saying, this is a scientific dispute. Sick Kids chastised her for signing the confidentiality clause and denied that she'd asked for legal help. She maintains she did. Apotex threatened to sue her. Sick Kids did not provide legal assistance.

She went on a speaking tour to raise money for her legal defence fund – more than 200 doctors around the world came together to form Doctors for Research Integrity to help – and the next thing that happened is she found herself chastised in the media for becoming a self-promoter. 'I live like a monk. I live in a very ordinary little house in a very ordinary part of Toronto. Basically I work. I don't have children. I don't have a lot of expenses. All the money I earned on the speaking circuit went to Doctors for Research Integrity to help cover my legal costs.'

In the midst of this, she and colleagues began getting hate e-mail. It looked like a concerted campaign had been mounted to discredit her. She asked Sick Kids to investigate it and they found nothing. So she and some colleagues hired a computer forensic expert and they discovered the culprit – Koren.

'He kept denying it,' Olivieri says, 'but we caught him. Anonymous, harassing hate mail.'

When push came to shove, the administrators of Sick Kids

fired her. Not once, but twice, although the hospital denies this. They managed to cloud the issue in a great deal of confusion, saying that they'd originally wanted to move her thalassaemia work to another location and that she'd refused to go.

'The truth is,' one senior staff member there says, 'the bosses here were simply pissed off with a woman being this assertive.'

In the meantime, Koren's behaviour was roundly and publicly condemned, and considered by many at the hospital as sufficient grounds for dismissal. He was suspended in December 1999 but in April 2000 the hospital decided that he should remain suspended only until 1 June, the last two months without pay.

And then he was invited to return to work.

One of the first people with heavyweight credibility to jump to Olivieri's defence was the inimitable Dr Drummond Rennie of JAMA. Notorious for refusing even cups of coffee from the industry, Rennie is not one to hide his feelings.

'The good thing about the Nancy Olivieri story is that it brings starkly to the surface what goes on. First of all, the stupid signing of gag orders by researchers. Secondly, the influence of drug companies when they don't like the results. Thirdly, the brutal behaviour of institutions when those institutions believe they're getting a lot of money from a drug company. Fourthly, the power differential in all this. And fifthly, that if you squeeze a young researcher hard enough, she'll turn and she'll bite. We know this goes on, it's great when it comes out, because it tells people it mustn't go on.'

Admitting that no one really knows how prevalent this sort of thing is, he labels it, 'An entirely typical human story. You will always find betrayal, anger, self-advantage.'

Rennie says the issue isn't whether Olivieri is right or

wrong, it is that the moment she thought she was right, as soon as she thought there was a danger, there was a clear-cut course of action she needed to take.

'I don't worry about comments about science because I think scientists are permitted to have their scientific differences. Scientists can often disagree radically and angrily on important points of science. That's just and proper. And though I believe I know that scientists are influenced by money, even scientists influenced by money can legitimately disagree on a scientific question. But as the head of the trial, as a doctor with patients in the trial, if it is her belief that there is a danger, whether she is correct or not, she is morally bound, and actually in the law bound, to tell her patients. The issue is what she thought. Apotex can disagree with her, and they did. But they should have paid attention to her. They should have acknowledged her right and her duty to do what she did.'

The way he sees it, Apotex precipitated the crisis. 'A company that's in the business of research has to accept that things may go wrong. That's the basic issue. You can't just say, I'm going to shut down anything that doesn't go well. You've got to say, I don't know the result beforehand, otherwise why am I doing this study. Things can go wrong and you've got to expect that as a possibility. You can't just say it doesn't exist and we're going to draw away your funding because of it.'

He is equally outspoken about the hospital's role. 'The Hospital for Sick Children is a place with a remarkable reputation. But I think what has gone on there is a cesspit. A lot of people have behaved appallingly. Koren wasn't fired. Why? Because he's distinguished. It angers me a great deal, and I think it's proper to be angered by stuff like this. When you see a volcano erupting, you realize the centre of the earth is boiling magma. Where commercial interest comes in, science goes out the window. A company comes in and says, because the science isn't as we want, we're going to suppress it, and we'll ruin the career of that person who found it. It's wrong, it's absolutely, unspeakably wrong.'

Also rallying to Olivieri's cause were the two greatest living experts in the field of thalassaemia.

First was Sir David Weatherall, Regius Professor of Medicine at Oxford University and Director of Oxford's Institute of Molecular Medicine, who agrees that her scientific claims are valid. 'She has two concerns about this drug from her own work. One was that she found it is not maintaining its effect in a significant proportion of patients, significant being nearly half. And I think that two subsequent studies have proved that to be the case, so there's no question about that. On the second issue of whether it causes liver scarring, she's the only one who's actually ever done a controlled study to look at this. However, the numbers were small. This drug, before it's thrown out to the world, should have a more extensive prospective clinical trial. I think she was absolutely right in her stand against the company.'

Researchers, much like military planners, Weatherall points out, must always work on a worst-case scenario. 'As a clinical scientist, somebody who does research with patients, Olivieri is highly regarded by most of her colleagues and, to some, is considered the best in the field of thalassaemia. Her studies with this drug showed initial promise. But as she followed her patients, to her dismay, she found that nearly half of them were not continuing to respond. That's when Apotex tried to pull the shutters on her. Now, a doctor's first duty is to the patient population. I know this sounds trite, but her responsibility is to her patients and not to the bloody company. If you genuinely believe there's a problem, you have to disclose it. That's what she did.'

The second expert was Dr David Nathan, director of the Dana Farber Cancer Institute at Harvard University. 'There are two separate issues here. The first is how a researcher has been treated by her institutions. The second is Olivieri's science. And, in essence, it is only the first issue that really matters. The science is irrelevant. Whether Nancy is right or wrong, that will come out. But as soon as she concluded that the drug was dangerous and ineffectual, or at least much less effectual than she had originally told her patients, she had to act the way she did and, if she hadn't, her conduct would have been unethical. To her credit, after she got all the kudos from the scientific community for bringing this drug out of the cellar and showing how good it is, once she became suspicious of the drug, once she no longer had confidence in it, she told her patients and told the scientific community. She did exactly what she had to do. Which is when this all hit the fan.'

It is the secrecy clause, Nathan feels, that is the nucleus of the problem. 'The gag clause is a no-no. Confidentiality agreements are considered by many institutions, including Harvard, to be absolutely forbidden. In this case, Olivieri was something of an ingenue. She had never dealt with a drug company before. Nor did it help matters that the Hospital for Sick Children had a totally feckless system for monitoring what their researchers signed. Had the proper controls been in place, the incident might have been avoided. Then, too, had the hospital not been afraid of Sherman, they might have met their responsibility by correcting Olivieri's mistake in having signed the gag clause. They could have said to the drug company, it's too bad that we missed it and too bad if she signed it, but guess what, Mr Sherman, if you sue her you have to sue us.'

When Dan Soberman, the former Dean of Law at Queen's University looked at the gag clause, he decided, 'To the extent that such a clause prohibits disclosure of information about a medicine that might reasonably be believed by a researcher to cause harm to the health of a person taking that medicine, the clause is void. Period.'

Nathan is equally forthright. 'I don't care if she signed the Declaration of Independence. The judgmental mistake was to sign something that was stupid and outside of the policies. It was stupid of the hospital not to immediately say, sign it or not, we're fighting this. If they'd done that, the whole thing would have been over. Instead, the hospital beat up on her. They wanted to beat up on her, they wanted to drive her out. They wanted the Apotex money and they didn't like Nancy. Then they didn't control Koren's behaviour. He had a lot of open hostility to Nancy. The hospital was lethargic about investigating the hate mail. They didn't really care. It was Nancy and her colleagues who had to get the evidence. How embarrassing. How ridiculous. This is the hospital that helped to discover the genetic basis of cystic fibrosis. If they'd wanted to, they could certainly have found Koren.'

Nathan and Weatherall had both been brought in by the university and Sick Kids to try to find a solution. What they found instead was that both institutions had considered the options – blame Olivieri, which was the easy way out, or blame Apotex, which could have been the costliest way out – and both took the coward's way out. 'You always hope for common sense, but what happened in the Nancy Olivieri case was an abandonment of common sense by almost everybody. It became turf protection. Lack of wisdom. Nobody in the structure said, folks the game is over and you're going to do as I say.'

Nathan isn't sure how often these cases arise. He admits that it may happen much more than anyone knows, but finds these cases rare when you're dealing with an excellent drug company. 'If you look carefully at the Betty Dong case, it's a big company [Knoll] but not a great scientific company. The really good scientific companies, Merck, Novartis, they don't get into this. They've got a reputation to keep. Lilly, Pfizer, those people are big-leaguers and their scientific directors are superb scientists. When they do get into trouble, their chief executives are not combative businessmen like Barry Sherman. They're thoughtful people who are often ex-scientists. So I think it's rare. But there are an awful lot of drug companies, thousands of them swimming in the fringes of this thing.'

As for Sherman, Nathan contends, 'Apotex did something that most drug companies wouldn't do – they gave Nancy a sole source contract for the clinical trial. Sophisticated companies are much more careful. They don't want to be put into the hands of just one person, they want a group of three or four. That way, there's a group to ask, what does this data mean. With a sole source contract, if the one person comes to a conclusion that the company doesn't like, there's no way to deal with it. If they'd had a group of three or four people, Nancy could have dropped out and, if the other three didn't agree, the drug trials could have gone right on. But Barry Sherman is no Novartis.'

On his own account, Barry Sherman was being tracked down by the media. When the story reached CBS Television in New York, the programme *60 Minutes* took it up. Leslie Stahl interviewed Nancy Olivieri, who came across as the victim, and then interviewed Barry Sherman.

For a man who has shown such indisputable talent in business, he displayed abysmal media skills. When Leslie Stahl suggested that Apotex had launched a smear campaign against Olivieri, Sherman retorted on camera, 'That's completely absurd. She is the one who is conducting the smear campaign.' Then, as the crew changed tapes, and Sherman wrongly believed that the cameras were not rolling, he blurted out, 'She's nuts. Nuts.'

Stahl snapped, 'What did you just say to me? You just said she was nuts. You just said that to me. You looked at me and you said she was nuts.

Sherman realized he'd been caught out. 'I said to you . . .'

Stahl reminded him, 'You said she's nuts.'

'Hold on a sec,' Sherman pleaded. 'I said I'll say certain things to you off the record . . .'

'But that wasn't off the record,' Stahl retorted. 'We were rolling. The cameras were going. The point is that you are still saying these things and I am a reporter.'

Sherman pleaded that he was agitated. 'Given that I'm upset I might well say things that in a private conversation, off the record, that I would not say on . . .'

'But we're reporters,' Stahl reminded him. 'We're not your pals.'

It was an embarrassing lesson in the first commandment of broadcast interviews – there is no such thing as a dead mike or a camera not rolling.

In February 2000, the university and the Sick Kids hospital came to an agreement with Olivieri. While she was reinstated as an active member of the Sick Kids staff, she moved her office to Toronto Hospital, reporting to the Physician-in-Chief there. She retains full access to and responsibility for all of the patients she had been treating and continues to conduct her research. The terms of the settlement also include Sick Kids' agreement to indemnify her for any uncovered costs of legal actions brought by Apotex and to pay her legal and other costs up to C\$150,000 (£75,000).

The closest the hospital administrators ever came to any sort of public apology to Olivieri was a concession in a press release. 'The Hospital could have done a better job of providing her with support.'

Bizarrely, the release goes on to state, 'Over and over again the management of the Hospital backed her right to publish the material. They talked to people at Apotex and told them to back off.'

There's no proof that any such thing ever happened.

Despite the settlement, which recognizes, at least to some extent, that the university and hospital had acted foolishly, Nathan is still disturbed by the way they both tried to discredit Olivieri. 'Nancy's a highly regarded researcher who happens to be a feisty woman in what is traditionally a man's world. Scientific disputes can get personal and people who will stand up to the establishment are usually people with strong personalities who tend to generate reactions. It doesn't surprise me that they tried to discredit Nancy. Her stand was not popular. But then, if there's some battle that has to be fought, Nancy's right there to fight it.'

Nancy O. is, these days, back at work, smarting and nursing her wounds, and dispirited about the drug that Apotex has now taken to Europe for licensing.

'No one ever says to any of these people who claimed I was wrong, did you do systematic liver biopsies? They say, we never saw any signs of liver toxicity. But, did you take patient A and do a liver biopsy in 1989 before he started the drug and treat him for six years like I did and get a biopsy every single year? They'd have to say, no. Well, then, how many biopsies did you get on every patient? They'd have to say, one. Well, I say there's progression, so progression is at least two, right? You've got to have the first and the second and I had an average of four on every patient. You can't see progression if you don't look for progression. After a year and a half discrediting me, they're still having problems because nobody has ever been able to say, I did seventy-two biopsies just like Nancy did and there's nothing wrong with the drug.'

With European approval, L1 will find its way into clinics and hospitals around the world. 'As a result,' she says, 'I think people are going to die. We needed to continue the trials. We didn't want to stop the trials. They stopped the trials. We were perfectly willing, because at the time we didn't have any idea about the progression of liver fibrosis, we needed to continue the trials because we needed to know more. Every patient who had, with good faith, enrolled in these trials, wanted to continue on the oral agent. Apotex wouldn't continue.'

In the end, Olivieri believes, the tragedy will be the licensing of this drug, the indiscriminate use of this drug, the lack of biopsies to follow liver toxicity, the fact that patients are dying. But they're not necessarily going to die right away. She believes that, if patients stay on L1, some of them will die because of the drug, but the drug-related death will look exactly like the disease-related death and no one will realize it's the drug.

When the settlement was announced, everyone at the university and everyone at the Hospital for Sick Children hoped the affair would finally go away. That the world might forget how the university had allegedly been looking to the Apotex Foundation – one of the ten largest corporate donors in Canada – to help finance a building project with a C$20–30 million (£10–15 million) gift. And how Sick Kids needed to maintain its relationships with Gideon Koren and Michael Spino.

According to the *Globe and Mail*, 'Nancy Olivieri was hung out to dry, and children were put at risk, because the hospital and university were too hungry for Apotex's good will and, more to the point, its cash.'

Sick Kids' CEO Michael Strofolino always denied that Apotex money was at the heart of this.

In fact, it now appears that there was more at stake than just a C$20 million (£10 million) donation from Apotex to the university for a medical research building. The company's gift would have triggered a series of matching grants from the federal and provincial governments worth around C$50 million (£25 million) and private donations of about C$23 million (£11.5 million). That brings the total to C$93 million (£46.5 million).

Olivieri was seen as having got in the way of that.

Having mishandled the affair from the beginning – not just administratively but also in the media – the Hospital for Sick Children found itself in the midst of a full-blown public relations disaster. With few options left, Strofolino brought in an outside reviewer to investigate the situation, to assess what had gone wrong and to report back to the hospital's board of directors. That this was something the hospital administrators wanted to do is doubtful. They were almost certainly forced into it. Their public relations was so miserable and without something substantial to show the press, they would appear to have totally lost control. So they went for it.

But they made sure they hedged their bets.

The man they asked to head the review was Dr Arnold Naimark, Professor of Medicine and Physiology at the University of Manitoba and the university's former president.

Normally, reviewers are referred to as independent, and this one was no exception. At least, it was no exception in that Naimark was referred to as being independent. Not that there's any doubt about his credentials as a physician, scientist and educator. But Naimark brought baggage with him that should have been questioned. Instead of going to someone who was completely neutral, totally outside the world of academic medicine and hospital management, Strofolino went to someone who might be defined as 'one of the boys'.

During Naimark's term of office as President of the University of Manitoba, Apotex had donated C\$789,840 (£394,920) to the school. What's more, according to Naimark's own report, over the twelve-year period 1986–98, Apotex had donated C\$6,908,051 (£3.45 million) to the University of Manitoba. That Apotex or Barry Sherman might have donated money to nearly all universities with health sciences faculties – as Naimark would later claim – doesn't erase the fact that Naimark, directly or indirectly, still had a relationship with Apotex and/or Sherman.

Naimark also had a business relationship with a member of the Sick Kids' board, the same board he was being asked to sit in judgment of. Furthermore, he maintained very close ties to the Canadian pharmaceutical industry.

When asked why he didn't recuse himself, Naimark answered, 'My only role as Reviewer was to review the facts and circumstances giving rise to the L1 controversy and to report my findings to the board. It is crucial to understand that I was not a grievance arbitrator nor was I to render a judgment as to any matters in dispute between Apotex and Dr Olivieri. The board was concerned with matters related to the hospital, such as patient safety, conflicts of interest within the hospital, etc., and not with Apotex per se. The Review was seen by the hospital as background for a subsequent review and revision of the hospital's policies and procedures in relation to clinical trials research. Given the foregoing, the fact that I happened to be President during a period when Apotex made occasional donations to the University of Manitoba, as it has done to nearly all universities with health sciences faculties, was regarded by the board and by me as immaterial.'

A poignant reminder of what happens when academia chases drug company money, Naimark's report whitewashed the affair, showing contempt for independence right from the start. Olivieri, Brittenham and the others who knew the most intimate details of the University–Sick Kids–Apotex relationship refused to cooperate. In turn, Naimark displayed loathing for Olivieri, pushed conflicts of interest – such as Koren and Sick Kids with Spino and Apotex – out of consideration, and based many of his conclusions on the tainted evidence of Koren.

He also neglected to mention that, while he was President and Vice Chancellor of the University of Manitoba, a pharmaceutical company called Cangene had its offices on the campus and played a much-welcomed regular role in the scientific life of the university community.

Cangene is a subsidiary of Apotex.

A Cangene director is Michael Spino.

Cangene's chairman is Barry Sherman.

So the independent reviewer whom the Hospital for Sick Kids chose to judge Nancy Olivieri – the same independent reviewer who regarded challenges to his independence as immaterial – had once been, Barry Sherman's landlord.

CHAPTER NINE

Goliath Hates David

They've got the government conned.
(Warwick Smith, British Generic
Manufacturers' Association)

'Big Pharma in this country uses its muscle in quite a clever way,' contends Warwick Smith, executive director of the British Generic Manufacturers' Association. 'Just look at where the multinationals are based.'

He draws a little map on a pad, puts a circle where London should be, and then checks off a lot of little Xs nearby. 'The UK is one of the major world centres of pharmaceutical research, and do you see where the big companies are based? Right here.' He points to south-east England. 'Now, these companies have consistently said that they stay here because the government has policies and legislation that favours them. And they have consistently warned that, if those policies and that legislation were to change, they'd move out of the UK.'

He crumples up the paper, 'It's bollocks,' and throws it away. 'Where are they going to go? France? Germany? Never. South-east England is a good economic base, and the City of London is nearby and it's helpful to be doing business in English. But that's not why they stay. They've got the government conned. No one ever challenges them. The government buys into the scenario that Big Pharma has to be handled with kid gloves because that's what Big Pharma wants the government to believe. It's bluff and all you need is somebody with the balls to call their bluff.'

He nods several times to reinforce his point. 'The real reason Big Pharma is in south-east England is because of Heathrow Airport. Because Heathrow has more frequent international routes than any other airport in the world, including airports in the USA. That's why they're in south-east England. If some day the government got tough with them and called their bluff, they'd back down. It's Heathrow.'

A generic drug is a copycat version of a branded drug, permitted to come onto the market as soon as the branded drug goes off patent, but only on condition that the copycat is 'bio-equivalent' with the original. That means, the generic version must be more than just a chemical copy. It has to be as safe and effective as the branded drug and act in exactly the same way. It must contain an identical amount of the active ingredient and must be in the same dosage. A generic must also meet standards for 'bio-availability', meaning that it must deliver exactly the same amount of the active ingredient into the bloodstream and in very nearly the same time exactly, within a narrowly defined margin of difference.

However, where branded drugs and generic drugs are allowed to differ is, occasionally, in the inactive ingredients that are of no medicinal value – such as colouring and flavouring – and, always, in price.

Because the generic manufacturers have not had to undergo huge R&D expenses or vastly complicated clinical trials, building a generic drug costs considerably less than developing a branded drug. Where Schering-Plough, for instance, is said to have spent $300 million (£195 million) on researching, developing and bringing Claritin to market, Barr Laboratories has spent somewhere around $1 million (£650,000) getting its generic version ready.

Granted, the average consumer in the UK never sees the price of drugs, but the NHS has to pay for them – and taxpayers ultimately foot that bill – and the differentials can be startling. Thyroxine, a medication prescribed for overactive thyroid, is sold to the NHS at £8 per tablet. The generic version costs around 3.4 p per tablet.

Today in Britain, generics account for around 55 per cent of all drugs dispensed but only around 10 per cent of the NHS's drugs budget. The average cost of a branded prescription is £13.04, while the average cost of a generic prescription is £3.78.

If a prescription is written in the generic name of the drug – which is the way younger doctors are being taught to prescribe – pharmacists are permitted to dispense either the branded drug or the generic. If the prescription is written in the branded name, then no substitution is possible. Even if the branded drug is off patent and has been for twenty years, as long as a doctor writes the branded name, then that's what's given and that's what the NHS has to pay for.

'The government says it produces no controls to make anyone do what they don't want to do,' Smith contends. 'But they just happen to train doctors to write generically. Big Pharma hates that.'

It's not very fond, either, of the notion that the government has set a target of 72 per cent generic prescribing in the NHS.

In an attempt to stem the tide, Big Pharma pulls out the old chestnut – no profits, no investment in R&D – and never hesitates to warn, stack the deck against us and we'll go somewhere else.

'There's a saying,' Smith goes on, 'when you're up to your backside in alligators, it's difficult to remember you're there to drain the swamp. Well, when you're up to your backside in patents, most drug companies conveniently forget that patent law is not there to protect the patent holder. It's there to give companies an incentive to commit money to do research. As a society, we say to Big Pharma, if you commit all these funds and you invent new products which benefit society, then we will give you a monopoly on those products for twenty years. That's the quid pro quo. But it's a limited monopoly because if we give you 100 years, you'll keep making money out of that invention and you won't invent anything else. So a patent is really about stimulating research and not protecting products.'

Conversely, once a drug comes off patent, generics are all about keeping drug prices down, which, the way Big Pharma sees it, is a direct threat to their profits.

AstraZeneca owns the patent on one of the world's top-selling drugs. In the States the stomach ulcer treatment is called Prilosec. Everywhere else it's known as Losec. The generic name is omeprazole. The drug loses partial protection in 2001, but AstraZeneca claims that patents covering the use and formulation of the drug are protected until 2014. When three generic firms disagreed and announced, in early 2000, that they intended to challenge those patents, AstraZeneca fired back with three lawsuits. Considering that AstraZeneca relies on the drug for around $2 billion (£1.3 billion) a year – almost a third of its worldwide sales – it's understandable that it's not going to give up without a fight.

Included in its tactics is an alternative version of the drug. AstraZeneca claims it's a different drug that does the same thing, but does it better. But it built its original omeprazole market on the claim that the drug is 98–9 per cent effective. The question therefore becomes, what's so special about this new version? The answer has to be, it safeguards the market for another patent life.

At AstraZeneca, management sees this as a logical way for

a commercial company to behave. It has a huge market and it's protecting it.

The generic industry takes a different view. It says that what AstraZeneca is doing will not bring benefit to a single patient and therefore this is wasted R&D. Eager to get their hands on the molecule – and perhaps with a hint of sour grapes – the generic companies see millions being spent developing a molecule that may or may not be as good as omeprazole, and millions more which will have to be spent convincing everybody it's better than *omprazole*.

The numbers make an even stronger case.

Patients and healthcare systems around the world are paying $2.5 billion (£1.62 billion) a year for omeprazole. Once it comes off patent, generic competition will reduce that initially by, say, 50 per cent, and eventually by as much as perhaps 80 per cent. That immediately frees up at least $1.25 billion (£0.8 billion) from those same healthcare budgets to pay for the next innovative drug. Without the generic, $2.5 billion gets them nothing more than son-of-omeprazole.

But AstraZeneca has already made one bid to keep the cash cow going by moving the goalposts. It withdrew the capsule from the market and replaced it with a tablet. The two are interchangeable, otherwise the regulators would have demanded new clinical trials. But suddenly the generic industry can't compare its omeprazole capsule to AstraZeneca's capsule because it doesn't exist on the market any more. The regulatory authorities will not go back and look at something that was on the market previously, even though it wasn't withdrawn for safety or other reasons. And the companies can't make a generic tablet form because that's protected by a law that gives the branded company ten years of marketing exclusivity.

Big Pharma, knowing how and where to invest its lobbying budget, has the European Union to thank for this lifeline, which is summed up in two words – 'is marketed'.

In the States and now in Canada, generic companies are permitted to develop their versions of the drug while the original is still under patent. The thinking is that, this way, the generic company will be ready to sell its version as soon as the brand-name drug comes off patent. But in Europe, Big Pharma lobbied effectively to extend protection to the branded drug for however long it takes the generic firm to get approval.

The relevant European Union directive says that a generic copy must demonstrate essential similarity to a product that 'is marketed' in the EU. Because 'is marketed' happens to be in the present tense, it has been interpreted to mean that the branded product must still hold a licence in order for a generic product to get a licence. What the branded manufacturers therefore do, before patent protection ends, is withdraw the licence for the old product, obtain a new licence for the revised product and leave the generic industry with nothing to copy.

The generic industry has been trying to get the regulatory authorities to stand up and be counted on this. It wants the EU to say, if a company voluntarily withdraws a licence that has no safety issues, then the authorities should still be able to refer to it going forward. In other words, generic manufacturers should still be able to make that drug by showing bio-equivalence.

Unfortunately, Big Pharma speaks louder and carries a lot more political muscle. In the States, it contributes directly to political campaigns. Even foreign manufacturers, which are otherwise prohibited from contributing in the USA, get around the law by making contributions through their US subsidiaries. Glaxo, for example, while reassuring Parliament that it's British to the core, has been one of the largest foreign companies funnelling money through subsidiaries into US election campaigns. And it's all perfectly legal.

'You don't find them making huge campaign contributions

here,' Smith goes on, 'not the way they do in the States. But that's a UK cultural thing. Instead they do a lot of little sponsorship. One of the political parties holds a gala dinner at £5,000 a table, so a few of the big companies take tables. Or they sponsor the wine. Or they get themselves invited to sit on a task force. They're also very keen on social inclusion. When they've got a big plant somewhere, they support the local library, or build a theatre, or run a creche.'

Although, he says, they're not always very subtle. 'The most outrageous thing I see is the TransAtlantic Business Dialogue. It's a business-driven talking shop to facilitate trade between Europe and the USA. It's organized into different sectors and there's a pharmaceutical group. One year, they held a conference on patent law in Chicago. They flew three European Commissioners and their wives over there, put them up, fed them, took them on the boat around the lake and made certain they understood Big Pharma's patent concerns. For me, that's outrageous.'

Equally contemptible, he feels, are their lobbying techniques. They are well known for coming on strong and often. Although sometimes they get hoisted by their own petard. A few years ago, there was a vote in the European Parliament to allow a generic company to develop a drug that was still under patent protection. Smith went to see a British MEP on the afternoon of the vote. And as soon as he walked into the MEP's office, he was told, I'm voting your way. Smith wondered why. The MEP replied, because I'm getting pissed off with drug company people phoning me and telling me to vote their way. It seems that every pharmaceutical company had called every member of the European Parliament to remind them that they had to protect patent rights. In doing so, they'd annoyed the hell out of the MEPs. The vote went in favour of the generic company.

But Big Pharma clearly had another card to play. The

Commission in Brussels never implemented the European Parliament's decision.

Cyril Beck retired in 1992. 'I play golf these days with the same people who, back in those days, sued me all the time and tried to put me out of business.'

Now 70, with a white moustache and piercing eyes, he insists, 'Of course, it was much more gentlemanly here than it was in the States. In the States it was brutal.' And then the man considered to be the grandfather of the British generic drug industry smiles again. 'I sometimes play golf with them too.'

There was no British generic drug industry in 1951 when Beck graduated from pharmacy school at London University. Sure, drugs were coming off patent all the time and a few small firms were manufacturing their own brand of Phenobarbitone or codliver oil capsules, but that was about it. The big drug companies kept making their own drugs and nobody was in a position to challenge them.

Beck opened a small pharmacy in north-west London, ran it until he could open a second and then, over the course of the next ten years, he opened a third and a fourth. But he was always looking to do something else because he fancied himself an entrepreneur and there was nothing entrepreneurial about running a retail pharmacy. He kept a tiny office at the rear of that first pharmacy where he plotted his ascent into the world of big business and, as luck would have it, one day 'entrepreneurial' came to him.

A Dutch pharmacist walked in and asked Beck if he was interested in selling some products wholesale. In those days, drugs were cheaper in the UK than they were on the continent, so Beck became the buying agent for that Dutch pharmacist. He soon learned that Dutch druggists were ferrying over to England to buy Valium by the carload and decided there must be a way he could supply that market.

'I went along to Roche and said, if you sell Valium to me, I'll sell it to the Dutch pharmacists and this way you'll cut out all the small market traders. They thought that was great. Roche sold me enormous quantities of Valium, which went through me to a company in Holland for distribution there.'

Unfortunately, prices eventually equalized and Beck's 'parallel export' business disappeared.

In the meantime, he'd seen an article in the papers about some explosions at a British pharmaceutical factory.

'It was a company called May and Baker. Today they're part of Rhône-Poulenc. They marketed an antidepressant called Imipramine and in order to make it they needed an intermediate product called Iminodibenzol. The problem was that Iminodibenzol was volatile and kept blowing up. I figured I could supply the intermediate ready made for them. So I went to Italy and found a manufacturer who was prepared to make it for me. I sold it to May and Baker and found myself in the raw materials business.'

Needing a vehicle for his raw materials business, Beck bought a small company called Harris Pharmaceuticals. While building up that business, he began to think that, as long as he had raw materials, he might as well start manufacturing drugs too. He didn't have any manufacturing facilities, but he knew companies that did – the same ones that were buying raw materials from him – so he approached them and they began making products under his Harris Pharmaceuticals label.

From a raw materials business of ten people, he became a generic drug company of fifty people, soon added his own packaging and analytical unit and, by 1976, was important enough for Big Pharma to take notice.

He confirms, 'That's when the lawsuits started.'

Fighting the generic industry has always brought out the most ferocious side of Big Pharma. Drugs come off patent, generic companies circle overhead and whatever the branded companies have to do to keep the generics away is considered fair game.

'I got into a fight with Roche over Valium,' he goes on. 'Remember, they were my friends when we were exporting to Holland. And I wasn't even making the pills. That was being done by another company under licence to Roche. I was just importing the raw materials for them. But that didn't matter to Roche. They sued Harris Pharmaceuticals and they sued me personally, too.'

The judge decided the suit against Beck was no good, but ruled in Roche's favour against Harris. Beck appealed. In fact, he took it all the way up to the House of Lords.

'There was a principle involved. Then I looked at the numbers and realized this is silly. One kilo of the raw material made about 100,000 tablets. There wasn't enough money involved to keep appealing the judgment. So I dropped it.'

He used his money instead to buy a company in Scotland called Norton Pharmaceuticals, which gave him entrée into one of the largest drug wholesalers in the UK. It meant he could more easily sell his own generics. After a while he decided that Norton was a nicer-sounding name than Harris, so he changed the name.

'I didn't want to keep subcontracting my manufacturing, so I bought a tableting company in south London, which meant, as Norton, we were a fully integrated generic drug company.'

The first in Britain.

And the bull's eye on the target for Big Pharma.

'As more and more drugs came off patent, the battles grew tougher and tougher. They had the lawyers and the money to tie us up everywhere they could. They took us to court for everything. We were always in court fighting them. That was the tactic they used.'

It is still the tactic they use. If Big Pharma can delay a generic coming onto the market, the amount it spends on legal costs is minor compared with what it's making by maintaining the monopoly. At the same time, the generic company has to take on those costs and a significant risk with no guarantee of success. Under British law, even if the generic company wins, which these days it invariably does, it only gets reimbursed 70 per cent of its costs.

'They've always had more money than anybody else,' Beck asserts, 'and use it to bully everybody else. We had every right in the world to manufacture a generic once the drug was off patent, but that didn't stop them from trying to stop us. They were relentless. Once, they even sued to keep us from making our generic version in the same colour as their version.'

He raises his hands in defeat.

'That's the one time I didn't bother to fight. It was easier to change the colour.'

Generic drugs had a fairly low profile in the United States until 1984, not only because they were often misunderstood – the branded drug industry has habitually tried to imply that generics are not the same as the real thing and therefore not as safe – but because there were, in those days, a lot of hoops generic manufacturers had to jump through in order to get approval. It was a profitable business but not a greatly profitable one and, while investment in generic drugs was steady, it was not enthusiastic.

Congressman Henry Waxman, a Democrat from southern California, and Orrin Hatch, a Senator from Utah, vitalized the industry with their Drug Price Competition and Patent Restoration Act. Known as Waxman–Hatch, it starts from the principle that the branded drug has already made its way through clinical trials to be proven safe and efficient. Logically, then, as long as the generic version is an exact copy, it too is safe and efficient. Now, to get approval, generic manufacturers only have to file an 'abbreviated new drug application' (ANDA) demonstrating bio-equivalency with the brand-name pharmaceutical. Instead of taking three years to get to market, as long as they have the science right it means they can manage it in three months. Getting there faster and cheaper freed resources so that they could bring even more generics onto the market. Before Waxman–Hatch, a mere 19 per cent of the prescription drugs dispensed in the United States were generics. By the close of the century, just about half were generics. Before Waxman–Hatch, only around a third of the big-selling branded drugs would be copied. These days, almost every branded drug can expect some generic competition.

Generally speaking, within the first year after patent expiration, the generic is priced 25–40 per cent less than the original and can expect to grab 20–50 per cent of the market, although it varies with each drug. But then a strange thing happens to the price of the branded drug. With market share dropping, say, 30 per cent overnight, and continuing to decline rapidly towards 20 per cent within a few years, one would think Big Pharma would try to compete on price. Instead, the companies rely for a while on a hard-core market. They send their reps out to convince doctors to keep patients on the branded drug, advertise heavily to doctors – and, in the States, advertise heavily to patients too – and spin the idea that generics aren't the exact equal of the original. They then try to make up their turnover by raising the price of the branded drug by whatever percentage of market share they've lost, say 30 per cent.

Waxman–Hatch took care of Big Pharma, too. The law extended patent terms by the time spent in the FDA review process plus half the time spent in clinical testing. There were some limitations to these extensions but, on average, the law awarded an extra three years' protection to Big Pharma's innovator drugs.

It also forced Big Pharma to become that much more inventive in its fight to keep generics down.

Sometimes it does it in the simplest of ways. Zovirax was made by Glaxo Wellcome in Britain to treat cold sores. Half way through its patent life, the company discovered that it could be used to treat chicken pox. So it went to the regulators and added chicken pox as an indication. That's perfectly fair and perfectly within the law.

When the drug came off patent, four or five generic manufacturers filed applications to produce their own version, intending that it too could be used to treat cold sores and chicken pox. But Glaxo wouldn't stand for it and took the generic companies to court. Its case was that, while the drug could be indicated for cold sores, the data supporting the drug's use for chicken pox were still protected and, therefore, if the generic companies were going to market a generic version of Zovirax, they couldn't claim it was a treatment for chicken pox. The court agreed. And Glaxo reps duly reminded doctors that, if they were looking for a chicken pox drug, the generic wasn't authorized and only Zovirax would do.

Big Pharma triumphed again when it convinced politicians that it needed another patent extension – this time set at six months – for drugs that had already been approved but that might be additionally tested and approved for paediatric use. Glaxo was one of the first on line with its heartburn remedy Zantac. It proved it was okay for kids and got itself an extra six months' protection. It is estimated it spent $1 million (£650,000) testing the drug and, for that, will earn back $50 million (£32.5 million).

Ten years after the Waxman–Hatch Act, the nations of the world signed up to the Uruguay Round Agreements Act. That was the treaty which lengthened protection to twenty years but started the clock ticking on the date that the patent application is filed rather than seventeen years from the date that the patent is granted. It wasn't the best Big Pharma could have done, but it was better than the old way.

Around the same time, Big Pharma decided that the generic companies were cutting too deeply into its profits, so it plotted to beat them at their own game. Merck was first, setting up its own generic company, West Point Pharma. Bristol-Myers Squibb set up Apothecon, Rhône-Poulenc Rorer had Arcola Laboratories, Lilly had Dista, American Home Products had Elkins-Sinn, SmithKline Beecham had Penn Labs, and Bayer had Schein. By 1994, eight of the fifteen largest generic companies were owned by Big Pharma firms.

Six years later, only one remained, Geneva Pharmaceuticals, a subsidiary of Novartis.

They moved away from the market because it's such a different business and such a different business culture. In generics, for instance, the time-scales are special. Sales figures come up every hour. Research-based companies don't work like that. The style is incompatible. Big Pharma thought that, by buying into the generic industry, it could take a slice of the market. What it wound up doing was making profitable businesses less profitable. So it sold out, inadvertently creating larger generic companies which, in turn, are growing globally.

And it went right back to fighting in the way it knew best.

Many US states have laws on their books freely allowing pharmacists to substitute a generic drug when a brand-name drug is prescribed, unless the physician specifically says he does not want a generic substituted. To help things along, several major companies send their reps out with a little gift for doctors – prescription pads preprinted with the words 'no substitution'.

The big drug companies also joined forces on a state-by-state lobby. They aimed to convince politicians that, at best, pharmacists should not be given a free hand to substitute and, at worst, the drug formularies for state-funded programmes should be limited so that generics could not compete on an equal footing with the branded drug.

Novartis, for example, petitioned the state of Massachusetts to limit the generic versions of Neoral, its leading medication for organ transplant recipients and the company's largest-selling drug. Even though the patent had expired some years before, Novartis argued that automatic substitution should not be allowed. The state ruled that, unless a doctor wrote 'no substitution', the pharmacist could dispense the generic.

Dupont did much the same thing when its blood thinner Coumadin – which earns it $500 million (£325 million) a year – went head to head against Barr Laboratories' generic version Warfarin. In this case, Dupont argued that Coumadin was in the special classification of 'narrow therapeutic index' (NTI). That means there is almost no margin of error in the dose. The drug can be dangerous if it is even slightly too high and ineffective if it is even slightly too low. Barr insisted that bio-equivalency meant Warfarin meets the NTI measure. The FDA even stepped into the fray. Associate Commissioner Dr Stuart Nightingale wrote in a fax to medical organizations and fifty state boards-of-pharmacy, 'There are no documented examples of a generic product manufactured to meet its approved specifications that could not be used interchangeably with the corresponding brand-name drug.'

Still Dupont lobbied for a policy of 'informed consent', which would prohibit substitution of NTI category drugs unless the doctor and the patient both agree. Some states already have such laws, others have been considering them.

Because prescribing drugs is a complicated matter, and several factors come into the equation, Big Pharma never hesitates to put doubt into doctors' minds – are you really willing to gamble with your patients' safety by trusting some generic company to meet the NTI requirements – and to make it as difficult as possible for people to get the equally safe but considerably less expensive generic version.

Then, too, even if the branded industry could have arranged a scandal to sink generic competition, it would never have come up with anything as good as the 1989 fiasco at the FDA.

Over the course of the previous year, some ANDAs seemed to be moving faster than others. When a few frustrated companies – notably Mylar and Barr – discovered their drugs were languishing in a system that didn't appear to be working, they demanded to know why. Federal investigators were called in, to uncover a scam where a handful of FDA employees were accepting bribes to approve certain drugs and thwart competing applications. The Commissioner at the time was forced to resign in disgrace and forty-two people, plus ten companies, were found guilty of criminal acts.

The damage done by the scandal to the generic industry was incalculable. Consumer trust plummeted. The branded industry jumped on that bandwagon with 'we told you so', further aggravating the situation. Even though most generic manufacturers were untouched by the scandal, the entire industry was bathed in damning headlines and suffered for years because of it.

The generic story of the new millennium was the blockbuster drug story of the 1980s – Prozac.

First introduced in 1988, it was hailed as the wonder drug of the decade and had a marked effect on 40 million lives. It is, perhaps, the single most successful drug in the history of medicine, at least since penicillin.

The development of the drug began in Britain in 1953, when psycho-pharmacologist John Gaddum suggested that a substance in the brain called serotonin played an essential role in human sanity. Within four years, the National Institutes of Health in Washington were devoting serious research to serotonin. That led drug companies in the 1960s to begin testing a new class of treatments, called selective serotonin reuptake inhibitors (SSRI). The Swedish company Astra was first on the market in 1981 with Zelmid, a drug withdrawn two years later for being toxic.

At the same time, scientists at Eli Lilly in Indiana were working on a project called '110140', which was a drug generically known as Fluoxetine. The FDA approved it in December 1987, and Lilly dubbed it Prozac.

As successful as Prozac was right from the start – its first full year on the market saw Eli Lilly sell 175 million of these green and white pills – it was never far from controversy. The FDA was accused of succumbing to pressure from Lilly for regulatory approval. Then, despite the agency's approval for the treatment only of chronic depression, Prozac was immediately prescribed for dozens of off-label uses, including PMS, bulimia and obsessive-compulsive disorders. Next, the price of the drug was questioned. It cost $2 (£1.30) per pill, when the market was filled with antidepressants at 10 cents (6p) a pill.

By 1990 it was the most famous prescription drug in the world. Prozac had even made it onto the cover of *Newsweek*. But a Harvard Medical School report in the February 1990 issue of the *American Journal of Psychiatry* reported six cases of what appeared to be Prozac-induced agitation leading to violence and suicide. The company denied that there was any link between the drug and suicide. The following year, the FDA agreed that no credible connection existed. Since then, more than 160 cases related to violence and suicide have been filed against Lilly. Most were dismissed. Some have been settled out of court, about which the company will say nothing. The few that went the distance saw Lilly winning them all.

In the meantime, the generic companies had been lining up, waiting for the moment when they could take their chunk of this market.

One of those companies is Barr Laboratories in New York. 'Around 1993 or so,' says Bruce Downey, Barr's CEO, 'it came to my attention that the original molecule patent on Fluoxetine was expiring in 1994. The problem was, there were two additional patents protecting Prozac. One was a "use" patent, which protects the use of Fluoxetine to treat mental illness, and that expires in 2001. Then there was this oddball patent, called a "mechanism of action" patent, which describes how Fluoxetine inhibits the reuptake serotonin. That expires in 2003. To me, that didn't sound as much like an invention as it did a description, so we had someone look at these two patents and the report came back that they might be vulnerable. We decided to challenge them in December 1995.'

The strength of Barr's case rested on that second patent, which Downey and his lawyers believed violated one of the principal rules of patent law – you only get one patent per idea.

'When you launch a patent challenge,' says Downey, 'there's a whole ritual you need to go through. You do the R&D for generic approval and file with the FDA. You tell them that you believe the patent on the product is either invalid or unenforceable and that you're going to challenge it. As soon as you make that certification to the FDA, you also send it to the patent holder. They then have forty-five days to sue you and, if they do, they get a thirty-month stay of FDA approval so that the court case can run its course. Regardless of the validity of the patent, they get thirty months.'

These challenges, Downey admits, are worth the effort only when the patent is weak and the prize is a blockbuster. 'There's no percentage in challenging strong patents. And if it's only a million-dollar product, the challenge wouldn't be economically feasible. But with Prozac, worth a couple of billion, if you can launch your generic even six months early, that can be worth hundreds of millions of dollars to the generic company.'

Needless to say, Lilly never intended to let Downey do

anything of the kind. It took his challenge to court, and also launched a tablet form of Prozac. Because he was challenging only the capsule form, this was a pretty strong defence against the possibility that he might win. 'It was a backup plan. If we'd won, they could have switched everyone over to the tablet and there wouldn't have been a market left for our capsule.'

Next, Lilly moved with its once-a-week pill. The idea here is to patent the delivery system – the time-release mechanism in the drug – then shift the market from a daily dose to a weekly dose, forcing Barr back to the drawing board to find another delivery system that would produce the same effect without violating this new patent.

And even then they weren't done.

Fluoxetine is a mixture of two isomers of the compound fluoxetine, one is active and one that isn't. The one that isn't active is theoretically the source of some of the drug's side-effects. So Lilly came up with a way of isolating the so-called positive isomer from the so-called negative isomer. Its idea was to get that single isomer approved, then switch people onto that compound.

'The key to generic use is substitution,' Downey continues. 'My Prozac won't be substitutable for the tablet form, the once-a-week form or the new compound. By the time we get there, that $2 billion might be down to a $200 million (£130 million) market with the $1.8 billion (£1.2 billion) moved to these other forms. Their reps are out there selling them now, convincing everyone that they're better. If they get their timing right, they introduce the new product, move the market and discontinue the old product so there's no product to substitute.'

In January 1999, the Federal District Court in Indianapolis, Indiana, granted summary judgment in favour of Lilly on Barr's claims against the two patents. Eighteen months later, on 10 August 2000, shares in Eli Lilly were halted on the

New York Stock Exchange awaiting an announcement. When it came, the shares plunged from $108.55 (£70.55) to $76 (£49.40), a loss of 29 per cent. And Barr's shares surged 68 per cent, from $45.75 (£29.74) to $77 (£50).

The US Court of Appeals for the Federal Circuit in Washington had overturned the original decision protecting Lilly's 'mechanism of action' patent. Barr would now be permitted to come onto the market with its version in 2001. At $2 billion (£1.3 billion) a year just in the USA, the decision had reasonably cost Lilly some 20 per cent of its global sales over those two years. Whether or not there is any market left for Barr is another matter.

In Britain, by contrast, the fight for generic Prozac wasn't a fight at all. It was a Sunday afternoon at an airport freight hangar.

The drug came off patent in the UK in early 2000, and Bioglan Pharmaceuticals was ready. But it took some doing because the law in the European Union is tipped in Big Pharma's favour. Unlike in the USA and, lately, Canada, where a generic manufacturer has the right to develop a drug still under patent – but cannot stockpile it in the country – European law prohibits a manufacturer from doing anything in the country while the drug is protected. The obvious result is that development – and, with it, investment and employment – leaves the country. In the case of Prozac, it had already come off patent in Germany, so Bioglan was free to go there.

'It's a crazy law,' notes Bioglan's generic chief, Lynda Foster. 'We can't work on a drug that is still under patent without being in violation of the patent holder's rights. This is not about selling the drug, this is not about infringing on their market, this is not about taking any money away from them, this is about getting our version ready to be on the market the day patent protection ends. This is about a law that forces us to invest and employ people outside the UK.'

It's about a law that was passed, obviously, because Big

Pharma sold politicians on the argument that it needed more time to exploit the market. Had Foster and Bioglan not found a way around it, Lilly might well have enjoyed another twelve to eighteen months of owning that market while the generic companies scrambled to copy the drug and get it approved.

Instead, Bioglan manufactured and stockpiled in Germany, and the minute the patent expired in the UK it shipped its version in.

'It all happened over a weekend,' Foster says. 'We flew the drug in from Germany on a Sunday, spent the day unloading the planes and loading the lorries. We got everything out so that our version was on sale first thing Monday morning.'

CHAPTER TEN

Playing Hardball

Garbage was a bit like a lucky dip because you never know what you're going to get.

(Paul Whybrow, undercover cop)

The first thing was always reconnaissance.

He drove his rented car out to the Spanish factory that afternoon, watched the main gate, noted that the guard shack was far enough away from the production facilities at the rear of the property, then followed the fence round to the back. He wanted to find a spot where he could safely park later that night and where he could most easily get over the fence.

He assured himself that access would be easy.

That's when he heard dogs barking.

Two German shepherds and a South African ridgeback raced to the fence. He waited to see if any others arrived. It was just the three. He reassured himself that access would still be easy and drove back into town to find the nearest butcher.

Much later, in the dead of night, now dressed in black with his face darkened too – the way you always see commandos in movies – he returned to the factory. Driving slowly and without headlights so as not to attract the guard's attention, he parked where he'd planned to, got out of his car and walked along the side of the factory towards the guard shack until he attracted the dogs' attention. When they barked and ran towards him, he tossed three steaks over the fence before retreating into the night. The dogs ripped the steaks apart and ate them quickly. An hour later, he rattled the fence at the rear of the factory. Nothing happened. There was no barking. The tranquillizers he'd laced the steaks with had done the job. So, now, while the three guard dogs slept, he climbed the fence.

Jimmying a window to get inside the plant was easy. He made his way through the offices and shop floors. He ripped labels off large chemical drums, found paperwork in files that he could take, and photographed the production facilities. On the way out, he stole several bags of office garbage.

Just as he got back to his car, the guard from the front gate started waving a flashlight at the factory. Perhaps he'd heard something. Perhaps he was wondering why the dogs were all asleep.

Paul Whybrow couldn't have cared less. It had taken him less than 25 minutes to get in and out. And, as the guard walked cautiously towards the factory, Whybrow disappeared into the night.

As the market for legitimate prescription drugs has grown to a colossal size, the market for illegal prescription drugs has grown alongside it.

These are illicit generics made by companies in direct violation of patent protection; counterfeit drugs that contain no active ingredients but are packaged and priced like the real thing; and substandard drugs that contain some active ingredients and are sold as the real thing but do not meet pharmocopoeial standards. Because it serves Big Pharma's interests, illegal prescription drugs get grouped together under the heading of counterfeits. When the word generic can be tossed into the pot, it deliberately tars legitimate generics with the same brush as counterfeits, trying to confuse the issues of bio-equivalence and counterfeit drugs to create the impression that the two words are interchangeable.

Of course they're not. The World Health Organization defines counterfeit drugs as those that are deliberately and fraudulently mislabelled with respect to identity and/or source. The only similarity between legitimate generics and counterfeits is that they both cost Big Pharma billions of dollars a year in lost revenue. Where legitimate generics and counterfeits are decidedly different is that counterfeits present serious health dangers to the public.

When a shipment of diethylene glycol, a chemical found in antifreeze, was deliberately mislabelled as glycerine, it was used to make cough syrup which was shipped to Haiti and killed eighty children. A few years before, the same solution was used to make counterfeit eye-drops that were administered to patients in Bombay. Fourteen people died.

When thousands of doses of a meningitis vaccine showed up in Niger, packaged to look like the genuine SmithKline Beecham product but actually nothing more than salt water, people died of meningitis.

When fake Microvlar oral contraceptives flooded the market in Brazil, dozens of women suffered unexpected pregnancies. In this case, the local subsidiary of the German pharmaceutical company Schering AG, which manufactures the pills, had produced a batch of look-alike placebos – 650,000 packages, each containing twenty-one lactose and sugar pills – to test out its new packaging equipment. The placebos were supposed to have been destroyed after the tests, but a criminal gang managed to steal them en route to the incinerator.

Statistics are difficult to compile and therefore not terribly reliable. Many years ago, the WHO reported that 7 per cent of the medicines sold in the world were counterfeit. The

International Federation of Pharmaceutical Manufacturers' Associations claims the correct figure could be as high as 10 per cent. A survey conducted by the WHO over a fifteen-year period, 1982–97, listed 751 incidents of counterfeit pharmaceuticals appearing on the market in 28 countries. Most of those counterfeits were said to have been manufactured in India, Pakistan, Indonesia, Thailand and the Middle East, but a source now says that perhaps a quarter of them came from Spain, Italy and Greece. Another report claims that substandard drugs are pouring into Africa from Vietnam, although it's not clear whether those counterfeits are produced by criminal gangs in Vietnam, or somewhere else and merely transshipped through South-east Asia.

Western health officials currently accuse China of being the largest producer of substandard medicines. While predictable denials come from Beijing, the Chinese continue to flood the Third World with their drugs. India also has plenty to answer for. An estimated 26,000 companies there manufacture pharmaceuticals, a huge percentage of them operating in factories that fail to meet even minimal standards of hygiene or safety. Those drugs regularly show up in pharmacies as far away as Mexico, a country said to be drowning in counterfeit medicines. One estimate is that fake drugs, mostly from India and China, make up 10 per cent of the lucrative Tijuana market. That's where Americans stream across the border from California to buy cut-price prescription drugs, medication not authorized for sale in the USA, or drugs for which they don't have a prescription. One batch of antibiotics, packaged in Mexico, was recently traced from Panama into Venezuela. When the sell-by date expired, the drugs showed up all over Latin America – including Tijuana – now in counterfeit packaging with an extra two years added to the expiry date.

In Indonesia, which has a huge counterfeit drug problem, 60 per cent of the market is supplied from Malaysia and Thailand by organized criminal gangs. In Pakistan, officials publicly admit that 2 per cent of the drug market is counterfeit. Experts privately agree that the truth is closer to 50 per cent. In Bangladesh, drugs worth $77 million (£50 million) are smuggled into the country every year, most of them outright fakes or substandard. *Time* magazine has suggested that up to half the medicines sold in sub-Saharan Africa could be fake.

In the USA and Canada, more and more counterfeit drugs are coming in through the mail, having been ordered over the Internet. The European Commission has categorized counterfeit drugs as one of the top ten most disturbing forms of high-tech crime. In Britain, counterfeit drugs have been seized alongside shipments of legitimate parallel imports from other European Union countries, especially Greece. Glaxo Wellcome became so concerned when manufacturers in India began copying a big-selling medication to treat urinary tract and respiratory infections – and then discovered that its best-selling Zantac was also easily counterfeited – it upped the stakes by designing entirely new packaging that was much costlier and more difficult to copy. Adding holograms and security seals has proven to be relatively effective. But it isn't always enough and usually works only when companies also send their reps out into the field to find fakes on pharmacy shelves and then spend money on ads to warn consumers.

As counterfeiters have become more adept at sidestepping those efforts, the multinationals have stepped up the fight. Twenty of the largest drug companies funded the Pharmaceutical Security Institute (PSI). Essentially a civilian police force, its agents are sent into the field to investigate clandestine manufacturers, to identify illegal traders, to gather samples for patent infringement cases and to liaise with law enforcement.

The PSI provides the industry's officially acknowledged spook.

Paul Whybrow was one of the agents the industry doesn't acknowledge.

Born in 1951 in Kent, England, Whybrow joined the British Merchant Navy right after school, sailed around the world on passenger liners for the next three years, came back to England and, not having any idea what he wanted to do with his life, got a job selling cars. That lasted nine years, until a strike by British miners, high interest rates and inflation combined to cripple the economy.

Needing work, he spotted a recruiting ad for the Port of London Authority Police, decided he wanted to be a detective and, at the age of 28, signed on. He completed the standard training courses but quickly discovered that the Port was not for him. He spent ten weeks patrolling the docks along the Thames River at Tilbury, checking seals on the back of lorries and, as they drove out the gate, getting his lungs filled with diesel fumes. As soon as he could manage it, he transferred to the City of London Police.

After two years of walking a beat, he moved into the Criminal Investigation Division as a detective. In 1984 he was assigned to the Fraud Squad. In those days, there were no professional undercover cops on the City force. Scotland Yard had a team of undercovers it loaned out to other forces, but these were mostly cops who knew how to buy stolen televisions off the back of a lorry. There wasn't anybody on any force who could play the role of a banker to negotiate a parcel of stolen bonds, or be a businessman interested in a stock scam.

The medium-height, dark-haired and fit Whybrow fell into it by accident. When an informant tipped off the Fraud Squad about a conman looking to unload Italian bank bonds worth $2 million (£1.3 million), somebody decided that Whybrow could look the part. He put his warrant card in his desk drawer, took some petty cash for cab fares and, without any backup, went to meet a pair of suspects at the Royal Garden Hotel in Kensington. Two weeks later, both suspects were in custody and the stolen bonds were recovered.

Because it worked the first time, Whybrow was sent undercover a second time. Within a few months, his superiors realized that he had a real talent for this. So they gave him a new identity, a passport to match, a credit card in his new name, a bank account in that name too, and an address. Just like that, the City of London Police had the first official undercover officer in the entire country specifically to deal with financial fraud.

'The problem was,' Whybrow says, 'no one at the time fully understood how to run an undercover operative. I'd work three or four weeks under my assumed persona and, when the case came down, they'd put me back on normal police duties. I wasn't taken out of circulation. In an ideal world I should have been. But this isn't an ideal world. It meant I had to learn how to be careful. Not paranoid, but careful.'

As far as he knows, he got burned only once. He was doing a job in Gibraltar and part of the script called for him to get arrested with his two targets. They were nabbed picking up £600,000. The idea was that the known fraudsters would lead him from that job to a much bigger one.

'We walked into the bank where we were to get the money and I went up to the manager to ask if the transfer had been made. That was the code. And sure enough, a few seconds later, the cops come through the doors. They cuffed us and hauled us off, including me, and put us in cells cut out of the Rock. The two targets kept telling me that someone stitched us up and I kept agreeing with them. The police interviewed them one by one, with me listening in from another room, then tossed us back in the cells together. Finally they brought us into the superintendent's office. He went through a big theatrical scene where he slammed our passports down on his desk and told us we were three very lucky gentlemen.

He said there just wasn't enough evidence to hold us. He said, "I suggest you walk out of this police station and get off this Rock before we find a good excuse to lock you up." We grabbed our passports, got into my hired car and drove to Malaga. We were supposed to meet again back in England to plan the bigger job.'

But it never happened. The informant who'd originally put Whybrow onto these two suddenly showed up with the news that he was a marked man. 'They'd somehow found out I was a copper. They told the informant they were going to get me. Sure enough, they called me for a meet but I didn't go. I never saw either of them again.'

Over the course of ten-plus years, Whybrow was someone else as he chased down stolen US government cheques that were being negotiated by the Camorra Mafia in Italy, as he helped recover huge amounts of counterfeit money, as he rounded up criminals living off the underground economy. There were times when his backups got lost, and times when his targets made sure he couldn't be followed, leaving him alone in situations with heavily armed and very determined criminals. But most of the time he found himself fighting the system.

'I wouldn't call it burn out because it wasn't, but I got to a point where I was very frustrated with budgetary constraints and bad management. Senior officers who'd never worked undercover couldn't understand how to manage an under-cover. And every undercover police officer you'll ever meet will tell you this. We all think we're a breed apart, but you're bound to feel different and special if you're travelling the world, dealing with top-class international criminals. In the case of some of my handlers, the biggest job they'd ever done was a burglary. They'd taken the exams and been promoted but they didn't understand someone doing undercover work at my level. They still wanted to talk to me as if I was investigating a petty cash theft.'

It came to a head the day Whybrow was paged by a target who wanted to meet him at the London Hilton. Whybrow went to his boss for petty cash. His boss asked why he had to meet the man now and why he needed money.

'I explained that I had to meet him because I was his man in the City and he asked to meet me. The governor wanted to know, how long are you going to be? I said, I don't know. He said, we don't have a lot of overtime this week. I told him it wasn't about that. He wanted to know what I was going to do with the petty cash. I said, I'll have to buy coffee or something and I need to get a taxi. He said, why take a cab when the Number 11 bus takes you straight up the Strand and from there you can pop around to the Hilton. I said, the last time this guy saw me I was driving a £62,000 Porsche, and you want me to arrive on a bus? That's the kind of thing I was up against. It pissed me off. I couldn't understand why I had to argue about a cab fare when I was putting my life on the line to catch criminals.'

So he decided to call it a day. 'I made a deliberate decision that it was time to go. It was easy because I knew there was a whole corporate world out there looking for people who could do what I did.' Within one week, Carratu International, one of Europe's leading private investigation agencies, offered him a job. He was taken to lunch by a man – call him Mr Jones – who said the firm needed someone to work undercover in its pharmaceutical division to collect evidence of counterfeit drugs and of patent and trademark infringements.

At Carratu, just as in so many private detective agencies, pharmaceuticals are a big money ticket.

'I started there on a Monday. By Tuesday I was in Barcelona doing an undercover job. Strictly front-door stuff. We were trying to prove that a company was infringing a drug called Captopril. This was for Bristol-Myers Squibb. I went to the plant on the pretext of being a buyer. All I was supposed to do was walk in the front door, give someone a list of my requirements and arrange to have a sample sent to me in England. Instead, I talked them into giving me a tour of the factory, white coat and safety glasses and all. I saw the Captopril being dispatched, obtained a sample the same day and came back to Jones on the Friday with everything he needed.'

After that, there were jobs for AstraZeneca, Pfizer, Glaxo Wellcome, Bayer and Roche.

After that there were also jobs that took him through the back door.

He insists that no one ever asks anyone to do anything illegal, but everyone knows what evidence is needed. 'They always say that they never condone anything illegal. But then, they've got to say that, don't they.'

Most jobs were routine and uneventful. During the day he'd go in the front door. At night he'd climb over the wall. He was never armed, except with tranquillizers for the dogs. The factory guards were armed, however, and occasionally shots were fired.

'You know what? The guards doing the shooting were just as scared as I was, except they were frightened that they were going to catch me. The last thing they wanted to do was nab me and have to deal with me. So they didn't shoot at me, they shot over my head to scare me away. They didn't know who they were chasing or how desperate I was or what I was after.'

What he was after were those drum labels which would tell his clients what chemicals were on hand and where they'd come from, who was shipping what to whom and what the manufacturing process looked like. So he stole labels and rifled desks and took photos and also grabbed as much garbage as he could.

'Garbage was a bit like a lucky dip because you never know what you're going to get. Inevitably, it's in black plastic bags, so you take it away from the scene. I've spent many many hours in hotel rooms with the floor covered in garbage. You rip the bags open, go through them, put the good stuff in a new bag and dispose of the worthless stuff wherever you can. You find invoices, letters, faxes, bank statements, customer lists, minutes of meetings, amazing intelligence. Ten years ago you could get whatever you needed out of someone's garbage. Today people know and they shred. That means you sometimes have to bring the garbage back to London and have the shreddies reconstituted. There are people who do just that, paste all those shreddies back together again. You collect whatever you have to, any way you have to, so that the client can make their case of patent infringement.'

For the next nine months, his work took him all over the world. Those years of police experience had fine-tuned his instincts – never paranoid, always careful. And here, budgets were not a problem. He used different names and had different front companies to back him up. When a client wanted him to check on an infringer in Beirut, he'd fly first to Cyprus, stay there a few days, then book onto a twenty-four-hour guided tour of Beirut. The boat sailed from Cyprus and, once in Beirut, passengers simply walked ashore without an Immigration check. The ship's captain held everyone's passport. Because there was never an entry stamp for Lebanon, he could come in and out without anyone suspecting he'd been there before. When the coach pulled up to the ship to take passengers on a tour, he'd slip away from the main party, rent a car and driver and do his own thing.

One of the front companies he used was registered in Malaysia. When his target, working for an infringing company, announced at a meeting in Switzerland that they were ready to do a deal, Whybrow realized that the infringer was nearly trapped. But the target said that, as luck would have it, he was going to be in Malaysia in three days' time and suggested they meet at Whybrow's offices there to close the deal. Whybrow immediately agreed, even though he didn't actually have an office in Malaysia.

He returned to England that night, spoke to the pharmaceutical company he was acting for, got its okay, and was strapped into a business-class seat on the following morning's flight to Malaysia. As soon as he arrived, he invented an office. Almost like a scene out of *The Sting*, he took over premises, decorated them with materials supplied by the pharmaceutical company to appear as if it was totally legit, and met his target. Once the bad guy and his associates had seen that Whybrow was who he said he was, and within forty-eight hours of arriving in Malaysia, the office set was struck and Whybrow was on his return business-class flight to London.

As if the world of counterfeit drugs and patent infringement isn't already murky enough, globalization has created an underworld of independent traders who move legal drugs back and forth across borders illegally. Most companies manufacture drugs specifically for export. All over Europe, for example, the multinationals cater to their home markets with one set of prices and then, because Eastern Europe is a huge market in size but a relatively poor one, they export a line of drugs – the same drugs they sell at home – priced lower for the East European market. What those freelance traders try to do is buy drugs destined for Eastern Europe and divert them back into Western Europe at home market prices.

One of Carratu's clients, the German giant Bayer Pharmaceuticals, started finding these so-called grey market drugs in pharmacies only a few blocks from its factory in Leverkusen. So Whybrow was dispatched to Switzerland to gather evidence against the culprit.

Normal surveillance on the target uncovered a way through which Whybrow – using one of his covers – could meet the man. Over the course of several weeks, Whybrow and the target began having lunch together. Whybrow gradually led their conversations around to business and, as trust built up, the target confessed that he'd been playing in this grey market. The way the target's business worked, he'd set up a company to do business in Russia, was buying medicine from Bayer and supposedly shipping it to Kazakhstan. At least, that's what Bayer had been led to believe. In reality, the products were never leaving Germany. They were being sold there through wholesalers and into the legitimate market.

Whybrow claimed to have a similar scheme set up through his non-existent Malaysian company. The target fell for it and suggested the two do a few joint ventures. To help it along, the target offered Whybrow the use of his offices in Switzerland. Over the next few weeks Whybrow directed faxes and contracts – all drawn up with Bayer's cooperation – to himself in care of the target's office.

Obviously, the target was reading the faxes and, just as obviously, he was believing what he read – that Whybrow was connected well enough to buy shipments from the multinationals that together they could divert.

The target now suggested they form a company together and open a bank account in Switzerland, over which the target himself would have signature authority. Bayer wired $25,000 (£16,250) into a Whybrow account in England, and Whybrow wired it straight out to the new company's account in Switzerland.

Everything was ready to go. Whybrow had even argued with the people at Bayer that, instead of closing down the target right away, they should allow one or two shipments to go through so that they could then track the people doing the target's bidding for him in Germany. But, at the very last minute, the whole thing was scrapped.

With hindsight, Whybrow wonders whether it was Bayer that got cold feet, or Jones. He thinks one possibility is that Jones stopped the job because Bayer didn't know what he was doing and if they found out, they would have been furious.

'He would have had to explain how we'd compromised the target. That's why I think he pulled the plug. I argued, if you genuinely want to catch this man, he's right there to be caught, right now. But he wouldn't do it. I guess he didn't have a way of explaining to the company exactly what he was doing.'

What Whybrow didn't know at the time is that Jones had a serious falling out with the management at Carratu. One day, just like that, Jones was gone. Whybrow, together with another ex-cop working at Carratu named Mick Flack, went to see Jones and found him very down in the dumps. They did what they could to encourage him, to assure him that he'd find another job somewhere. A few months later, Jones seemed to land on his feet, now dealing directly with Carratu's former client, Bayer AG.

Remembering the guys who'd stood by him, Jones wanted Whybrow and Flack to leave Carratu and form their own agency. He told them he was controlling all of Bayer's investigations, that he had a budget worth around £1.4 million for patent protection and that Carratu would never get a penny of it. He told them, 'You two start a business and you can have the lot.'

They were reluctant at first, but the offer was simply too good to turn down. So Whybrow and Flack left Carratu, set up a company called Temple Associates in Covent Garden, and went back to work for Jones.

One of the first cases Jones put Whybrow on to was the Canadian company Apotex. 'As far as Jones was concerned, Barry Sherman was a real thorn in his side. He was obsessed with Sherman, convinced that he was a major infringer, and he wanted him taken down. I'd been out to Canada on behalf of Carratu, gone through the front door of Apotex and had an interview. Mick and I then went out to Canada together, and sat around watching the trucks going into the loading bays at the rear of the plant. We dressed in overalls and carried clipboards and walked around the loading bays to see what was coming in and going out. Sometimes we even carried a box with some stuff in it, just in case someone asked us what we were doing there. We could tell them we were making a delivery to Mr Johnson. Make up any name. You'd be amazed at how much you can get away with if you look the part.'

Not far from the Apotex loading bay was an area with picnic tables where employees would have lunch. So Whybrow and Flack sat there eating hot dogs for a couple of days, always taking notes.

'Maybe we did a week's surveillance around the back. But the security is pretty tight at Apotex and you can forget about getting in there after hours. In Italy and Spain the places are made out of cardboard and string. But Apotex was good.'

They reported back to Jones that they didn't yet have what he wanted. He asked them to try to get a mole inside the company, and they felt they could arrange that. But that wasn't enough for Jones. Now he came to England to meet with Whybrow and Flack.

'We had lunch together outside at a country pub.' Whybrow alleges, 'And all the time, Jones is thinking about how he can get Sherman. This is no longer just business, this is personal. He doesn't just want to compromise him in a corporate way. He's talking about playing hardball with Barry Sherman. It was very direct. He said to us, We have to get this bastard Sherman. He said to us, What are we going to do about him? Let's take him out of the game. Take him out. Mick and I both knew enough not to say anything. He could have been wired. We weren't going to commit ourselves to anything. But Jones was suggesting everything.'

According to Whybrow and Flack, the conversation then went like this:

Jones: 'What can we do?'

Whybrow: 'What do you want us to do?'

Jones: 'What about your contacts with the police in Canada? Could you get him stopped?'

Whybrow: 'Anything's possible.'

Jones: 'Let's say he had half a kilo in his boot.'

Neither Whybrow nor Flack said anything.

Jones: 'What's his sexual preferences? Little girls? Or even under-aged boys?'

Again, neither Whybrow nor Flack would get drawn into this. But Whybrow insists that Jones was adamant.

Jones: 'We've got to take him off the scene. Got to take him out.'

On the face of it, Whybrow says, Jones might have thought they'd do it. After all, he was paying them £500 a day, and for that money they at least looked like they were interested. But he maintains there was never any question of doing it. 'We figured we'd go out there for a few days, then ring him from Canada and say, sorry, it can't be done. There are, after all, some things we're simply not going to do. You do have the draw the line. But we'd have gone out there and made like we're trying to do it and charge him three grand for it.'

In fairness to Jones, he adds, the closest he came to possibly suggesting that Whybrow and Flack break the law was saying that he wanted them to do 'whatever it takes'. According to Whybrow, Jones had always been a bit wild, and even slightly reckless, but he never said to them, do it. He never asked them to commit a crime.

Whybrow thinks now it was more like a fishing expedition. 'He was looking to find out from us what we could do. He wanted Sherman taken out but I don't know what his solution was. He might not even have had one. Even if he did, it wasn't going to be easy because Sherman is a very sharp operator.'

While all this was going on, Mick Flack was working some informants for Jones and Bayer in Cyprus.

The target there was a manufacturer named Pittas who, Jones believed, was one of Europe's major pharmaceutical infringers. Flack's contacts were a marine surveyor he called Lefty, who had access to the port at Limassol, and Lefty's cousin, who worked at the airport at Larnaca. Between the two of them, they covered just about anything leaving Cyprus, including everything shipped out of Pittas' factory.

Even though it was Flack's dossier, Whybrow had gone out there with him on several occasions. Now, in mid-February 1996, Lefty had contacted Flack to say he had some good documents to show that Pittas was still infringing. Flack got Lefty to send a sample along. It looked promising and so Flack asked Jones if he wanted anything done about it. Jones told him to go out to Cyprus right away.

Whybrow was working a small deal for a US bank in London where one of the managers had been compromised by a Russian. Flack told Whybrow he was running over to Cyprus and asked if he wanted to come along. The weather was terrible and snow seemed imminent. A couple of days in the sun appealed to Whybrow, so he said, sure.

Flack was already booked on a flight. Whybrow followed the next day. The two had rooms at the Four Seasons in Limassol but there was a lot of building work across the street and it was too noisy there. They moved to a hotel next door. There they encountered insurmountable troubles with the plumbing – the toilets wouldn't flush – and for the third time in three days they changed hotels again.

Lefty's documents weren't as good as Flack had hoped, so he pressed him for more. Lefty's response was to set up a meeting with a chain-smoking, gold-bracelet-bedecked character called Georgio. And that's when Whybrow says he started to smell a rat.

'He gave us the documents and left. But they were pretty useless. Lefty then told us that he had to pick up more documents from somebody's office the next day. We kept asking, are they going to be better and he kept assuring us they were. He said the guy who had the documents couldn't get them to us, that we had to go to him. So we hired a car, drove up to the offices, went in, some guy gave us more documents and we left. On the way out, I noticed there was some broken glass on the floor. But I didn't think anything of it. We just went back to the hotel, looked through these documents, there were some that were okay, packed them in my suitcase, checked out and drove to the airport. As far as we were concerned, that was the end of it.'

It was now late on Wednesday night, 14 February 1996. The airport was pretty much deserted. They parked the hire car, checked in and headed for the gate. That's when Flack remembered he still had the car keys. What they normally would have done is what they'd done hundreds of times before – wait until they got home to shove the keys into an envelope, address it to Avis and post them back. But, because they had half an hour before the plane left, Flack looked around, spotted the Avis desk about 100 yards away, told Whybrow to go through and took the keys back.

When he didn't find anybody at the Avis desk, Flack banged on the counter. The clerk, sleeping in the back room, woke up and took the keys. But, just as Flack turned around to leave, the fellow called him back. He told Flack he had to wait a minute because there was a problem with the car. Flack stood there while the fellow made a phone call.

Meanwhile, Whybrow was waiting for him at the gate. When the flight was called, he got onto the plane. He told himself that Flack would be there any minute.

The stewardess came through the cabin with orange juice.

Whybrow took one and settled down to read his news-paper. Then the stewardess returned to do a head count. Now Whybrow realized something was wrong. 'Once that happens, your instincts tell you not to get off the plane. I wasn't going to look for him because so much can happen on that island. I knew to stay put.'

The cabin crew started to shut the door. Just before they got it closed, someone knocked on it. They opened it and a man came onto the plane. He looked around, then went straight to Whybrow and asked to see his passport. He looked at it, gave it back to Whybrow, got off the plane and, again, the stewardess counted heads.

All this time the engines were running.

The crew went to shut the door and, just like the first time, before they could get it closed, someone banged on it.

Now several men came onto the plane, went straight for Whybrow and dragged him away.

A police car was parked at the bottom of the steps, its headlights shining on the underbelly of the plane. Flack was standing there, guarded by two men. The police had the cargo bay opened, and Whybrow's bag was pulled off. They put it in the car's headlights, opened it and yanked out the papers Lefty's contact had given them.

One of the cops asked Whybrow, 'What are these papers?'

He answered, 'Business documents.'

The cop said, 'These are stolen and you are both under arrest.'

Whybrow and Flack were handcuffed and taken to the police station at the airport. They were left sitting in the CID office under police guard, without water or food, all night. Late the next morning, an officer arrived from Limassol, bundled them into a car and drove around the countryside for what seemed like several hours until he found a woman hoeing her garden. She turned out to be a magistrate and was the one to sign the papers which kept them in custody.

Whybrow was then taken to Limassol Central Police Station. Flack was driven somewhere else. And for the next twenty-three days, without ever being charged, they were held in solitary confinement.

The cell was very small and had no light. They were not allowed to wash or to shave. The bed was one plank of wood, the blanket was filthy and moth-eaten. There was a Coke bottle in the corner that served as a urinal. If they needed a toilet, they had to wait until one of the guards took them to it. The food was mainly stale bread.

Sometime around the seventh day, a lawyer showed up. He was British, from London, and the first thing he told Whybrow was 'I'm from the B people. I've been sent to help you. Is there anything you need?'

Whybrow knew that B meant Bayer.

This lawyer arranged for a local attorney to take the case. Whybrow says he later learned that Bayer paid the local attorney £12,000 for each of them. But the local lawyer was never seen by either of them again. It was only later that Whybrow also learned how Lefty had been compromised by someone close to Pittas and, to save his own butt, had handed Pittas the two operatives from Bayer.

It was another week before Whybrow was able to get word out of the jail that they needed another lawyer. This time a young Cypriot attorney named Nicos Clarrides showed up and took over their case. But justice moves slowly in Cyprus and the two stayed on remand, waiting for a hearing from the night they were arrested until 20 June.

Because there was no statute for industrial espionage in Cyprus, they were then charged with burglary and conspiracy to undermine the economy of the island to the tune of $70 million (£45.5 million).

Both Whybrow and Flack went into shock. 'Our lawyer came to us and warned, you'll get seven years if you try to contest this and it doesn't matter what you say because this is now political. Our lawyer said there really wasn't much he could do. He said the only way he could help was if we pled guilty to the burglary. He said, they want to have you labelled as criminals who have come to Cyprus to undermine the economy. But if you plead guilty to the burglary, which is set at only £44, he said he'd do his utmost best to get the conspiracy charge dropped.'

The £44 was for the broken glass that was supposed to prove forced entry, which Whybrow had seen on the way out of the office the night they got the papers. 'Mick and I felt that, as much as it goes against the grain, we'd take the burglary charge. By this time, we're in prison together. I figured we'd already done four months and that if we pleaded to the burglary we'd be going home. So that's what we did. Then there was that terrible period of waiting for them to drop the conspiracy charge. That must have been three weeks.'

When they finally had their hearing, they walked into court thinking they'd be going home that day. Even their attorney said that for a £44 burglary they probably only should have done three weeks. So Whybrow and Flack sat in the courtroom thinking it was all over, until they heard the prosecutor outline their crime. He told the judge how the two had flown in separately and changed hotels three times. He never said the hotels were 20 yards apart and they had a good excuse each time. He made it sound as if they were simply trying to stay one step ahead of the police.

The judge sentenced them to eighteen months.

They were thrown back into prison.

Clarrides tried to assure them that they would win on appeal. But, until then, they were stuck in their cells. No toilet paper. No doors on toilets. No glass in any of the cells. Bare bars. Temperatures up to 32 degrees during the day and not much cooler at night. Boiled courgettes and fatty old meat for food. Nothing to do all day.

The prisoner in the cell next to Whybrow ate the light bulb. There was nothing left in his cell that he could use to do harm to himself, so he unscrewed the light bulb and ate it to kill himself. When that didn't work, he somehow got hold of battery fluid and drank that.

At night, the Iranian drug traffickers who were there would start chanting, then slashing themselves with little pieces of flint they sharpened on the floor. Down the cellblock were Russian hitmen who walked around scowling at everybody. They were all ex-special forces soldiers – Cyprus is infested with Russians – who were serving life terms for shooting people in the back of the head.

The only other Brits were three soldiers who'd raped and then murdered a Scandinavian tour guide. They'd chopped her up and had buried her in the sand.

Whybrow shakes his head. 'Those are the guys you had to sit and laugh and joke with. The guys you played Monopoly with. They expect you to be their friends. They spoke English and they were reasonably clean. It was them or the Iranian drug dealers or the Russian hitmen. At least with the Brits you could talk about cricket.'

Their appeal was heard on 23 September and the three-judge panel reduced their sentence to nine months. With a little bit of remission time, they were out three days later.

Handcuffed again Whybrow and Flack were put on a plane to Zurich. Whybrow had lost 3 stone. Flack had lost 4. Both were also totally hooked on Mogadon, sleeping pills that the guards handed out every night like candy. It was the only way they could cut out the noise. The British soldiers put the sleeping pills under their tongues and pretend to swallow them – because the guards had to see you take them – and then went back to their cells, spat them out and saved them up so they could bomb out at weekends.

From Zurich, Whybrow and Flack were flown to London. Flack went into a deep depression. Whybrow heard his wife of twenty-eight years say she was leaving him.

A few weeks later, Jones made contact.

He begged Whybrow not to throw this stuff back at him. He said that there was a willingness to help, but warned that it had to be managed in a professional way. He said there might even be a job at the end of it for the two of them. 'All I ask', he said, 'is that you don't throw stuff back at me.'

Whybrow agreed to a face-to-face meeting.

It never happened and he's never seen Jones again.

He was, however, contacted by a lawyer who said he was representing Bayer, hinting that the company wanted to settle with him, somehow to make it all right. That lawyer arranged a meeting with people who were apparently Bayer's corporate lawyers in London.

Whybrow then discovered that, as soon as the arrest hit the papers, someone claiming to be from Bayer had contacted his wife and Flack's wife and told them that, if they kept their mouths shut, they'd be taken care of. The media cottoned on to the wives immediately, but they refused to talk.

'We were all told', Whybrow insists, 'that we would be looked after. That's why we felt they owed us. Not because we got nicked working for them. Those are professional risks. They could have compensated us for going to prison. But our wives had been warned not to mention the word Bayer to anybody and they didn't. They kept their part of the bargain and so did we. We could have said that in court in Cyprus. That's all Pittas wanted to hear. He wanted us to say we were working for Bayer. He wanted to hear someone say that Bayer had instructed us to take covert actions against him. But we didn't. All we wanted to be recompensed for was keeping our mouths shut. We were asked a million times who we were working for and we kept our mouths shut. That's why Bayer owed us.'

In Whybrow's mind, there's no doubt that Bayer, or at least someone acting for Bayer, paid all their legal bills. When Whybrow met with the lawyers and told them the story, they seemed shocked. He told them about the way he'd operated, and about how he'd set up a company in Switzerland with a $25,000 bank account to trap an infringer. He told them about the jobs he'd done for Jones and, to prove he was one of them, he even showed them his Bayer ID card.

Now the lawyers really got nervous.

They told him that, as a sign of good faith, if he returned that ID card to them, they would see that he was taken care of. So, in front of a witness, he handed them the card.

'That's right, because I had a witness, I handed it back to them. It never even touched the table. They scooped it up, and you could see the look of relief on their faces. That's when they got aggressive. How do we know about this and about that? I showed them all the papers. They wanted copies of the papers but I wouldn't give them any. They offered to buy them. In return for all papers and a total gag on what we did for Bayer, they offered us about £12,500. Mick and I both said no. We said that was an insult. And guess what, they decided they didn't know who we were, that they'd never heard of us, and we've never heard from them since.'

Whybrow is married again and runs his own agency, but doesn't do any pharmaceutical work. Flack is out of the business entirely. Jones ran a pub for a while – Whybrow believes Bayer may have bought it for him – but got out of that and moved to Germany, where he now lives within walking distance of Bayer's main office.

The infringers are still infringing.

And, one presumes, Bayer is still doing whatever it has to.

CHAPTER ELEVEN

Whatever it Takes

The physicians' role as God is diminishing all the time.
(Duncan Moore, analyst)

'The US market is the critical market for the pharmaceutical industry,' says Morgan Stanley Dean Witter's star analyst Duncan Moore. 'That's where you've got the highest rate of receptivity to new products, and also the highest prices. What's more, it's a market that has demonstratively shifted away from being entirely professional to becoming consumer driven. The physicians' role as God is diminishing all the time.'

Because drug companies in the States can directly target consumers through advertising, the patient's input into treatment is playing an increasingly important role in drug company marketing. The result is an expanded market.

'Much of the value that is created by new pharmaceutical products is value which is recognized by the consumer and not so readily by the payer-provider industry.'

Moore says that, if you had a stomach ulcer in the 1960s, it was usually removed by surgery and that was very expensive. When Tagamet came along, you could get treatment for your ulcer for a relatively modest cost and avoid surgery.

'Clearly, the insurance industry in the US and the government-sponsored health systems in Europe benefited enormously from that. Tagamet and Zantac, between them, got the incidence of stomach ulcer surgery down to virtually nothing.'

Now, with the advent of proton pump inhibitors, the cost of treating acid disease has gone up dramatically.

'But you and I, instead of having to spend four weeks in pain waiting for the ulcer to be cured by Zantac or Tagamet now only have to endure two weeks of pain if we take a proton pump inhibitor. It's more effective but more costly. There is a benefit to the consumer but none to whoever pays the healthcare bills. The drug companies recognize this consumer angle to prescription pharmaceuticals and have targeted their marketing to the consumer rather than just to the healthcare professional.

'It will happen in Britain,' he promises, 'despite the best efforts of the governments that pay for healthcare.'

And although he doubts that direct-to-consumer advertising will happen in Europe he feels government resistance becomes irrelevant as we become increasingly computer literate.

'Educated people are already finding out about diseases and treatments on the Internet. They're already no longer entirely dependent on the physician.'

So, in essence, direct-to-consumer marketing has already come to Europe and, as a result, drug prices are rising to reflect increased marketing costs.

'If you're a Glaxo and you're the only company promoting a migraine drug, then obviously it doesn't cost you a huge amount of money to have quite a high awareness of your product. When there are four companies doing exactly the same with direct-to-consumer marketing, then the cost of making the same relative noise goes up. That's happening in most categories. Costs are going up as healthcare becomes more and more a consumer product.'

*   *   *

Big Pharma knew it was coming, because it'd been lobbying for it for years. But when it happened, when the FDA finally lifted the ban on direct-to-consumer advertising (DTCA) on television in August 1997, the drug companies still weren't sure how the public would react to it.

DTCA had been around for years. The first prescription drug ad directly aimed at the public was to sell Eli Lilly's new anti-arthritic drug Oraflex in 1982. The company's claim that Oraflex prevented arthritic progression turned it into a $1 million-a-week drug. But, five months after it hit the market, the drug was pulled because of renal failures and deaths. It turned out that there had been such a serious failure to report problems before FDA approval that prosecutions followed, including that of a British medical director working in the United States. There was also litigation in the UK. The FDA put a halt to DTCA for two and a half years in order to revise its guidelines and tighten controls. It set all sorts of limitations on what could and could not be said, straight-jacketing advertisers with all sorts of rules, regulations and FDA scrutiny.

Now, in August 1997, Big Pharma could advertise products by name, could make claims about a drug's efficacy and didn't have to fully list side-effects. The main precautionary notes that once had to be included were reduced to a mention somewhere that only doctors could prescribe the drug and a website address or freephone number where the public could get more information.

The companies had been advertising to doctors for ever and knew how to market cholesterol-lowering drugs and antidepressants to physicians. Selling to the public, in what would soon become a marketing free-for-all, was a very different game. To begin with, the public had no understanding of the science. Pharmaceuticals would have to be sold like breakfast cereals. But, unlike breakfast cereals, the public couldn't just go out and buy the stuff. All ad campaigns are crafted to create or reinforce a need for a product and then create a response. In this case, the need would have to be explained in a language that the average person could understand and the response would have to be, 'go see your doctor about this'. So Big Pharma, not having any idea how this would work, stuck its toes into the water with a series of ads for a small number of relatively benign drugs.

And the response was far beyond anything that the drug companies could ever have hoped for.

The floodgates were open.

Patients already taking drugs asked their doctors for a change in prescription to the advertised drugs. Patients not taking drugs decided they needed drugs and went to their doctors to get them. Doctors, being in business and needing to keep their clients happy, began prescribing more drugs. And ad spending soared to over $100 million (£65 million) a month, an increase of 500 per cent in just three years.

Schering-Plough hired Joan Lunden, the former host of *Good Morning America*, to help sell Claritin, making her the first TV celebrity to endorse a prescription drug. It added a vacation in Hawaii contest to the campaign. Within six months of the FDA ruling, Claritin was the number one prescription drug being advertised, its sales having risen by almost a third. Other allergy drugs fought back with ad campaigns and showed huge increases in sales – Hoechst Marion Roussel's Allegra doubled, Pfizer's Zyrtec rose 56 per cent. Merck took out full-page newspaper ads plugging its cholesterol-lowering drug Zocor and offering customers a money-back guarantee. Glaxo advertised its stop-smoking treatment, Zyban. Astra advertised its treatment for stomach problems, Prilosec. SmithKline advertised its antidepressant Paxil.

Certain categories of drugs lend themselves more easily to ads – at least they sell better when advertised. Those include lifestyle drugs, such as Viagra and Rogaine, which promises to grow hair; instant gratification drugs, such as allergy treatments, analgesics for pain and cures for stomach problems; and fear of the future antidotes, medications that reduce high blood pressure or high cholesterol and therefore comfort consumers into thinking that they are reducing the risk of heart attacks.

Within six months of the FDA ruling and counting only the seven most heavily advertised health problems – cholesterol, smoking, osteoporosis, hair loss, ulcers, menopause and depression – 3.2 million more Americans had gone to see their doctor than in the six months prior to the FDA ruling, which was an increase of 22 per cent.

Within a year, a Harris Poll survey for Harvard University's School of Public Health reported that almost 30 per cent of the patients taking a prescription drug had spoken to their doctor about a drug they'd seen advertised. Although, of the same people surveyed, only around 12 per cent actually received a prescription for the advertised drug. That led critics of DTCA to conclude that one very real effect of the FDA ruling was to increase visits to doctors by people asking for drugs that their doctors didn't feel they needed.

'Direct-to-consumer advertising for certain drugs has had a dramatic impact in volumes of prescriptions and expenditures,' observes Dr Steve Schondelmeyer at the University of Minnesota's Prime Institute. 'But even more than the impact on drug expenditures, it creates added costs in the healthcare system. I've talked to many physicians who tell me that the number of visits by patients just enquiring about a drug that they've seen advertised has gone up dramatically. Now, some of those patients might have needed treatment and they weren't getting it, so that's fine. But a number of those patients didn't need treatment. They're the "worried well". The ad induced a visit that wasn't necessary. So the drug companies, advertising for their benefit, are creating additional costs in the healthcare system. Then, with some of those people who

232

don't need any treatment, the doc figures, oh well, maybe a little something isn't going to hurt them so I'll give them a prescription anyway. It's difficult to argue that this is acceptable.'

It is precisely the prescribing to the worried well that has made DTCA the overwhelming success it has been.

'The drug companies are banking on a synergy between the direct-to-consumer and the direct-to-provider advertising,' notes Dr Eric Rose, a member of the University of Washington School of Medicine faculty who has extensively researched pharmaceutical marketing and the drug company–physician relationship. 'The patient sees ads with the name Lipitor and a picture of someone running happily in the grass. The doc sees ads for Lipitor which proclaim, better than Nevacore, 20 milligrams a day, and have some simple little graphs. What the drug company is hoping is that when the patient mentions Lipitor, that triggers the doctor's decision.'

There is also, Rose says, the any-banana-in-the-bunch syndrome. 'If the patient mentions a specific drug and there really is no significant difference among different drugs in a given category, then the doctor is more likely to choose the one that the patient has mentioned just because he's more likely to want to satisfy the patient.'

Drug company market research shows that when people go to their doctor and ask for a specific prescription, as long as the patient's analysis is correct and the medication is needed, the doctor tends to prescribe it. But there are times when the need for medication is less clear-cut and doctors are still willing to meet patient expectations.

'Especially', Rose says, 'where that will foster compliance with other aspects of treatment that the physician feels are also important. The practice of medicine is, after all, salesmanship and negotiation. It is trying to get someone to agree to do something that's going to keep that person healthy.'

A patient paying a doctor for a visit creates a business–client relationship and, as such, it is understandable that the client would want to have some say in the results of that visit. Asking for a particular drug or treatment might well be part of the process. And the doctor involved might well feel that she needs to satisfy her client.

In an NHS-type situation, where the patient doesn't pay for the visit or the prescribed drugs, the relationship is different. It probably doesn't affect the medicine, but it certainly would affect other aspects of the doctor–patient relationship, such as trust.

Many doctors in the USA report that much of what gets fed back to them by patients who learn about drugs through DCTA rarely applies to their specific case. That DCTA has led to unnecessary concerns about some drugs and misguided notions about others. That it has also given a bias to the more expensive drugs – those advertised – and created some doubts in the minds of patients about the efficacy of less expensive, older drugs, especially generics.

A spokesperson for PhRMA, the industry's Washington lobby, insists that advertising gets patients to consult their physician, it doesn't dictate the result of that consultation, and it doesn't necessarily mean that those patients are going to wind up taking the advertised drugs. Yet while the industry measures the success of DTCA by claiming that people are going to see their doctors in record numbers to talk about their health because ads have made them aware of problems they need to deal with – and see that as a good thing – there is another side to this that some physicians feel is not such a good thing. It is that the criteria necessary for an informed choice do not appear in an ad, because if they did the information would be far beyond the understanding of the average person.

Responding to the PhRMA, Public Citizen's Health Research Group has stated categorically, 'We are aware of no valid scientific evidence that suggests DTC prescription drug advertising leads to better health outcomes for the public.'

On the contrary, the group believes that the prevailing evidence shows clearly that DTCA may induce needless economic hardship and perhaps physical harm to consumers.

Now that the genie is out of the bottle, it is near-impossible for anyone to control the genie's behaviour.

Eric Rose feels that, 'You can either try to regulate the drug companies' marketing efforts and encounter a tidal wave of resistance, or the profession can prevail upon itself to behave in a professional manner. The responsibility is 100 per cent with docs to educate themselves about the promotional techniques of these companies and to insulate themselves at least from the effects of them. I wouldn't go so far as to say that it's unacceptable for docs to expose themselves knowingly to any type of promotional presentation, but I think it's unconscionable not to check how that content jives with the peer-reviewed medical literature.'

Drug companies argue that advertising isn't really advertising, it's education. That by making the public more aware of illnesses and treatments, they're also making people more conscious of their own health and, perhaps, getting them to discuss it with their physicians. They argue that when patients are educated about health, they are healthier consumers.

To suggest that direct-to-consumer advertising is educational is, according to Dr Christophe Kopp, a GP and editor at the independent French drug bulletin *La Revue Prescrire*, 'Like counting how many angels can dance on the head of a pin'. He says he spends a lot of his time deconstructing misinformation from ads and resisting patient requests for hyped-up and costly drugs. As for the argument that DTCA of prescription drugs 'empowers people' and that 'reluctant doctors are just paternalistic', he insists, 'That's simple demagoguery'.

Merck had turned its promotional guns away from Mevacor in favour of Zocor, its new anti-cholesterol drug, to do battle with Warner-Lambert's Lipitor. When Bristol-Myers Squibb came in with Pravachol, ads worth $126 million (£82 million) over two years earned it only the third place slot. It abandoned the campaign, raising the question, if those ads were merely about providing information to the public, why were they stopped? But no one at BMS cared to answer the question. Two phone calls to the company, one in the USA, one in the UK, elicited the response 'We'll have to get back to you on that one,' but nothing more.

It is apparent that drug companies spend the vast sums of money on advertising only when ads result in more prescriptions being written. The patient is being turned not into an educated consumer but rather into a foot soldier in Big Pharma's battle to get doctors to prescribe.

Why else, for example, would the companies spend money trashing competitors that have already been ruled dangerous?

When the FDA announced in 1997 that studies were showing how phenolphthalein, the active ingredient in many over-the-counter laxatives, presented a cancer risk for humans, Bayer recalled stocks of its phenolphthalein laxative Phillips' Gelcaps. Within a day or so, Schering-Plough was running full-page ads in *USA Today* and the *New York Times* reiterating the FDA's findings, noting that a Novartis laxative contained phenolphthalein and that Schering's laxative did not. Its product contained bisacodyl, which was itself being looked at by the FDA, but the ads didn't mention that.

Also not loudly publicized by the drug companies are those side-effects of DCTA – for example, wasting doctors' time with unnecessary visits. One drug-marketing research firm found that, while patient visits increased overall 2 per cent in the ten months following the FDA ruling, patient visits just for allergies – in the wake of the Claritin, Allegra and Zyrtec campaigns – increased by 10 per cent. A survey of 1,000 adults, commissioned by *Time* magazine in association with *Health* magazine, found that one-third of the consumers who saw a drug company ad mentioned the drug to their doctor.

Now factor in increased prescribing, a certain percentage of which is obviously not warranted. In 1998, Claritin's US sales climbed to $1.9 billion (£1.2 billion), this after Schering-Plough spent $136 million (£88 million) advertising the drug.

And, because the advertised drugs are almost always the most expensive ones, drug costs rose an estimated 12–15 per cent during the first year of DCTA alone. *Time* magazine demonstrated this by showing that nearly 30 per cent of the people they surveyed said that if a doctor did not give them the drug they wanted – as opposed to no prescription or a prescription for another drug – they would consider switching doctors.

Research has also shown that scientifically unsupported information that appears in drug advertising has greater influence on prescribing decisions than the scientific literature.

The watershed study was done in 1982 by Dr Jerry Avorn at Harvard University. Eighty-five doctors in the Boston area were presented with drug company ads and scientifically peer-reviewed literature on two classes of drugs – propoxyphene-based analgesics, which were supposed to be the most advanced on the market for reducing pain, and cerebral vasodilators, which supposedly brought more oxygen to the brain and were therefore said to be a practical way of treating senile dementia.

Both classes of drugs were heavily touted by their respective companies and made to look effective. The scientific literature, in contrast, showed propoxyphene-based analgesics to be no more effective than aspirin and cerebral vasodilators not at all effective in treating dementia. When first approached, 68 per cent of the doctors in the test sample rated drug company marketing as only minimally important in influencing their prescribing, while 62 per cent said scientific papers were very important. But, when Avorn and his team questioned them about the two classes of drugs, 50–70 per cent of the time the doctors repeated information that came only from drug company promotional materials. Avorn's conclusion was simple – clever promotion, even when it belies the medical literature, can fool a majority of doctors.

With the exception of the United States and New Zealand, most western countries limit prescription drug advertising to professional medical and pharmaceutical journals. Direct-to-consumer advertising is not permitted in Britain or, for that matter, anywhere in the European Union. Drug companies get around the embargo by designing DTCA to appear as anything but an ad for a drug. Instead, they advertise diseases – the pharmaceutical version of an infomercial – and hint that the cure is the company's unnamed drug.

In September 1998, Novartis took a three-quarter-page ad in the *Guardian* under the headline 'Living with Heart Disease'. The copy reminded the public that Novartis was a world-leading life sciences company and, as such, was developing treatments to help people suffering from hypertension and to reduce the risk of heart attack. The ad didn't name a product – that would have been illegal – but the very obvious implication was that anyone interested in knowing the name of the drug and, consequently, getting a prescription for it, needed only to apply to their own GP.

Comments Dr Joel Lexchin, a Canadian physician who has been highly critical of DTCA, 'This is a very common tactic that companies use even in advertising to physicians. They either make vague general statements like the one in this ad and let people draw their own, usually erroneous, conclusions or they cite relative risk reductions rather than absolute risk reductions in order to make the product look much more impressive.'

Canada represents a good-sized secondary market where DTCA is not permitted but drug companies expect a Canadian audience as a free bonus for a skilfully bought campaign. It's because the majority of Canadians live along the US border and are bombarded by US media. They can watch US television, listen to US radio, read American newspapers and American magazines. So, whether they want to be or not, they are an addition to the US catchment area for advertising. And they are perfectly free to visit their doctor and ask for a prescription for a drug that they've seen advertised illegally but unstoppably in Canada.

In the Third World, where regulatory agencies are inefficient and have little power, companies headquartered in Europe and North America get away with things that are much too dubious to try at home.

To sell Prozac in Pakistan, Eli Lilly provided doctors with a brochure to hand out to patients. Inside was a questionnaire – listing vague symptoms such as sleeping too little or too much – so that consumers literally could diagnose themselves with depression. Anyone passing the test was encouraged to take one capsule of Prozac every day.

Because Pakistan, like many developing countries, doesn't enforce prescription-only regulations, anyone can easily buy Prozac, or any other prescription medicine. Professional medical associations in Pakistan labelled the promotion deplorable.

Another company looking to sell into the Pakistan market – where more than 200,000 children die from diarrhoea every year – heavily advertised its anti-diarrhoea drug as suitable for all cases. When the government there realized that the drug's advertised use might be harmful to patients and, in any case, manifestly contravened World Health Organization advice on treatment of the illness, the company withdrew the ad.

The trade magazine *Medical Marketing & Media* gave the game away in its November 1995 issue when it confessed, 'In the old marketing model, pharmaceutical companies created patient demand by influencing doctors to write prescriptions. In DTC promotion, companies listen to the patient, respond to their needs, and hope to increase sales by driving consumers to a doctor's office and requesting their product.'

Public Citizen asks, if the purpose of DTCA is to educate and inform the public about drugs, why isn't the information complete and accurate? Because, when it comes to that, the industry has a pretty miserable record for being completely accurate in its advertising.

The University of California at Los Angeles conducted a study in 1992 on 109 ads, randomly selected from major medical journals. After putting together a panel of recognized specialists, they asked each doctor on the panel to evaluate those ads that related to his or her particular field of medicine. A majority of the doctors decided that thirty of the ads should not have been published because of serious medical inaccuracies and thirty-seven required major revisions in order to make them accurate. What's more, only nine of the ads were considered in keeping with FDA regulations on medical advertising. That meant, 100 of the 109 were in some way in violation of those same FDA regulations.

If they advertise that way to doctors, who presumably have some way of deciphering what's being said and, with some effort, discovering the truth, what then of the unsuspecting public?

AdBusters, a magazine out of Vancouver, British Columbia, has an international reputation for debunking advertising. It dissected a Bristol-Myers Squibb ad for Pravachol.

The ad featured a picture of Darryl Sittler – a Canadian sports icon – and his family, and was headlined, 'Darryl Sittler knows about the risks of heart attacks – so should you.'

The copy read, 'Darryl lost his father to a heart attack. He believes in knowing your cholesterol risk. One out of three first heart attack victims die not knowing their risk. One particular medication, with a good diet and lifestyle, can reduce the risk of first heart attacks by 31 per cent and second heart attacks by 62 per cent. Call now, if not for you but your family.'

No product is named, giving the ad the look of a public service announcement. There is also free-phone number for the 'Heart Attack Prevention Line'. Bristol-Myers Squibb's name appears only in small print at the bottom.

AdBusters attacks the ad in three areas.

First, the technique. Here's a sports star who seems to be in great shape and the inference is, if he's worried about having a heart attack, the rest of us who aren't in such great shape should be terrified. Making that sort of association is a common ploy.

Second, the inference that there's an easy way to become less susceptible to a heart attack. All any of us have to do to become 31 per cent less likely to have a first heart attack is to take this medication, eat plenty of vegetables and jog. Not only does this oversimplify a problem that is both complex and important, the statement is not supported by any evidence that it is, even in its simplicity, true.

Third, the use of the figure of 31 per cent. This comes from a study published in the *New England Journal of Medicine* in 1995 which looked at 6,600 men from western Scotland. The average age was fifty-five. All had high cholesterol. Some 45 per cent smoked. Half the group took Pravachol. The other half took the placebo. The *NEJM* results noted that those taking the placebo had a 7.9 per cent chance of a first heart attack. Those taking Pravachol every day for five years had only a 5.5 per cent chance of a first heart attack.

The difference therefore is 2.4 per cent. The way Bristol-Myers came up with 31 per cent was by dividing the 2.4 per cent difference in risk by the placebo group's 7.9 per cent.

AdBusters calculated that a 55-year-old woman with high cholesterol but no other risk factors has a 3 per cent chance of a heart attack in the next five years. By taking Pravachol every day for five years, she might reduce her risk by 31 per cent – although you can't tell that from the survey because it didn't look at 55-year-old women with high cholesterol – which brings the 3 per cent figure down to 2 per cent, or a benefit to only 1 per cent of 55-year-old women.

But that's not what the ad suggests.

It implies that Pravachol increases everyone's chances of avoiding a first heart attack by one-third.

How many Pravachol prescriptions would it have sold to North Americans if it said, 'for Scottish males with high cholesterol, half of whom smoke, a medication which costs approximately $4,000 for five years of therapy, with a good diet and lifestyle, can reduce the risk of a first heart attack by just over 2 per cent'?

Wyeth-Ayerst promoted its antidepressant Effexor in a newspaper campaign with headlines such as 'I got my mommy back' and 'I got my marriage back'. By suggesting that life could get better for children and other family members as soon as a depressed adult seeks treatment, this reinforces the notion that there is a pill for every ill. If this was genuinely intended to educate, shouldn't there be some mention of the fact that there could be equally effective, less expensive alternatives?

'People who may or may not be healthy but don't believe that they're healthy are being encouraged to see their doctor because they've been encouraged to think they might have a problem,' says Dr Peter Mansfield, the Australian physician who founded the Medical Lobby for Appropriate Marketing (MaLAM). 'They've made up their mind on the basis of the advertising, which of course has been designed to persuade them that something might be wrong. The doctors are then under a lot of pressure to do what their patients want. Drug companies know that doctors are always looking for simple solutions, that we're under pressure to see a lot of people in a short period of time, that we're looking for something we can do for people and do quickly.'

When Eli Lilly started promoting its cancer drug Evista for reducing the risk of breast cancer, AstraZeneca – maker of Nolvadex, the only drug approved by the FDA to promote itself as proven to reduce the risk of breast cancer – filed an injunction under the Lanham Act, which prohibits false advertising. The court agreed with AstraZeneca's claim that the dissemination of false information creates a 'grave public health risk'.

In a press release acknowledging the court's decision, AstraZeneca noted, 'It is imperative that the public and physicians be able to trust the information presented to them by pharmaceutical companies.'

To sell Prilosec, an Astra–Merck joint venture, ads were used that had the effect of striking fear into anyone with a stomach ailment. 'People who have heartburn two or more times a week probably do not have ordinary heartburn, but the potentially serious condition of gastro-oesophageal reflux disease.' Then, too, they may also just be eating too much.

Similarly, Merck opted sell Fosamax, a drug aimed at the post-menopausal market, with the headline 'Thanks to Fosamax and its power to rebuild bone, Susan Brenner is still paddling her own canoe after 50'. There was a picture of a nice-looking, presumably healthy, fifty-ish woman next to a lake at sunset. The text went on to say that meno-pausal women may have osteoporosis and because of that are susceptible to breaking bones. What it didn't say was that statistics show that most osteoporotic fractures occur not at fifty but after the age of seventy-five. Nor did it provide any hint of what happens when a woman of fifty takes Fosamax for the next twenty-five years. There may not be a long-term study available to show what happens or if there is, and the results are negative, Merck may have a reason for not saying. But the hint is, women will be better off for taking the drug. In fact, there are long-term studies of oestrogen, which is also prescribed to prevent fractures by increasing post-menopausal bone mass, and they indicate that the effect of the drug is reversed after use is discontinued, and show no long-term gain if used for less than ten–fifteen years.

When Eli Lilly started advertising its antidepressant Prozac, it already had a huge share of the market. The ads were designed to expand that market. Its 'Welcome Back' ads were aimed at people not being helped for depression and who would, through Prozac, be welcomed back to a normal state of mind.

The text tried to demystify public perceptions of tranquillizers while all the time reassuring potential customers that Prozac is not a tranquillizer. 'It won't take away your personality. Depression can do that, but Prozac can't.'

When Pharmacia & Upjohn's Rogaine went from prescription-only to over-the-counter status, meaning that anyone in the United States could simply walk into a store and buy it, ads for the product took on the look of a shampoo ad. 'Hair care you need . . . right now.' Obviously, from a marketing standpoint, it's easier to sell a general beauty care product than a medicine.

The Mexican Prescription Drug Industry Association (AMIF) followed that lead with a series of large newspaper advertisements in late 1996 telling consumers to insist that the medicines prescribed by their physicians should not be substituted with generics by the pharmacist. It showed a pregnant woman saying that, for her health and for the health of her future child, she always follows her doctor's recommendations.

The point of the ad is to suggest that generic substitution could be harmful during pregnancy. But at no point does AMIF provide any scientifically acknowledged proof of that claim, obviously because it is not true.

In 1995, the magazine *Consumer Reports* sent twenty-eight ads for prescription drugs for evaluation to thirty-two medical specialists. The experts judged that only about half the ads presented a balanced view of effectiveness, potential benefits and risks. Only about half the ads spelled out side-effects in the body of the ad, as opposed to putting it at the bottom in minuscule, nearly unreadable print. Eleven of the ads were judged by at least one member of the panel to be more harmful than helpful. And one-third of the ads contained errors of fact or made claims that could not be scientifically defended.

After an ad for Cortaid ran in *Parade* magazine containing this claim – 'Only Cortaid is recommended most by doctors. That's because Cortaid stops the persistent itching, then goes beyond to help heal the blotchy, allergic skin rash. Trust the brand doctors prefer over all other brands' – a man in Washington DC wrote to the CEO of Pharmacia & Upjohn, makers of Cortaid.

He said in his letter, 'I assume the statements about doctors' preferences and recommendations were based on one or more surveys of doctors. I would be obliged if you could send me information about the survey(s) on which these statements were based, including the specific questions that were asked about preferences and recommendations for Cortaid, the statistical results for those questions, and details of the survey design(s), including sample sizes, method of data collection, and survey response rates.'

The reply, from a brand group director, was right to the point, 'While the statement you cited from the advertisement is correct and we have substantiation for the claims made in the statement, it is not our practice to publicly disclose the information you have requested absent a compelling business need to do so.'

The question is not what will happen *if* DTCA ever comes

to Britain. It is, instead, what will happen *when* it comes to Britain, because it surely will.

The opening gambit took place in the autumn of 1999 when Pharmacia & Upjohn – which had just begun marketing its new incontinence treatment in the UK – bought TV spots for a 'disease awareness campaign'. It's been very active with such campaigns in the States where, to give it its due, it has helped millions of American women come to terms with what is sometimes regarded as an embarrassing illness.

The campaign in Britain was endorsed by a number of professional organizations and had the blessing of various patient groups. And everybody at every stage tried to make it perfectly clear that this was not about advertising, it was about education. That, of course, is precisely what the American drug companies, the professional organizations and patient groups said throughout the early 1990s as disease awareness campaigns broke down FDA resistance to DTCA.

Faced with a European market expanding at just 5 per cent a year without DCTA, and the US market expanding at 12 per cent a year with DCTA, AstraZeneca has already run a disease awareness campaign in France. Glaxo was said to have been considering one in the UK for its flu drug Relenza when it ran up against staunch criticism from the National Institute for Clinical Excellence. A company executive admits that the possibility of disease awareness campaigns has been discussed in connection with other drugs.

The push for it is coming from Big Pharma.

Anyone in Britain who thinks it won't happen in the UK needs merely to look at Australia, where DTCA is not permitted and yet drug companies have worked their way around the ban.

In June 1997, Roche was the centre of controversy for a campaign related to its antidepressant Aurorix. The company bought a full-page ad in the 24 May issue of the *Sydney Morning Herald*'s 'Good Weekend' magazine, advising patients who might be taking an antidepressant and also experiencing sexual problems to consult their physician. The ad implied that there was a cause-and-effect relationship between some antidepressants and sexual problems. Neither Roche nor Aurorix was mentioned in the ad, but the artwork used in this ad replicated the artwork that Roche was using in Aurorix ads aimed at physicians in medical journals. There, claims were made such as, 'Aurorix has been shown to improve sexual desire by 42 per cent and anorgasmia by 28 per cent.'

Roche was clearly hoping to link the consumer health informational ad to the medical journal ads so that, when a patient came in to discuss antidepressants and sexual health, the doctor would immediately turn to Aurorix. It appeared to be also making claims for Aurorix that were not necessarily substantiated. For its efforts, Roche was heavily criticized for violating the rule that 'no linkage could be made between the advertisement and a specific prescription only product'. But the criticism came after the ads had run and, consequently, after both the public and the doctors got the message.

Big Pharma with its global power can be guaranteed to chip away at rules and regulations that currently prevent drug companies from selling more prescription drugs, spending whatever they have to to drive home the point that this is only about educating the public and therefore a worthwhile end that justifies the means.

In the meantime, where drug companies can't advertise directly to consumers, they promote directly to consumers. They get stories placed in newspapers that are often little more than in-house releases. They look for publicity from patient groups that they form for every disease for which they sell drugs. The Viral Hepatitis Prevention Board helps promote awareness of the need for vaccinations against hepatitis B and is largely backed by SmithKline, which happens to make a hepatitis B vaccine.

Companies sponsor 'awareness weeks' – Influenza Awareness Week, Meningitis Awareness Week, Cholesterol Awareness Week – pick a health problem and flood the papers with news stories in the hope that some awareness of the company product will rub off. It's understandable, for instance, why Glaxo would gladly team up with the Migraine Foundation to fund Migraine Awareness Week at a time when the company is promoting a migraine drug. This is not to suggest that there is anything dishonest in promotion stunts such as 'awareness weeks', but it is difficult to take the corporate view that this is only about education.

Then, even if the Medicines Control Agency thinks it can somehow largely control the promotional activities of Big Pharma in Britain, what happens when a pharmaceutical company outside the UK buys ad time on CNN, or in the *International Herald Tribune*, or in the international editions of *Time* and *Newsweek*, or on Internet sites, all of which are available in Britain.

A little more difficult, but not necessarily impossible in Britain, is Big Pharma's backdoor approach.

After the Minister of Health for British Columbia discovered that 300 pharmacies were selling prescription information, including doctors' names and their prescribing habits, to an international drug-marketing company – which in turn sold on the information to Big Pharma – he actually ordered a rewrite of the by-laws of the College of Pharmacists making the practice unacceptable.

A similar ban has also been extended to Quebec. But the marketing firm in question says it continues to collect such information from 3,000 pharmacies, all willing participants in the programme, from across the other provinces.

An argument can be made that the pharmacies and drug-store chains that sell this information should know better.

That they might say to themselves, if someone walked in off the street and asked these same questions, would we give it to them? The answer, clearly, would be no. Equally, the argument can be made that they're simply responding to market conditions and there wouldn't be a market for such information if the drug companies themselves hadn't created it.

In parts of the States, a similar tactic has emerged. A large chain running supermarket drug stores uses a company to manage its prescription database. That company then acts as a marketing middleman, selling information from the pharmacy database – with the pharmacy's permission – to drug companies that then target customers with direct mail. The letters are personalized and made to appear as if they come from the pharmacist.

The most spectacular effect of globalization in the Internet era is the evaporation of geographical boundaries. In some areas they are merely fading fast, in other areas they are already gone. DTCA of pharmaceuticals is one of those areas where they have totally disappeared.

After sexually related sites, health sites are said to be among the top three most popular Internet destinations. What you find when you get there is anything and everything. In 1995 hardly any pharmaceutical company had its own website. Now they all do. There are also online pharmacies to meet the increased demand for product, especially lifestyle products, which have shifted across the line from physician driven to consumer driven. There is information on every disease imaginable, on every treatment imaginable, on every drug imaginable. There is advice and there is chicanery.

There's also plenty of DTCA, available to anyone in the UK with a modem. And in this case Britain has fudged a little, by allowing certain direct-to-consumer information to be put up on a website.

The *British Medical Journal* website is a good example. It is also a prime example of how the web creates an arena for opposing agendas. While usually condemning drug company marketing on its editorial pages, the journal has recently begun to accept drug company ads on its website. The Medicines Control Agency has ruled that the use of the website for drug company marketing is acceptable because the intended audience is doctors. However, access to the website is free and open to anyone and the *BMJ* reports that around 5 per cent of hits are from members of the public. The journal's rationale is that advertising allows it to provide a huge, searchable database of high-quality information on all aspects of medicine free to everyone. But when you put that in the context of its editorial opinions, it suggests that, if consumers can see the ads on the website, some might draw the conclusion that the drug must be good, otherwise the *BMJ* wouldn't have a commercial relationship with it.

A study in *Scrip* magazine found that the net is not yet a major force for driving sales, which might be why the government leaves DTCA alone on the net. People have to go looking for a site. It's not like television, which comes right into someone's home and gets to people who are not actively seeking information on a topic. Also, television by its nature more easily creates emotional images that have been shown to create behaviour change. That's why it is the most powerful – and economically viable – advertising medium in the world.

But, by 2010 or so, television and the Internet will have digitally fused into one. At that point, effective and influential DTCA by the drug companies on the net will be an uncontrollable reality.

There has always been a market for pharmaceuticals purchased without a prescription and for drugs not approved by a regulatory agency. In the past, however, obtaining them has meant buying from a local smuggler or going offshore. Now, the Internet brings you right to the source. All of a sudden the borders don't exist, and anything you want can be found with the click of a mouse.

For Americans looking for cheaper prescription drugs, it's no longer necessary to travel to Canada or Mexico. The cheaper drugs are right on the web. For a Briton who wants drugs the local GP won't prescribe – Viagra, Prozac and diet drugs are the most prevalently offered – they are easily obtainable on the web. Because the drug itself can't be transmitted, once it's ordered and paid for – which brings up the real risk of credit card fraud – the pills have to come into the country in a traditional manner.

A package addressed from somewhere in Europe is rarely looked at by Customs' officers. A package from New Zealand labelled 'gift – no commercial value' probably won't get looked at either. Even if it does, recipients can always say they have no idea who sent it or why, re-order and play the percentage game that the next one will get through.

'One of the things we discovered,' says Kevin Della-Colli, who runs the US Customs Cyber-Smuggling Center in Washington DC, 'is that when you order 1,000 units, the company may ship it in 100-unit batches, thinking two may get seized and 800 pills will get through.'

Part of the problem is that the net has eliminated the middleman.

'In the past, we'd always go after the person who filled up the trunk of his car with 1,000 Valium tablets and we'd prosecute that person as a smuggler. But the smuggler has disappeared from the picture thanks to the Internet.'

He concedes that a lot of pharmaceuticals sold on the net might be legitimate. 'Other countries have different ways of dispensing prescription medication, and different laws in respect to how it can be transported or sold. They might not be doing anything illegal in say Thailand by offering these drugs for sale. And we have no way of preventing anyone from going to a website and ordering prescription medicine.'

Some of the sites offering pharmaceuticals for sale are perfectly legitimate, are licensed and will function only under the strictest controls. Some of the sites say that they will mis-describe a package in such a way as to make it difficult for US Customs to find it.

'When you buy off the Internet, how do you know what you're getting? You may be dealing with a company two blocks away, or in Thailand, in Amsterdam especially for steroids, in Mexico, in New Zealand or in Indonesia. You have no way of knowing. And these companies aren't necessarily selling pre-wrapped blister pack boxes. Some of them are sending you a zip-lock bag filled with little blue pills or little green pills. The pills may be real. They may be counterfeit. They may be product that has passed its sell-by date. Or they may be shipments stolen overseas that are being offloaded on the net. There's no way of telling, and there is a real public health risk.'

The packaging of Internet drugs raises an interesting point.

In many cases, they are in fact properly packaged. At least they appear to be. Counterfeit drugs sometimes come in counterfeit packaging, too. But there is also a market for legally manufactured goods being re-imported. It's not unheard of for drugs on sale in a foreign country to wind up being sold to anyone, anywhere, on the Internet. This is not to say that the drug companies themselves are actually doing that. But they do keep track of sales around the world. And you need look no further than Tijuana to start asking questions.

In the Mexican border town just south of San Diego, pharmacies will sell you anything, in any quantity, and without any paperwork. It is, of course, illegal to take undeclared drugs back into the United States. But anyone who's ever tried to drive back into the USA through the Customs checkpoint late on a Sunday afternoon knows what a real traffic jam can look like.

Every car is stopped. But very few are ever checked. Customs simply doesn't have the staff to look closely at more than a very tiny percentage of the people coming through.

The quantity of prescription drugs purchased in Tijuana and taken back into the States is huge. That's because drugs are cheaper there, because some people want drugs their doctor won't prescribe and because there are drugs available in Mexico, especially AIDS drugs, that are not licensed in the USA.

But when you look at the drugs that are cheaper and you look at the ones that are bought without prescriptions, and you realize they're real – that they're the actual product of a Big Pharma drug company – the question has to be, doesn't the Big Pharma drug company know where these drugs are going?

If they were counterfeit, Big Pharma would go after them because drug companies vehemently protect their patents and wouldn't want somebody marketing imitation or fake products. So you have to assume that the same Big Pharma companies that have desperately fought parallel importing legislation wherever it's come up are actually playing the game themselves.

If it's not the drug companies selling direct to wholesalers in Tijuana and in cyberspace, it's the drug companies selling to wholesalers who are then reselling the drugs. When they see someone in a two-bit town selling enough Viagra to turn on half of southern California, what do they do about it?

They pretend it's not happening.

Either they do know what's happening with their product, or they should know because they have every reason to know. Prescription drugs are not like normal products. If you ship a load of jeans somewhere, no one has to track them around the world until they're sold. But if you ship out a load of prescription drug products, there has to be a paper trail until they reach the consumer.

CHAPTER TWELVE

Targeting the Doctors

At the heart of the relationship between drug companies and doctors lies a critical contradiction.
(Dr Peter Mansfield of MaLAM)

Drug companies and doctors are joined at the hip by their closely related interests, but closely related doesn't mean identical, and the two often find themselves, decidedly and deliberately, pulling in different directions.

Where agendas meet, science is served. Yet good science is not necessarily good business, any more than the best business will automatically produce the best science. In a perfect world, doctors and drug companies would have only one agenda – the advancement of their patients' health. But this is far from a perfect world. Whereas every doctor's first and foremost responsibility is – by oath and by law – to his or her patients, every drug company's primary obligation is, by design, to its shareholders and employees.

Their ultimate objectives are fundamentally different. And that difference manifests itself every time a doctor writes a prescription.

If diagnosis is the art of medicine, then the selection of

treatment is the application of that art. But for doctors who've been practising for just fifteen years, an estimated 75–90 per cent of the drugs available have come onto the market since they went to medical school. It means that they have no formal training in the function and utilization of those drugs. Whatever they know about them is down to whatever they have taken it upon themselves to learn. This homework, which is absolutely essential in order to stay abreast of the accelerated pace of modern medicine, is an important part of the profession that the patient never sees.

To keep up to date, doctors today are spoiled for choice. Literally thousands of journals, magazines, newspapers, research papers and reviews are regularly published to cover every conceivable aspect of medicine, down to the most minuscule specialization. Every day of the week, including weekends, there are dozens of lectures, Continuing Medical Education (CME) seminars and professional association congresses that doctors can attend. Add to that hundreds of medical sites easily available on the Internet. Stanford University's 'High Wire Press', for example, has an online archive of nearly 150,000 free full-text articles and half a million pay-per-view articles.

But not all information is created equal. In this case it runs the gamut from good to bad, from evidence-based truth to honest errors of fact, deliberate manipulation of facts, statistical mumbo-jumbo, half-truths and outright lies. Doctors are forced to sort through this minefield and somehow make sense of it. After all, lives are at stake. At the same time, a drug company's ability to control the information that a doctor receives can affect the bottom line. After all, profits are at stake.

'At the heart of the relationship between drug companies and doctors', says Dr Peter Mansfield of MaLAM, 'lies a critical contradiction. Drug companies know very well that their marketing is influential but they won't admit that it's harmful. Doctors know very well that it's harmful but they won't admit that it's influential.'

Enter here the drug company representative.

An informal polling of the top forty pharmaceutical companies suggests that they globally employ around 100,000 full-time sales reps and are the bread and butter of another 10,000–15,000 people employed independently as direct-to-physician marketing specialists. Although personal selling is the most expensive way of promoting prescription medicines, it remains the industry's choice because it is the most effective. As 80 per cent of a drug's market is said to come from 20 per cent of prescribers, a small increase in prescribers translates into a much larger increase in market share. That's why the drug companies commit $15–20 billion (£10–13 billion) a year worldwide to the effort, a figure that roughly translates into one drug company rep for every nine-to-eleven practising physicians in the industrialized West. Put another way, the figure usually bandied about is that Big Pharma budgets its direct selling marketing efforts at $8,000–13,000 (£5,200–8,400) per physician.

Company reps – officially known in the trade as 'detailers' – are the modern-day descendants of the snake-oil salesmen of the 1850s. But, unlike their ancestors, they are probably the most highly trained professional salespersons of any industry. So much so, for instance, that in Britain, within two years of joining a company, apprentice detailers must pass a comprehensive industry-wide accreditation exam or look for other work. Some of their training is science based – many of them come to the job with university-level science degrees – which makes sense, because the rep has to be able to understand how drugs perform. But the business of detailing is not about science, it is about peddling drugs to doctors.

At Merck, the career brochure explains that a sales rep's role is 'to effectively promote Merck products through a needs-based selling approach. Representatives provide accurate information to physicians and other healthcare personnel so that Merck products will be prescribed when indicated.' Among the skills the company looks for are 'sales and persuasion skills, communication, leadership, planning and organization, self-motivation and initiative'.

At Eli Lilly, reps are given the goal of 'achieving sales growth in their respective territories'. They may also be called on to conduct market analysis, 'with a focus on key growth areas, product/market trends, and key influencers'. Included in the list of Lilly's requisite skills are communication and interpersonal skills, negotiation skills, project selling and a 'return on investment mentality'.

At Bayer, 'the Sales Representative will be responsible for supporting and achieving the sales target objectives within the assigned territory . . . will also assess prospective and existing customers/business opportunities to ensure optimal utilization of resources . . . [and] will collaborate with other Sales Representatives on an ongoing basis to assess business opportunities for the development and presentation of the annual territory business plan, actively pursue new business opportunities, as well as record and maintain an accurate customer list for the assigned territory'.

Not surprisingly, an emphasis in rep training is placed on sophisticated selling techniques, including videotaped role-playing. Once out in the field, reps may be assigned to look after a list of physicians or to work a list of hospital residents and pharmacists. The more experienced they get, the more likely they are to be further trained to work in a specific therapeutic area – say, coronary care, or oncology, or arthritis and anti-inflammatory disease management – to match the specialized interests of more senior physicians. Reps are also matched, where possible, with their clients by personality type. A low-key conservative doctor is less likely to get along with a hard-driving flamboyant rep, so that doctor is placed on the list of a more suitable rep.

Much to the ire of the industry, a former Abbott Laboratories representative has recently been widely quoted as saying, 'Prescription drugs are marketed now as if they are cosmetics or candy.'

'It simply isn't true,' snaps a Wyeth executive. 'We are regulated by government and industry authorities, and because we are employees of a company, we are subject to the rules of the company as well. If we violate accepted practices, a lot of people will have a lot to say about it. But the last word really belongs to the doctors. If they don't trust us, we won't get back in to see them and they won't prescribe our drugs. They are the ultimate gatekeeper.'

Dr Alastair Benbow, Vice President and Medical Director at SmithKline Beecham, agrees. 'We have to be pragmatic because the time doctors have for all the information they need is limited. If they have a drug company representative in front of them with whom they have built up a relationship over a period of time, and they trust that person's judgement because they've found that the information is balanced and useful, then getting information from a drug company representative is perfectly acceptable. After all, you only need to make one mistake as a representative. If you lie or mislead a doctor, you're not going to be invited back, nor should you be.'

SmithKline has about 350 reps in the UK. The number of visits each rep must make varies, but generally speaking they call on four to eight doctors in a day and the average visit lasts around 11 minutes.

'Doctors need to be up to speed with all the rights and wrongs of prescribing a particular therapy,' Benbow continues. 'We think we know our drugs best. We think we can best educate and inform doctors about new medicines. We also want to ensure that our medicines are used correctly.

It's in nobody's interest to have somebody using the wrong dose, or prescribing a drug inappropriately.'

To back up their reps, SmithKline operates a Medical Information Department (MID), an after-sales service helpline that a doctor can ring to ask questions about a specific drug or treatment. In the UK, SmithKline's MID takes 26,000 calls a year and responds to about 6,000 written requests. Additional backup is provided by a team of staff physicians to handle clinically orientated questions. But then, all of the major drug companies operate similar programmes in all their markets, always relying on the rep to be their conduit between the doctor and the company, creating the image of an enlightened relationship in which the company is a full partner in healthcare solutions.

The only problem with all of this is at the very root of it – the reason Big Pharma spends an estimated one-third of its marketing budget on reps. That is, to sell more drugs.

'Physicians are human, they can be influenced,' notes Dr Ashley Wazana, a researcher at Montreal's McGill University and author of the study 'Physicians and the Pharmaceutical Industry'. The paper leaves no doubt that drug companies know what they're doing and do it because their investment reaps returns. Especially worrying is the argument that, although doctors recognize drug companies are trying to influence their prescribing, many of those same doctors continue to believe that they are beyond being influenced.

'People are often so busy that they're willing to get their information from the most convenient source regardless of considerations of who prepared what,' says Dr Eric Rose of the University of Washington School of Medicine. 'The drug companies know that it won't take much to make a doc favour one drug or another. If you've blasted a doc with advertising that includes the starting dose, and the doc sees that everywhere he looks, in every piece of mail he gets, in every magazine he reads, then when he's in the middle of a busy clinic day and he knows that there are three different similar medications he can prescribe and he remembers the starting dose of one right off the top of his head, maybe that's the one he's going to prescribe. It's subtle and the effects are not necessarily pernicious, not necessarily harmful to the patient, but doctors are supposed to make their decisions based purely upon the best scientific data, not what's easiest to remember but what's best for the patient.'

The industry responds that its critics are confusing the issue by suggesting that, just because some information is easy to obtain, the quality of it – in other words, its accuracy – must be questionable.

'Not true,' says that executive from Wyeth. 'We make it easy because it's in our commercial interests to do that. At the same time, it's totally obvious that supplying anything but high-quality information would be stupid because it's incompatible with our commercial interests. There is so much scientific literature readily available, if we told anything but the truth, we'd be exposed immediately. On top of that, the legal ramifications of unethical sales promotion could be catastrophic. Believe me, any detailer who lies to a doctor-client in the morning is not going to have any doctor-clients by lunchtime. These are intelligent people we're dealing with and if the element of trust is breached, if they don't believe what the detailer is saying about a drug, if they think we're trying to pull the wool over their eyes, they're not going to prescribe the drug or ever let that detailer come back. Who loses if we don't supply the highest-quality, most accurate information? We do.'

It's an articulate defence, but belies the fact that salespeople don't need to resort to untruths when a partial truth will do. The used-car salesman whose jalopy doesn't have a reverse gear, stresses the advantages of driving forward.

This defence also ignores the industry's reliance on 'the myth of progress'. Reps are coached to play up the newness of a drug and how advancements in medicine are making lives better. And it is absolutely true that advancements in medicine are making lives better. But the newest drug isn't necessarily the best drug, any more than newest means the most effective or the cheapest.

Warner-Lambert launched Lipitor, its me-too cholesterol-lowering drug in 1997, to go head to head against Merck's complete domination of that market with Zocor. Lipitor's unique selling point was that it was more potent than Zocor and new. A beefed-up rep force hit 81,000 doctors' offices every month for several months. New won, and toppled Zocor from the top of the cholesterol-lowering bestseller list.

Finally, the defence flies in the face of the scientific evidence. Studies conducted over a thirty-year span that have looked at drug company reps and their sales pitches all seem to draw the same conclusion – that there is a deliberate lack of balance in the information companies supply to doctors and, because of that, doctors who rely on drug companies for their information are more prone to inappropriate prescribing.

A survey of faculty and house staff at hospitals in Minnesota and Wisconsin revealed that more than a quarter of the doctors had changed prescriptions at least once in the preceding twelve months after a conversation with a drug rep.

A survey at the University Hospitals of Cleveland found that doctors who attended drug company-sponsored meetings, or had meals with drug reps, or had received research funds from drug companies or had been paid by drug companies for a speaking engagement, were more likely to ask a hospital to add drugs to the formulary and that, in most cases, those drugs had little or no advantage over drugs already on the formulary.

A survey of ninety-six British GPs revealed that 90 per cent of them had attended a pharmaceutical company-sponsored meeting. Only 17 per cent of those who attended felt the event was a valuable experience.

A survey of over a hundred statements recorded during thirteen drug company presentations revealed that 11 per cent of the statements were inaccurate in favour of the promoted drug.

A study at the University of South Australia's School of Pharmacy recorded sixteen pitches made by drug reps to doctors and compared their claims with the data in the Australian Approved Product Information (AAPI). Contraindications – side-effects and conditions under which the drug should not be used – were not mentioned in the presentations. Thirteen of the sixteen pitches contained inaccuracies, which included the promotion of off-label uses or non-authorized applications of the drug. And where supplementary literature, such as comparative product information and scientific data, was given to doctors along with the company's promotional literature, those materials were usually incomplete and sometimes inaccurate.

A survey of primary care physicians revealed that 34 per cent doubted drug company representatives had sufficient knowledge of the products on offer; 65 per cent felt reps did not sufficiently explain side-effects; and 57 per cent believed reps often 'extended the indications' of drugs, meaning that the rep either promised more than the drug might reasonably be expected to deliver or tried to promote off-label benefits.

Another similar survey found that physicians who saw drug company reps more than once a week were statistically more likely to prescribe higher-priced drugs.

Yet another study, this one published in the *Journal of the American Medical Association*, looked at sixteen previous studies and reiterated that doctors who regularly saw drug company reps were more likely to engage in 'non-rational' prescribing than doctors who did not see reps.

The French medical journal *La Revue Prescrire* established an anonymous network of GPs and hospital pharmacists to monitor the information that drug company reps were

providing. After each detailer's visit, the doctors and pharmacists were asked to fill in a form, noting whether the information given on drug indications and doses differed from
the official data sheet; whether side-effects, contraindications
and interactions were mentioned; what evidence the rep
used on which to base claims; and whether any incentives
were offered, such as gifts or payment for participation in a
clinical trial.

Eight years' worth of data led *La Revue Prescrire* to conclude
in 1999 that, in 27 per cent of drug rep visits, indications
did not correspond with the scientific literature; that 15
per cent of the time the stated dosage was not correct;
and that 76 per cent of the time side-effects were not mentioned. What's more, off-label use was a common selling
technique, meaning that reps made claims that were either
not backed up by clinical research or simply invented to
suit their own purpose. For example, a contraceptive pill
was lauded for its off-label benefit of curing acne, a drug
used to treat attention failure in the elderly was described as
a suitable stimulant for anyone, and a medication prescribed
for benign liver symptoms was touted as a cure for bad
breath.

'From medical school on,' observed the magazine *Consumer
Reports*, 'physicians are taught to regard medical school faculty, medical journals and professional meetings as sources of
unbiased information. Pharmaceutical companies have found
ingenious ways to influence all three. In the process, the
distinction between promotion and true scientific exchange
has been blurred and, in some cases, totally erased.'

There's no doubt that, when it comes to toothpaste, dish-
washer powder and running shoes, marketing influences consumer decisions. And yet surveys show that doctors almost
overwhelmingly insist that, when it comes to their prescribing
habits, they rely more heavily on scientific training and
objective literature than on marketing. Surveys also show that

most doctors feel they are immune to commercial manipulation.

At least to some extent, that sense of immunity is a direct result of drug company spin. The best marketing always reinforces empowerment – the salesperson is the equivalent of the magician who forces a card on an unsuspecting member of the audience. If doctors feel that the choice of any particular drug is their good idea, they're more likely to prescribe it. And as every magician knows, the less the audience realizes it's being manipulated, the greater the trick.

It is estimated that as many as 85 per cent of primary care physicians see drug company reps three to six times per week. Concerned that so many doctors were devoting so much time to drug company promotion, in July 1999 the *British Medical Journal* took a firm stance against detailers.

In 'Reasons for not Seeing Drug Representatives', a *BMJ* editorial reminded physicians, 'Their job is primarily to sell their company's product. They are an important part of the pharmaceutical industry's promotion methods, and they are highly successful in altering doctors' prescribing habits.'

Cited was a survey in Northern Ireland which demonstrated that prescriptions of various drugs increased in the wake of drug reps' visits. 'At the time that new drugs are licensed,' the *BMJ* editorial went on, 'there are often no published comparisons with existing standard treatments and rarely any economic evaluations. Thus the really useful information is often unavailable at this stage, and by the time it is, the sales force has moved on to talk about other, newer products.'

The author of the *BMJ*'s editorial was Dr David Griffith, a consultant geriatrician at Mayday University Hospital in England. 'There is a plethora of very good information available to doctors today,' he said in an interview, 'it's just a question of taking the time to access it. Yes, getting information from a drug company representative may be the easiest way of all, but easiest is not necessarily best, the quality of the information is questionable and seeing drug reps in order to save time is a cop out. I'd be very surprised if they actually lied about a product. But I know they are selective with their facts and economical with information. I believe drug company representatives and the bias that they bring to healthcare is disadvantageous to healthcare.'

Letters poured in to the editor of the *BMJ* in response to Griffith's editorial.

Dr Harvey Rees, a senior registrar in psychiatry in Bristol, warned, 'It is naive to suggest doctors underestimate the goals of drug companies in promoting their products within a highly competitive market.'

Dr Chris Sedergreen, a family physician from British Columbia, reported on a conversation with a drug rep twenty-five years before. 'During a particularly sumptuous dinner and no doubt emboldened by generous helpings of Beaujolais I told him, "You know, Allan, your product really isn't any better than anyone else's," to which he replied "I know, but as long as you go on prescribing it I can go on taking you out for dinners like this."'

Dr Steven Reidbord, the medical director of an outpatient psychiatry clinic in San Francisco wondered, 'Would companies spend so much if these efforts didn't work?'

Dr David Evan Morris, a GP from Wales, reported on a conversation in which a detailer added to a particular drug's benefits its nutritional value. Morris questioned that claim. The drug rep replied, 'If you prescribe enough of it, my family get to eat better!'

Gert Hubertus, a medical rep from East Sussex, was fast to point out, 'I like to think that the service I give to doctors is valuable. I meet whatever educational needs I can, and I make sure I know all about my product and competitors. In return the doctors (my customers), time permitting, listen to my argument.' He went on to say, 'It is not rocket science, there is no need to do gigantic multi-centre analyses of prescribing data, and nor is it an industry secret. Reps influence doctors. I, however, do not believe for one moment that doctors are so unprofessional as to allow their habits to be influenced in a way that is detrimental to the health of their patients.'

Another drug rep, Melissa Gorgei, joined the debate. 'I have never misrepresented a feature of my drug, nor have I ever knocked another product. I can assure you, however, that there are those reps who do engage in these types of practices. Just like any other field, though, the pharmaceutical industry has both good and bad seeds.'

SmithKline's Alastair Benbow takes a different tack. 'Should the representative be a doctor's only source of information? Absolutely not. If a doctor chooses not to see company reps, and gets the relevant information he needs from other sources, great. But the reality is that many doctors don't take the time, or don't have the time, to get their information from other sources. Therefore we provide a very valuable service.'

When pressed about the collision of interests between the medical side of Big Pharma and the commercial side, Benbow says, 'There's no doubt that commercial people are more interested in the short-term view and the scientific side of the business, I think, always needs to take the longer-term, broader view. As a guardian of the research and medical side of the business, it's my responsibility to say to the commercial people, this is in the broader interest and we need to get that information out there. We have a duty as scientists to inform and educate the commercial parts of the organization, to say, forget the here and now and the fast buck you want to make, what we want to do is good science, and good research done in an appropriate way will sell. Sure, there is a constant pulling and pushing in certain directions. There are commercial tensions within the business and you cannot just flick a switch to change them. I think it is quite possible for the two sides to be married up but you have to keep working at informing and educating them.'

There was a time when drug companies incentivized their reps with per sale bonuses. Contrary to what many industry critics believe, it doesn't appear to be done that way any more. Reps have a base salary, which can be topped up with performance-related incentives, but the additional income tends to be relatively small in proportion to the base. That might be because the companies see a major difference between drug reps and salespeople. According to them, if you're a used-car salesman, you know whether you've sold somebody a car. If you're a rep who visits a doctor to detail your product, the doctor may or may not prescribe the drug, you have no way of knowing. So they train their salespeople – and pay them accordingly – to approach the job as one that wields influence rather than clinches a sale.

Now the incentive can be much more satisfying than a small bonus.

'Our representatives' motivations', admits Benbow, 'are strongest when they believe that they can really make a difference, when we're able to get across the message to them that they are changing people's lives.'

He cites the example of a new therapy his company is bringing onto the market to treat type II diabetes. 'The representatives have all been trained over the past eighteen months on diabetes. Sure, along the way, we hope to sell a lot of medicine and make money out of it. This is a commercial venture. But there are 1 million diabetics in the UK and probably another million people who are undiagnosed diabetics. We need to educate the population so that those million undiagnosed diabetics can get whatever treatment they need. When the reps believe that they are playing an important role like this, that it's not just about the fast buck and the blockbuster drug, that they have a product which can make a difference in people's lives, then they're enthused and surely that's got to be a good thing.'

In the end, he concludes, it all comes down to one basic truth – that a detailer is only as good as the product. 'If the product is not particularly effective or has a poor safety profile, then no amount of detailing will influence that. As a profession, we are science data driven. Unless the science and data are good, you haven't got a chance.'

Most drug reps freely admit that they keep a diary or profile dossier on their doctors, recording various degrees of information, from the names and birth dates of a doctor's children, up to golf handicaps, favourite movies, favourite music, foods the doctor doesn't like and restaurants the doctor's spouse does. These diaries also give space to the people working in the doctor's office – with the names and birth dates of their children as well – because so much can depend on the staff, such as whether or not the rep can actually get in to see the doctor.

Although many drug companies themselves deny that they keep databases on doctors' personal lives, there is sufficient reason to believe that such things exist and, in a few cases, they are worthy of the CIA.

One doctor, using an online Internet forum, warned his colleagues that he'd seen a drug rep's database and that it contained detailed listings for 900 doctors. Among the fields were age, medications prescribed – broken down into per week, per month, per year – general prescribing habits, plus undergraduate and medical school records, in addition to the usual family and friends information such as names, birth dates, hobbies and even pets.

The rep explained to this doctor how she once did a search by birthdays in April, limited it to physicians aged thirty-five to sixty-five, then further limited it to the number of prescriptions written for one of her company's drugs. When she'd whittled it all down to a single name, she threw a surprise office lunch party for the doctor. When asked how she'd managed to get her information on doctors' prescribing habits, she confessed that her company bought it from certain pharmacies.

Obviously, it makes sense that drug reps who have worked a territory for a long time get to know their doctors quite well. And the better the database, the better the company can target those doctors for promotional reasons. Those who see drug reps are reminded through mailings that the company appreciates their time. Those who don't see drug reps are encouraged through mailings perhaps to rethink their stance. Company literature of all sorts – including personalized 'Dear Doctor' letters – shows up in just about every physician's mailbox just about every day. More and more, snail-mailings are being supplemented by regular e-mailings.

Databases decide who gets what unsolicited non-peer-reviewed journals. And who gets what Christmas greeting. Sometimes that's just a card. Sometimes it's more. One company, with a new osteoporosis drug, sent candy to high-prescribing doctors on their database, whether they saw company reps or not, and, so that those physicians got the point, it was white chocolate in the shape of the top end of a hipbone.

Sweets notwithstanding, feeding doctors is a tried and true drug company method for starting, then maintaining, relationships. It starts, usually, when doctors are in their first year of hospital residency, when reps juggling briefcases, pizzas and litre bottles of Coke are one of the most common images in the medical profession. They target residents because young doctors haven't yet established prescribing habits – it's the 'get 'em young' syndrome – understanding that once prescribing habits have been formed, they're very hard to break.

Disturbingly, there is anecdotal evidence to suggest that

these impromptu lunches have become such a powerful weapon that some young doctors have actually turned to drug reps for treatment advice, finding 'the pizzaman' more easily accessible than the physician in charge.

One doctor in Atlanta, Georgia, was so incensed at how demonically effective these reps were at beguiling residents, he described pizza as 'the most efficacious marketing tool ever devised'.

Various hospitals have reacted in various ways. Some allow the reps free rein. Some allow limited access to residents, confining them to certain hours or to a table somewhere out of the way for their brochures. Some have outright banned drug reps, albeit not without consequences. When the director of the student residency programme for internal medicine at McMaster University in Hamilton, Ontario, Canada, announced that the pizzas were finished and that his residents were off-limits, two companies demonstrated their displeasure. One threatened to withdraw industry funding of certain projects, the other denied a request to support a residency research project.

One trend is towards 'information management', in which hospitals allow drug reps to make presentations on a regular basis – but without pizza or anything else on offer – and then follow those presentations with a briefing by a non-biased pharmacologist. He compares what the drug rep said with the peer-reviewed literature, discusses what issues the rep has significantly ignored and explains what other medications are available that may work better and also be cheaper.

Perhaps not surprisingly, the more senior the physician, the better the food. Where pizzas are not appropriate, bottles of wine and champagne may be. Flowers and cakes have been known to show up for birthdays, and more than one physician's nurse has found a drug rep waiting for the office to open with a bagel breakfast.

Reps also show up lugging cartons of product samples.

In the United States, where healthcare is largely private, some doctors say they see drug reps only for the samples, so that they can administer expensive drugs to patients who can't otherwise afford to pay for them.

In Britain, where most prescriptions are on the NHS, and in other countries where the national healthcare plan meets the cost of expensive drugs, doctors who see reps to stock their office pharmacies with drugs say the samples come in handy in emergencies or at times when pharmacies are either closed or not convenient.

Samples, of course, can be used for the drug company's original intention – to put patients on a trial so that the doctors can see first hand how the drug works. That's fine. But often what happens is that a doctor decides to administer the sample because it's readily available, instead of administering an equally effective, less expensive but less accessible drug. When that happens, the doctor is playing right into the drug companies' hands. It stands to reason that, once a patient is started on a treatment, both the physician and the patient are usually reluctant to switch drugs. Which is why drug company reps also like to leave samples at hospital pharmacies. It costs nothing to hand out enough expensive drugs to treat a patient for a week, knowing that, once the patient has left the hospital, the treatment will be continued and paid for over the next however-many months.

In Japan, Big Pharma has it best of all. Retail prices are set by the government – something the drug companies normally hate – but doctors there are not only licensed to prescribe drugs, but also licensed to sell them. They buy from wholesalers – with drug company discounts added in to encourage prescribing – and then resell those drugs to their patients, pocketing the difference. Needless to say, reps are more than welcome to drop by with samples of the newest, most expensive drugs because the system encourages the doctors to use the newest, most expensive drugs.

In South Africa, when legislation was proposed that would prohibit drug companies from handing out free samples, some doctors began insisting that drug company reps pay a visit fee just like any patient. It was, they said, to compensate them for their time and to make up for the lack of free samples. The trend hasn't caught on and, in fact, has been condemned as unacceptable by both the South African Medical Association and the Interim National Medical and Dental Council. But it shows one way reps have been able to link a monetary value to the company–doctor relationship.

Another is through Continuing Medical Education.

As government healthcare budgets are slashed and insurance-based healthcare systems fight to keep costs down, CME has suffered. It's still required for various board certifications and for access to some hospitals, and it's encouraged for self-advancement, so Big Pharma has moved quickly to fill that void. Under the guise of CME, it reinforces the message of the marketers by offering physicians a straight trade-off: we drug companies will pay for the lectures and seminars that earn you, the doctors, CME credits, and pay for the food, and maybe throw in golf, or sailing, or skiing, or whatever; you physicians agree to allow us to set the curriculum, to select the speakers and – as long as we're not too obvious about promoting our own drugs – to convince you that you're being educated without any strings attached.

At no time does anyone add that, in exchange for our hospitality, we'd like you to prescribe our product. It doesn't need to be mentioned. Everyone understands. As one executive at Aventis admitted, 'Continuing Medical Education is now determined by what the marketing department wants, not what the doctors need.'

The pharmaceutical industry's own code of ethics preaches restraint. Most of the serious professional brotherhoods also try to define what's acceptable. The American Medical Association, the British Medical Association, the Canadian Medical

Association and the Australian Medical Association agree that CME has to be about education. So the drug companies make sure there is just enough science for the doctors to feel that everyone is complying with professional standards. The associations say that this is not supposed to be a mini-vacation. But that doesn't mean these events aren't held in mini-vacation type settings. The associations say that, at no point during a CME experience, should the sponsoring drug company exert control over the content in any speaker's presentation. So the drug companies talk about 'hands-off sponsorship', to suggest that they're not exercising visible control over content, while they hire speakers they can count on to be favourable to the company's products.

Bluntly put, drug companies run junkets cloaked as education to sell their drugs to doctors, much the same way that casinos offer complimentary airfares and hotel suites to bring high-rollers to the tables while all the time insisting that they discourage compulsive gambling.

Furthermore, drug company generosity is so readily available to doctors seeking freebees that, according to the *Lancet*, one British doctor in a senior post at a teaching hospital actually managed to spend fifty days during 1998 away from his desk and patients as a drug company guest, travelling to the United States, the Middle East, the Orient and no fewer than a dozen European countries.

This is not to condemn all CME as a lark, and it's again down to SmithKline's Alastair Benbow to show that there is definitely another side to the coin.

'We do events which have a very significant educational component and many of them are on weekends because that's generally the only time that people are available. We don't pay them to play golf. We work them really hard. The doctors will arrive on a Friday night, they'll have lectures that night, have lectures and workshops on Saturday, and they'll work on Sunday until the time they leave. There is a process by which an independent body looks at the educational content of a particular meeting and approves it so that the doctors can get postgraduate educational points. What's more, no spouses are allowed. Anyway, in the UK, you're not allowed to invite spouses along. That's not to say that no companies do that, but when they do they are breaking the regulations. Yes, I'm sure there are small companies who are getting away with a much lower standard. They're doing it because they're fighting for market share. Maybe those small companies haven't got the infrastructure or wherewithal to provide the level of education that is necessary. And what they do harms all of us. But if you look around Big Pharma, I'm sure you'll find that Continuing Medical Education is taken seriously.'

In Britain, for example, rules have been laid down that the cost of drug company hospitality 'should not exceed anything a doctor would not have normally spent'.

But nobody quite knows what that means.

When Fisons Pharmaceuticals invited doctors to two- and three-day meetings in Portugal and Barcelona to promote a pair of products, the UK Prescription Medicines Code of Practice Authority (PMCPA) – the arm's-length watchdog of the Association of the British Pharmaceutical Industry – decided it had gone too far. The cost per head for the junket ran to £1,100–1,500, a sum that the company argued was not lavish. But the PMCPA decided it was too much for the very limited educational content of the meetings and slapped Fisons' corporate wrists.

In Spring 1999, AstraZeneca hosted a pair of two-day meetings in Cambridge called 'Dispensing – Towards the Millennium'. They brought 101 doctors in for a Thursday lunch, meetings until Thursday evening dinner, Friday morning meetings and Friday lunch. All expenses including travel and accommodation – one night in student digs – were met by AstraZeneca. The second meeting took place because the first one was overbooked. It was identical and fifty-two doctors attended. Postgraduate education allowances were awarded to the attending physicians. Among the subjects discussed were asthma and migraine, two areas in which the company has a commercial interest. The cost per head, not including travel, came to £144. Did that exceed what a doctor would have normally spent on a tiny room with a single bed and a school dinner? One doctor thought so and complained. The PMCPA ruled that AstraZeneca had complied with the rules.

All it cost the company to better educate 153 satisfied doctors was £22,032 plus everyone's travel bills.

One major pharmaceutical company regularly invites a group of French cardiologists as its guest to the annual meeting of the American College of Cardiologists. Guests are selected because they're heavy prescribers of the company's drugs. In 2000, the doctors were flown from France to Los Angeles, put up at a beachside hotel, wined, dined and Disneyland-ed for six days. There were side trips to Tijuana and Las Vegas. Yes, they had carte blanche to all of the various professional meetings and lectures. And, yes, the doctors were encouraged to attend. But those professional meetings and lectures were in English, without translation facilities, and most of the French cardiologists didn't speak enough English to understand what was being said.

Four weeks later, some of those same doctors turned up at a CME weekend staged by another Big Pharma company, this time with spouses in tow, at an exclusive French Riviera hotel. Unlike Los Angeles, the lecture was in French and attendance was mandatory. But sitting in a conference room for three hours on the Saturday morning was hardly a steep price to pay for a weekend of lunches, dinners and pool parties.

Again, it was by invitation only to high prescribers.

'There was a study done in the United States,' explains Canadian Dr Joel Lexchin, 'where they looked at what happened to prescribing after twenty doctors were flown by a drug company to a meeting in some resort area. When these people got home, the prescribing of that product took off. It's simple, whether you call it Continuing Medical Education or you call it marketing, the more a doctor has to do with drug company people, the more likely that doctor is to prescribe the company's drugs and to request that those drugs are put onto his hospital formulary. This isn't saying that the drugs are bad, but are they the best value for the money? If doctors don't think they're being influenced by drug company hospitality, under whatever guise, then they're being incredibly naïve. After all, the drug companies aren't stupid, they don't spend their money on things that don't work.'

Nor do they waste their money on meetings that doctors won't attend. The rule of thumb is, the more glamorous the hospitality, the longer the list of doctors willing to show up. The fact that high-end glamorous hospitality might be against the pharmaceutical industry's own codes of practice is rarely a problem.

Lexchin continues, 'Companies still break the rules and get away with it because one of the things about voluntary regulation, which is the main form of regulating drug company promotion, is that the associations don't do any active monitoring, they wait for complaints. Now, if I'm flown for free to a meeting, I'm hardly likely to complain that the drug company that flew me there is breaking the rules.'

When Pfizer's idea of CME upset Joshua Sharfstein, a Massachusetts physician, he complained about it in a letter to the *New England Journal of Medicine*. In response, the company got defensive. Sharfstein explained how he'd come across a small poster on a bulletin board in the hospital where he works, proclaiming 'Pfizer Night Returns'. It was an invitation to physicians to meet a new team of Pfizer reps at a Boston billiards parlour. The theme of the evening was, 'Rack 'em up & Toss 'em down.' Sharfstein felt that such an event was unethical and contrary to the AMA's guidelines, which allowed modest meals and trinkets only insofar as they benefit patients and are related to the physician's work. He couldn't see how beer and billiards qualified.

'For aggressive drug-company representatives,' he wrote, 'such inappropriate promotions, which also violate the Pharmaceutical Manufacturers Association's code of ethical marketing practices, may be just a way of doing business. But for doctors, they violate a basic principle: that we are advocates for our patients and not on the make for ourselves.'

Refusing to admit that the company had been caught red-handed, Dr Joseph Feczko, speaking for Pfizer, shot back a reply. 'There were three slide presentations that we believe provided useful medical information to attendees.'

Wary not to fall into the same trap, Merck took a different approach. Pharmacist Larry Sasich at the watchdog group Public Citizen says that his son, a resident at a hospital in St Louis, was invited to attend a continuing education programme for the company's latest asthma drug. It was the summer of 1999, in the middle of the quest by Mark McGwire of the St Louis Cardinals to beat Roger Maris's 61 home run record. By sheer coincidence, the CME programme fell on a Sunday when the Cardinals were playing a double-header at home. So, Sasich notes, Merck invited the doctors to Busch Stadium, hosted a tailgate barbecue before the game, gave them plenty to eat during the game and delivered their spiel about asthma and the drug between games.

Occasionally, CME events create headlines. When Bristol-Myers Squibb announced a weekend programme on AIDS therapy that it was sponsoring at a very plush resort in Ontario, one doctor complained about it to the College of Physicians and Surgeons of Ontario. While the College recognized that this might violate its own guidelines, it had to admit that it was powerless to act. So the doctor told the media about it and, in the face of negative publicity, BMS agreed that a change of venue, to a hotel in downtown Toronto, was more suitable.

One company hired a PR firm to invite 300 doctors for a weekend in the Bahamas to discuss off-label uses for their product. This was a clear violation of everybody's rules, and the junket was cancelled. Instead, the company invited doctors to visit the corporate offices, 100 showed up, and the off-label discussion happened informally there.

Then, too, not all CME programmes are events.

One drug company sent literature on antihistamines to doctors, along with forms that they were asked to fill out in exchange for CME credit. The forms were both a test of the doctors' understanding of the literature, and an anthology of the doctors' experiences prescribing the drug. In other words, they didn't get the CME credit unless they completed the form and they couldn't complete the form unless they prescribed the drug.

A variation on that theme are 'Product Familiarization Programs' (PFP), which are little more than glorified sales pitches disguised as post-marketing studies. Shortly after the regulatory board has approved the drug but before it's brought to market, a group of potential prescribers are brought together in an attempt to establish a large customer base on which to launch the drug. To help doctors compile whatever statistics the company pretended to want in one particular PFP, the company supplied each doctor with a brand new fax machine, paid for a line to be installed for it, and then paid for the line rental.

Because drug companies are always looking inside the medical profession for celebrities to endorse their products – well-known or very successful physicians – another gimmick is the public speaking clinic. Here, doctors who show a friendly bent towards the company are whisked away to some resort to attend a two-day workshop in the art of public speaking. The drug company then certifies these doctors to be official spokespersons at events and meetings set up by the drug company. To the doctors in the audience of those events, these doctors are leaders in the field and frequently peer-reviewers. It is almost never disclosed either that these doctors have been trained by the drug company or that they are receiving an honorarium for their appearance.

The physician's desk was littered with drug company logo-ed pens, calendars, calculators, note pads, flashlights, golf balls, chocolates, rulers and letter openers.

The question was, 'Where did you get all this stuff?'

His answer, 'They give it to you.'

'Who?'

'The drug companies. The reps. They always hand you something.'

'And what do you do for them.'

'Nothing.'

'Then why do they give this stuff to you?'

'Don't ask me, ask them.'

So the same question was asked of an American Home Products marketing fellow minding a stand filled with corporate trinkets at a huge pharmaceutical fair.

'Why do you give all this stuff away?'

'They're harmless reminder items.'

'By harmless, you mean they're not bribes?'

'Bribes are absolutely not our style. That's not what this is all about. If you're insinuating that we expect something in return, you're dead wrong. If we give a doc a coffee mug that has our logo on it, it's just a friendly gesture to remind him who we are. If we give him a cheap plastic ruler that has our drug's name and dosage information on it, that just makes it easier for him to remember how much to prescribe.'

'What about tickets to football games . . . aide-mémoire?'

He shrugs, 'It keeps the door open.'

Wyeth-Ayerst broke the mould with 'Travel for Knowledge', a 'frequent flier' programme designed specifically to promote Inderal LA, the company's hypertension drug. A physician writing fifty prescriptions would be awarded a round-trip airline ticket to any destination in the United States. By the time the programme was stopped, more than 20,000 doctors had subscribed. Wyeth-Ayerst was subsequently fined nearly $1 million (£650,000) by federal and state authorities for its efforts.

A variation on the theme was Connaught Pharmaceuticals' 'Very Important Purchaser (VIP)' programme, with points awarded for each purchase of a company vaccine. Those points could then be exchanged for cash or gifts.

Some years ago, ten companies banded together to form 'The Physicians' Computer Network', which they'd designed to deal with many day-to-day office tasks. In exchange for agreeing to review thirty-two e-mailed promotional messages per month and making their prescribing information available to the ten companies, the doctors were given $35,000 (£22,750) worth of computer hardware.

Along the same lines, one company offered high-prescribing doctors office equipment, including laser printers and fax machines.

Another company, Searle of Canada, took the novel approach of linking drug sales with altruism. Every time a doctor prescribed Searle's oral contraceptives, the company made a contribution to a charity for battered women.

Believing that charity begins at home, Roche Pharmaceuticals paid physicians $1,200 (£780) if they prescribed the company's antibiotic Rocephin to twenty patients. They'd hoped to pass it off as a research project to test the efficacy of the drug by asking physicians what type of infection they were treating and the result of that treatment. The game was up when US Senate hearings revealed that the payments were not coming out of the R&D budget but from the marketing department.

More recently, accusations were lodged in the Spanish parliament against Abbott Laboratories for bribing doctors in an almost identical way. At issue was $2.7 million (£1.75 million) allegedly paid as gifts, trips and cash.

Today most countries have tightened up their guidelines when it comes to gifts from drug companies. The American Medical Association says they have to be 'of minimal value'. The Canadian Medical Association says no gifts. The Australians have amended their rules to say that gifts must be either brand-name reminders or somehow otherwise related to medical education. Any hospitality to doctors must be subordinate to an educational function. Almost as soon as the rules were adopted, the *Sydney Morning Herald* reported that ICI had offered doctors a choice of a $1,000 (£650) travel voucher, ten dinners for two at $120 (£78) each, or ten bottles of champagne for providing certain information which would assist that company in promoting its drugs. So as not to leave out the doctor's staff, there were also $130 (£85) perfume packs presented to the doctors' receptionists.

In Britain, abuses had piled up through the 1980s as drug companies flouted self-regulation. So Parliament banned expensive gifts, including medical equipment and foreign trips. Inexpensive gifts are permitted, as long as they're relevant to the practice of medicine or pharmacy and that the cost to the company does not exceed £4.99. The one exception, recently agreed, is a scientific textbook with a value up to £30. Parliament put an end to mountain bikes, stereos and photographic equipment, although in most countries items like that show up as raffle prizes. Doctors who qualify – which means they've filled in a few forms that pretend to be a survey – have their name thrown into the tombola. Still, one doctor who eventually stopped seeing drug reps noted in a letter to the *BMJ* that, by the time he called it quits, his entire black bag was filled with equipment supplied by drug companies.

Besides the fact that gifts of any size – including trinkets – give the impression of influence, the cost of the pen, pad, calculator, weekend of golf, scientific textbook, whatever, is ultimately passed on to the public, hidden inside the price of the drugs.

'Many doctors are insulted when you tell them they can be influenced,' Dr Eric Rose concedes, 'especially by a ballpoint pen or a coffee mug. And yet, in a survey of 100 third-year medical students, 85 per cent thought it was inappropriate for a public official to accept a $50 (£32.50) gift from a contractor, but less than 50 per cent thought it inappropriate for a physician to receive the same gift from a pharmaceutical company.'

Rose personally finds it absurd that somebody with a doctorate in medical science would willingly give up an hour to listen to somebody who doesn't necessarily know what they're talking about just so that he or she can get a plastic pocketbook protector and a souvenir ballpoint pen.

'A drug company's job is to make products that are safe and effective and, at the same time, to make money for their stockholders. That's what they're supposed to do, which is why I don't point a finger at them for marketing drugs the way they do. No, I can't blame a predatory animal for acting like a predatory animal. I put the onus on doctors. They're the ones I blame. It's the docs who have a fiduciary responsibility to their patients to be objective and impartial and not be bribed.'

That's why he doesn't see drug reps.

That's why Dr David Griffith, the author of the *BMJ* editorial, stopped seeing drug reps, too. 'We may not earn as much as doctors in America, but we have a decent salary, more than enough that we can afford to buy our own ballpoint pens.'

That's why a very successful internist on Long Island stopped seeing them as well. 'There was a never-ending line of people trying to sell me stuff. A few of them knew what they were talking about, especially the ones who had studied to be pharmacists. But the majority of them had simply rehearsed a routine. They were reciting a script to me. I couldn't justify the time they wasted so I cut them off. I told my secretary, no more.'

At least he thought he did. 'They kept coming, trying to get in to see me and, when they were told no, they left their promotional aids anyway. Not just leaflets and tear-sheets of articles but all the usual trinkets. They did whatever they could to bribe their way past the front door. They continued to show up with candy and other goodies.'

Eventually, he says, most of them got the message. Leaflets, brochures and tear-sheets continued to show up in the mail, along with non-peer-reviewed magazines touting the company's drugs, but the doorstep visits slowed to a trickle.

Except they didn't get turned off completely.

Alarmed at losing an important prescriber, Big Pharma sent in the big guns.

Someone arrived at the office one morning asking for an appointment with the doctor, and offered another physician's name as a referral. The new patient filled in the usual questionnaire and was worked into the appointment schedule. The doctor cordially greeted his new patient, who quickly confessed this wasn't really a medical visit.

'The company had upped the stakes,' he recalls. 'This rep was wearing a short skirt and a frilly blouse, she had a lot of hair and a big smile. She wanted to know why I stopped seeing her company's reps and if I would allow her to stop by every now and then, just to say hello. I threw her out. But you know what amazed me? Some of my male colleagues who'd also announced they wouldn't see reps, a few of those jerks fell for it. Sex sells. Far be it for a pharmaceutical company to let a doctor escape for the sake of a short skirt.'

So the question becomes, if you walk into a physician's office and find the desk littered with drug company logo-ed pens, calendars, calculators, note pads, flashlights, golf balls, chocolates, rulers and letter openers, what should you do?

Joel Lexchin answers right away, 'I would walk out. But then, I know where to go to get another opinion. Short of that, I would certainly be more sceptical of what that person prescribes for me.'

Peter Mansfield draws a medical analogy. 'If you look at the way drug companies market their products directly to doctors and think of those ways as risk factors, in the same way we think of cholesterol and blood pressure being risk factors in heart attacks, then trusting in drug company information is a more powerful risk factor for inappropriate belief. And if you see inappropriate belief as a heart attack, then trust in drug companies is a bigger factor than cholesterol.'

In other words, he says, stuff with drug company logos scattered around a doctor's office is cause for real concern. 'Yes, and I think a patient should express that concern. It's only the doctors who don't seem to be aware that there's a problem. For whatever reason, many doctors just don't understand that this whole issue of trust, which is so vital in the doctor–patient relationship, is being undermined.'

Eric Rose is equally frank. 'What patients should be worried about is not how many trinkets are on the doctor's desk, rather the source of that doctor's information. I think a very legitimate question for a patient to ask a doctor is, how do you keep up with new developments in medicine? There's nothing wrong with asking that and I don't think any doc should demur to answer that. Hopefully, the answer will involve peer-reviewed literature and other scientifically sound sources of information. If a doc says, sure I see drugs reps and I read all these magazines that come to my house even though I never subscribe to them, and look at all the neat stuff they give me, then you might want to reconsider your relationship with that doctor.'

Epilogue

The global pharmaceutical industry has emerged from the twentieth century as a hugely powerful economic force.

Granted, it is filled with highly intelligent, highly motivated people who, with monumental dedication, are trying to change the world, trying to make this planet a healthier one and, in so doing, without any doubt, enriching each of our lives.

Granted, too, as a result of such dedication, we are the first people on the planet who can be cured of disease. Our ancestors could be comforted, have their pain relieved and made to feel better. But we can be healed. That journey started, perhaps, with penicillin and has, in the space of a very short period of time, come all the way to the mapping of the human genome. We are, therefore, possibly the last generation to live three score years and ten. Our grandchildren could easily live to twice that. And if they do, that will be testament to the men and women who have dedicated their lives to finding and developing the science that unlocks the keys and opens the doors of better health.

But, in the pursuit of good, there has been evil.

If the recklessness of some people in this industry were mirrored in, say, the airline business, we would surely stop flying.

If the dishonesty – or at least the reliance on quasi-truths –

of some people in this industry were mirrored in the financial sector, we would not entrust our money there.

If the greed of some people in this industry were mirrored in our elected officials, what little respect politicians can still command would evaporate.

No, this industry is not like any other. Because we cannot stop taking medication we are asked to tolerate recklessness in the name of progress, to accept dishonesty in the name of research and development, and to turn a blind eye to greed in the name of shareholder satisfaction.

We are also faced with the sad truth that there is no indication, anywhere, that things will get any better.

The National Health Service is almost certainly the single largest purchaser of pharmaceuticals in the world. For the year 2001, the overall NHS budget is put at £48 billion, around 14 per cent of which is for drugs. That's roughly £6.7 billion. That's also nearly 50 per cent more than is spent on salaries.

A little-known sector of the NHS is its army of pharmaceutical advisers who, under the auspices of each health authority, attempt to keep prescribing costs down. These 250–300 men and women – all of whom must have a degree in pharmacology and at least three years' experience in primary care – are the closest that the NHS can come to an antidote for the thousands of detailers who visit doctors and hospitals all over the country to boost Big Pharma's sales.

'The reception we get', explains one, 'is not quite as cordial as the reception given to the detailers. We don't have pens and rulers and sweets to hand out. We're the people trying to convince doctors to change their prescribing habits. We're the ones who have to tell them either that they're spending too much or that they could spend less. We are often the people the doctor is too busy to see.'

Even though drugs in Britain are among the least expensive in the world, and even though the NHS has plans to ensure that seventy-two out of every hundred prescriptions will be for a generic drug, rather than the more expensive branded product, drug costs are rising at about 8 per cent a year and will continue to rise at that rate for the next few years.

Simple maths suggests that, based on drug costs alone, the NHS could be broke by the year 2020. That's if everything remains the same. Unfortunately, the demise of the NHS could be hastened by several additional factors.

First, drug prices in the UK are held down by the regulation of profits. Getting around that is no more difficult than paying more for better accountants than the government can afford.

Second, drug prices are under threat in the United States. A bill there that allows cheaper pharmaceuticals to be imported into the USA will have the immediate effect of reducing some prescription costs in America. Consequently, Big Pharma's profits will have to be sustained through price rises in other markets. Britain is a sitting-duck candidate.

And third, Big Pharma's assault on the ban against direct-to-consumer advertising in Britain and the EU is guaranteed, eventually, to succeed. Whether it's the slow-drip leak of the Internet or of satellite television, in due time Britain will be flooded by DTCA. Doctors intent on prescribing generics will be short-circuited and the NHS's ability to keep drug expenditure increases down to a mere 8 per cent will be neutralized.

Even then, if this was only about money, we might still be willing to pay for a CEO's ego and lust for corporate power. However, questions might reasonably be raised when the boards of directors of two giant drug companies – SmithKline Beecham and Glaxo Wellcome – put together their personal salary, bonus and stock option packages, awarding them-selves total remuneration enough to rival the overall profit of the entire UK generic drug industry.

And what about one's suspicions of an industry that feels the need to hire two lobbyists for every law-maker in Washington?

Or one's belief in an industry that has the gall to ask us to feel good about huge sums spent on R&D when that same industry spends even more money on marketing its products to us?

Or our pride in ourselves as a society when one of the most powerful influences in that society turns its back on the less fortunate who simply cannot afford to pay artificially high prices for essential medicines?

Should any of us fully trust – as we are asked to do – any corporation with our health when that same corporation is quick to remind its shareholders where its true allegiance lies.

No doubt, there are responsible voices in the industry who want to earn the public's respect – not just for the science, but for every aspect of the industry, especially the way it does business.

Sadly, those voices seem few and far between.

Instead, all too often, the noise the industry makes sounds more like chants of 'kill the messenger'.

'You have a lot to answer for,' came my criticism.

The senior marketing executive at one of the world's largest pharmaceutical companies responded simply, 'We're in business.'

'You're different.'

'Not as far as our shareholders are concerned.'

'Ask the people who can't afford to pay 10 bucks for a pill that costs 10 cents.'

'Don't tell me that the glass is half empty when it's almost full.'

'I'm telling you that people are dying.'

'The truth of the matter is that, thanks to us, people are living.'

I suggested, 'The truth of the matter is that good people sometimes, collectively, do evil things and, in this case, the overriding theme is collective corporate greed.'

He warned, 'You realize, I'm sure, that if you come after us, we'll come after you.'

'What does that mean?'

'You're welcome to interpret that any way you care to.'

'How about if I care to quote you as threatening me.'

Now he suggested, 'I wouldn't if I were you.'

And I warned, 'But you're not me.'

Acknowledgements

For their cooperation and input, I am grateful to many people in several parts of the world.

In the United Kingdom, my appreciation goes to: Cyril Beck, former Chairman of Norton Pharmaceuticals; Dr Alastair Benbow at SmithKline Beecham; Jon Close; Guy Dehn at Public Concern at Work; Linda Foster of Bioglan; Dr Martin Goldman at Pharmax; Dr David Griffith; Richard Jennings of Cambridge University; Richard Liwicki of Oxford University; Dr Andrew Millar; Duncan Moore of Morgan Stanley Dean Witter; Warwick Smith of the British Generic Manufacturers' Association; Sir David Weatherall of Oxford University; Dr Frank Wells; Paul Whybrow; and Dr Gavin Yamey of the *British Medical Journal*.

In Australia, thanks go to Dr Graeme Laver and to Dr Peter Mansfield of MaLAM.

In Canada, I am indebted to: Dr Nancy Olivieri; Barry Sherman and Jack Kay of Apotex; Professor Trudo Lemmons; Dr Joel Lexchin; Jim Keon of the Canadian Drug Manufacturers' Association; Dr Michele Brill-Edwards; attorney Lori Stoltz; and Dr Arnold Naimark.

In the United States, I wish to thank: Dr Alex Arrow; Dean Boyd, Phil Reed and Kevin Della-Colli at US Customs; Bruce Downey and Carol Cox at Barr Laboratories; attorneys Ezequiel Camerini, Mark Kleiman, Peter Reichertz, Dan Sigelman, D'Lisa

Simmons and Mike Williams; Jim Griffin of the US Justice Department; Dr John Gueriguian; Dr Susan Horwitz at Einstein College of Medicine; Dr Sheldon Krimsky at Tufts University; Dr Robert Misbin; Russell Mokhiber at Corporate Crime Reporter; Dr David Nathan of the Dana Farber Cancer Institute; Eugene Reed; Dr Drummond Rennie of the *Journal of the American Medical Association*; Dr Eric Rose of the University of Washington School of Medicine; Dr Michael Ryan of Georgetown University; Dr Larry Sasich of Public Citizen; Dr Stephen Schondelmeyer of the Prime Institute; Dr David Shimm; Dr P. Roy Vagelos; Richard Walden of Operation USA; Diane Walker at the Food and Drug Administration; Dr Monroe Wall; and Bob Weisman of Multinational Monitor.

Likewise in the United States, I am grateful to several members of Congress and their staff, in particular: the Honorable Marion Berry; the Honorable Henry Waxman; the Honorable Bernard Sanders; Paul Kim; Dustin May; and Tate Heuer.

Additionally, I owe thanks to various sources of input via: the American Medical Association, the British Medical Association, the Canadian Medical Association, the UK Medicines Control Agency, the European Agency for the Evaluation of Medicinal Products, the General Medical Council of the United Kingdom, the UK National Institute for Clinical Excellence, the Royal Pharmaceutical Society of Great Britain, the UK Ministry of Health, the British Prescription Medicines Code of Practice Authority; Doctors for Research Integrity, the Hospital for Sick Children and the University of Toronto; the editors of *La Revue Prescrire* in Paris, the *Lancet*, the *New England Journal of Medicine* and the *Canadian Medical Association Journal*; the International Federation of Pharmaceutical Manufacturers' Associations; the Pharmaceutical Research and Manufacturers' Association; the National Association of Pharmaceutical Manufacturers; Médecins sans Frontières; the US Department of Health and Human Services Food and Drug Administration; American

Home Products; AstraZeneca; Aventis; Bayer; Bristol-Myers Squibb; Glaxo Wellcome; Hoffman-Laroche; HMR; Eli Lilly and Company; Merck & Co; Novartis; Parke-Davis; Pfizer; Pharmacia & UpJohn; Schering-Plough; Searle; SmithKline Beecham; Sanofi-Winthrop; Warner-Lambert; Wyeth-Ayerst; the Technology Vision Group; and Cipla Pharmaceuticals.

The sheer abundance of information available on the world-wide web is such that no serious researcher can afford to disregard it. While it goes witht saying that the quality of the material available online runs the gamut from richly outstanding to totally unreliable, I wish to acknowledge my appreciation to the individuals who participate in and the organizations who make information and sources available on four exceptional sites: the E-Drug discussion group (www.healthnet.org), MaLAM (www.camtech.net.au/malam), Médicins sans Frontières (www.msf.org), and Health Action International (www.haiweb.org).

Finally, many special thanks to Katharine Young, Helen Gummer and Glen Saville at Simon & Schuster, to Nick Webb for understanding this project right from the beginning, to Alan Williams for his erudition and advice, to Liz Paton for her copyediting, to my agent Milly Marmur and, as always, to La Benayoun.

Select Bibliography

BOOKS

Abraham, John, *Science, Politics and the Pharmaceutical Industry: Controversy and Bias in Drug Regulation*, St Martins Press, New York, 1995.

Arno, Peter S. and Feiden, Karyn L., *Against the Odds: the Story of AIDS Drug Development, Politics and Profits*, HarperCollins, New York, 1992.

Barlow, Maude and Campbell, Bruce, *Take Back the Nation*, Key Porter Books, Toronto, 1991.

Basara, Lisa Ruby and Montagne, Michael, *Searching for Magic Bullets: Orphan Drugs, Consumer Activism and Pharmaceutical Development*, Haworth Press, New York, 1994.

Beauchamp, Tom L. and Bowie, Norman E., eds., *Ethical Theory and Business*, Prentice Hall, New Jersey, 1993.

Bian, Tonda R., *Drug Lords: America's Pharmaceutical Cartel*, No Barriers Publishing, Michigan, 1997.

Bogner, W. and Thomas, H., *Drugs to Market: Creating Value and Advantage in the Pharmaceutical Industry*, Pergamon, London, 1996.

Bork, Robert H., *The Antitrust Paradox*, Basic Books, New York, 1978.

Burkholz, Herbert, *The FDA Follies*, Basic Books, New York, 1994.

Cookson, William, *The Gene Hunters*, Aurum Press, London, 1994.

Danzon, P. M., *Pharmaceutical Price Regulation: National Policies versus Global Interests*, American Enterprise Institute Press, Washington DC, 1997.

Davis, P., *Managing Medicines: Public Policy and Therapeutic Drugs*, Open University Press, Buckingham, 1997.

Drake, Donald and Uhlman, Marian, *Making Medicine – Making Money*, Andrews & McMeel, Kansas City, 1993.

Gambardella, Alfonso, *Science and Innovation: the US Pharmaceutical Industry during the 1980s*, Cambridge University Press, New York, 1995.

Helms, Robert B., ed., *Competitive Strategies in the Pharmaceutical Industry*, American Enterprise Institute Press, Washington DC, 1996.

Helms, Robert B., ed., *Drug Development and Marketing*, American Enterprise Institute Press, Washington DC, 1975.

Hurtig, Mel, *The Betrayal of Canada*, Stoddart Publishing, Toronto, 1991.

Kenney, M., *Bio-Technology: the University–Industrial Complex*, Yale University Press, New Haven, 1986.

Kwitney, Jonathan, *Acceptable Risks*, Simon & Schuster, New York, 1992.

Lapierre, Dominique, *Beyond Love*, Century, London, 1991.

McCormick, Joseph B., Fisher-Hoch, Susan, and Horvitz, Leslie Alan, *Virus Hunters of the CDC*, Turner Publishing, Atlanta, 1996.

McDonald, Marci, *Yankee Doodle Dandy*, Stoddart Publishing, Toronto, 1995.

Maren, Michael, *The Road to Hell: the Ravaging Effects of Foreign Aid and International Charity*, Free Press, New York, 1997.

Mintzes, Barbara, *Blurring the Boundaries: New Trends in Drug Promotion*, HAI, Amsterdam, 1998.

Mokhiber, Russell and Weissman, Robert, *Corporate Predators: the Hunt for Mega-Profits and the Attack on Democracy*, Common Courage Press, Maine, 1999.

Peters, C. J. and Olshaker, Mark, *Virus Hunter*, Anchor Books, New York, 1997.

Preston, Richard, *The Hot Zone*, Doubleday, New York, 1994.

Rachlis, Michael and Kushner, Carol, *Strong Medicine*, Harper-Collins, Toronto, 1994.

Robinson, Jeffrey, *The Manipulators: Unmasking the Hidden Persuaders*, Pocket Books, London, 1999.

Ryan, Michael P., *Knowledge Diplomacy: Global Competition and the Politics of Intellectual Property*, Brookings Institution Press, Washington DC, 1998.

Schweitzer, S., *Pharmaceutical Economics and Policy*, Oxford University Press, New York, 1997.

Sjöström, H. and Nilsson, R., *Thalidomide and the Power of the Drug Companies*, Penguin Books, London, 1972.

Smith, H., *Principles and Methods of Pharmacy Management*, Lea and Febiger, Philadelphia, 1975.

Spece, R., Shimm, D. and Buchanan, A., eds., *Conflict of Interest in Clinical Medicine and Biomedical Research*, Oxford University Press, New York, 1996.

Sullivan, Donald L., *Consumer's Guide to Generic Drugs*, Berkley Books, New York, 1996.

Sunday Times Insight Team, *Suffer the Children: the Story of Thalidomide*, André Deutsch, London, 1979.

Sutherland, M., *Advertising and the Mind of the Consumer: What Works, What Doesn't and Why*, Allen & Unwin, London, 1993.

Watson, James D., *The Double Helix*, Penguin Books, London, 1997.

Werth, Barry, *The Billion Dollar Molecule: One Company's Quest for the Perfect Drug*, Touchstone, New York, 1994.

Young, James Harvey, *The Toadstool Millionaires: a Social History of Patent Medicines in America before Federal Regulations*, Princeton University Press, New Jersey, 1972.

NEWSPAPERS AND NEWS AGENCIES

Advertising Age

29 September 1993: Freeman, L., 'Consumer Ads for Rx Drugs Take off'.

Associated Press

21 September 2000: 'Senator's Roles Prompt Hypocrisy Cry'.

18 September 2000: 'Bayer Makes Tentative Deal in Probe'.

15 September 2000: 'Lawsuits Accuse Ritalin Makers'.

4 July 2000: Galewitz, Phil, 'Pharmaceutical Giant Glaxo Hits Setbacks on Road to No.1'.

22 May 2000: Moulson, Geir, 'Aids Strategy Needs to Look Beyond Price-Cutting, Africans Say'.

16 May 2000: Neergaard, Lauran, 'FDA Prepares to Overhaul Warnings'.

16 May 2000: 'American Home Products Investigated'.

3 May 2000: Holland, Jesse J., 'Medical Research Deaths Probed'.

18 January 2000: Galewitz, Phil, 'Drug-Company Mergers Could Raise Prices for Consumers'.

29 December 1999: Gullo, Karen, 'Drugs in Research Lightly Monitored'.

17 June 1999: Galewitz, Phil, 'Drugmaker Ads Can Backfire'.

24 May 1999: 'Diet Drug Company Accused of Funding Favorable Journal Articles'.

Boston Globe

11 June 2000: Zuckoff, Mitchell, 'Prozac – New Directions – Science, Money Drive a Makeover'.

12 May 2000: Rosenberg, Ronald, 'Transplant Drug Makers Request Refused by State'.

26 January 1999: Sager, Alan and Socolar, Deborah, 'A Fairer Prescription Plan'.

26 December 1999: Anderson, C., 'Drug Firms Said to Pay Less in Taxes'.

27 November 1999: Hoffmann, V., 'Health Groups Say Poor Nations Need Access to Generic Drugs'.

6 March 1999: Knox, R. A., 'Drug-Coverage Crisis Hurting Elderly'.

4 January 1999: Trager, Ellen Lutch, 'Cheaper Rx's for Seniors'.

7 April 1998: Zuckoff, Mitchell, et al., 'Public Research – Private Profit: Tax Dollars Fuel University Spinoffs'.

7 April 1998: Zuckoff, Mitchell, et al., 'Public Research – Private Profit: UMass Nearly Cut out of Lucrative "Pharming" Market'.

7 April 1998: Globe Spotlight Team, 'Public Research – Private Profit: MIT Unrivaled in Reaping Rewards of Its Inventions'.

7 April 1998: O'Neill, Gerard, et al., 'Public Research – Private Profit: Self-Dealing Scientists'.

7 April 1998: Globe Spotlight Team, 'Public Research – Private Profit: A "Helper" Who Calls the Shots and Holds the Money'.

5 April 1998: Dembner, Alice, et al., 'Public Handouts Enrich Drug Makers, Scientists'.

Cape Times (South Africa)
10 May 2000: 'Manufacturers Coin Billions on Aids Drug'.

Chicago Tribune
27 March 1999: 'FDA Allows Qualified Use of Warner-Lambert Diabetes Drug'.

US Federal Register
8 October 1998: 'Food and Drug Administration – List of Drug Products That Have Been Withdrawn or Removed from the Market for Reasons of Safety or Effectiveness'.

Financial Times

30 July 2000: Pilling, David, 'Malaria Study Given $40m'.

17 July 2000: Pilling, David, 'Glaxo Wins Malarone Approval'.

17 June 2000: 'Breast Cancer Drugs Recommended'.

6 May 2000: 'Ovarian Cancer Treatment Drug Gets Go-Ahead'.

3 May 2000: 'Clinical Body Looks at More Cancer Drugs'.

27 March 1999: 'FDA May Restrict Rezulin'.

15 March 1999: 'Consolidation Enters More Frantic Phase – Pharmaceutical Companies Face Increasing Pressures to Merge'.

14 June 1998: 'Biotech Sues Sacked Employee – Company Alleges Former Head of Clinical Trials Breached Confidentiality Agreement'.

5 May 1998: 'Agency Releases Details about Biotech Report'.

1 May 1998: 'The Changing Fortunes of British Biotech. Fateful Phone Call that Unbottled Dr Millar's Tale'.

28 April 1998: 'Millar's Motives in British Biotech Disclosures'.

27 April 1998: 'Sacked Director Says Biotech Board Upgraded Status of Trials'.

26 April 1998: 'Sacked Biotech Boss Reveals Doubts'.

Guardian

2 August 2000: Palast, Gregory, 'Keep Taking Our Tablets – No One Else's'.

17 June 2000: 'NHS "Should Use Best Breast Cancer Drugs"'.

6 May 2000: 'Ovarian Cancer Drug Cleared for Wider Use'.

12 April 2000: 'Controls Eased on "Too Costly" Cancer Drugs'.

18 August 1999: Boseley, Sarah, 'Drug Firm's TV Adverts Test Industry Rules'.

27 July 1999: Boseley, Sarah, 'Drug Trials Risk to Patients'.

Hartford Courant (Connecticut)

11 April 2000: Kauffman, Matthew and Julien, Andrew, 'Industry Cash a Potent Habit'.

9 April 2000: Kauffman, Matthew and Julien, Andrew, 'Surge in Corporate Cash Taints Integrity of Academic Science'.

Independent

17 June 2000: 'Postcode Lottery for New Breast Cancer Drug'.

12 April 2000: 'NHS Restrictions on Cancer Drug Due to Be Lifted'.

27 January 2000: 'One in Three Authorities in Breach of Cancer Guidelines'.

Indianapolis Star

22 April 2000: Swiatek, Jeff, 'Lilly's Legal Strategy Disarmed Prozac Lawyers Secret Deals, Hardball Tactics Limited Drugmaker's Liability for Top-Selling Antidepressant'.

International Herald Tribune

18 November 1998: de Aenlle, Conrad, 'Mergers Give Industry Boost in Developing New Products'.

2 July 1997: Elliott, S., 'Anti-Depressant Makes Sunny Pitch to Public'.

Le Monde Diplomatique

July 1999: Maréchal, Jean-Paul, 'Making Merchandise of Biodiversity'.

Los Angeles Times

31 January 1999: Bernstein, S., 'Drug Makers Face Evolving Marketplace'.

MaLAM Newsletter

March/April 1999: 'Memoirs of Methods Used to Sell Drugs'.

July/August 1997: Sweet, M., 'Healthy Profits – An Overview of Promotion in Australia'.

The Medical Post (Toronto)

8 September 1998: Wysong, Pippa, 'Time with Drug Reps Affects Prescribing'.

21 January 1997: Jeffrey, Susan, 'Research Conflict – Doctor May Be in Legal Battle after Reporting Negative Findings of Drug Company Study'.

New York Times

27 August 2000: Peterson, Melody, 'What's Black and White and Sells Medicine?'

23 July 2000: Stolberg, Sheryl Gay and Gerth, Jeff, 'In a Drug's Journey to Market, Discovery Is Just the First of Many Steps'.

23 July 2000: Stolberg, Sheryl Gay and Gerth, Jeff, 'Holding Down the Competition – How Companies Stall Generics and Keep Themselves Healthy'.

18 July 2000: Goode, Erica, 'Once Again, Prozac Takes Center Stage, in Furor'.

17 June 2000: McNeil, Donald G., Jr, 'Prices for Medicine Are Exorbitant in Africa, Study Says'.

21 May 2000: McNeil, Donald G., Jr, 'Medicine Merchants – Drug Companies and the Third World. A Case Study in Neglect'.

18 May 2000: McNeil, Donald G., Jr, 'Patent Holders Fight Proposal on Generic AIDS Drugs for Poor'.

23 April 2000: Gerth, Jeff and Stolberg, Sheryl Gay, 'Medicine Merchants – Drug Companies Profit from Research Supported by Taxpayers'.

23 April 2000: 'From the Lab to the Pharmacy'.

29 October 1999: Steinhauer, Jennifer, 'Rising Cost of Drugs Take a Bigger Share of Health Insurance Outlays'.

8 October 1999: Morrow, David J., 'Fen-Phen Maker to Pay Billions in Settlement of Diet-Injury Cases'.

29 June 1999: Abelson, Reed, 'Among US Donations, Tons of Worthless Drugs'.

16 June 1999: Toner, Robin, 'Drug Coverage Dominates Fight Brewing on Medicine'.

16 May 1999: Eichenwald, K. and Kolata, G., 'Drug Trials Hide Conflicts for Doctors'.

11 January 1999: Zuger, Abigail, 'Fever Pitch – Getting Doctors to Prescribe Is Big Business'.

17 November 1998: Freudenheim, Milt, 'Influencing Doctor's Orders'.

11 September 1997: Freudenheim, Milt, 'Cleaning out the Medicine Cabinet – Prescription Drug Makers Reconsider Generics'.

24 June 1997: Freudenheim, Milt, 'Lilly Cuts Distribution Unit's Book Value by $2.4 Billion'.

8 October 1996: Freudenheim, Milt, 'Not Quite What Doctor Ordered – Drug Substitutions Add to Discord over Managed Care'.

4 October 1994: Altman, Lawrence K., 'Some Authors in Medical Journals May Be Paid by "Spin Doctors"'.

18 November 1991: Freudenheim, M., 'Merck Reports Major Shift in Its Marketing on Drugs'.

Philadelphia Inquirer

16 June 1999: Greve, Frank, 'Drug Donations – A Bitter Pill?' Some Medications Shipped Abroad Provide More Relief for the Manufacturers Than for Those Who Are Suffering'.

20 April 1999: Collins, Huntly, 'Drug Firm's CEO Showed a New Way'.

18 August 1997: Gelles, J., 'Critics Warn Ads for Prescription Drugs Are Flawed'.

Pittsburgh Post-Gazette

8 March 1998: 'Drug Makers Guard Patents Lawsuits, Other Delaying Tactics Make It Tough for Generics to Break Brand-Name Grip'.

PR Newswire
6 July 2000: Publication of Glaxo SmithKline Merger Documentation.

Reuters
15 May 2000: 'AstraZeneca Sues US Generic Drug Makers'.
17 July 1998: 'Researchers Say Drug Companies, Politics Cheat Mental Health Research'.

San Jose Mercury News
16 May 1999: Krieger, Lisa M., 'Patients Feeling Squeezed'.

Scotland on Sunday
16 January 2000: 'Executive Denying Women Access to New Cancer Drugs'.

Scotsman
17 June 2000: 'Cancer Patients to Get Drug Following English Ruling'.
12 April 2000: 'Doubt over Access to Cancer Drugs for Scots'.
12 April 2000: 'Drugs Worth Paying for'.

Sunday Mirror (UK)
3 July 1994, 'Thalidomide Dad's Tragedy'.

Sunday Times (UK)
16 July 2000: Rogers, Lois, 'Doctors Cut down Patients' Drug Doses to Save on Costs'.

Sydney Morning Herald
25 October 1997: Sweet, Melissa, 'Healthy Profits'.

Times Higher Education Supplement (UK)
22 October 1999: 'Wellcome Pioneers'.

22 October 1999: 'Canada Tempts US with Cut-Price Fees'.

Tallahassee Times-Union
21 March 2000: Pendleton, Randolph, 'Medicaid Pill Prices at Issue. Legislators Debate Restrictions on Expensive Drugs as Costs Soar'.

Tampa Tribune
20 March 2000: Forgrieve, Janet, 'Buying Science'.

Toronto Globe and Mail
2 November 1998: 'Salvage Group Tackles Sick Kids' Image Disaster'.
7 September 1998: Letter to the Editor: 'To Tell the Truth'.
28 August 1998: 'Researchers at Sick Kids Threaten to Leave'.
21 August 1998: 'Sick Kids Plans External Review of Clinical Trials'.
13 August 1998: Taylor, P., 'A Doctor Takes on a Drug Company'.
8 January 1998: Immen, W., 'Heart-Drug Supporters Financed by Makers – Study Links Research to Doctors' Funding'.
20 March 1997: Berger, P., 'The Industry Is Acting Improperly in Promoting HIV Drugs'.
20 May 1996: McKenna, B., 'Generics Press Ottawa for Relief'.
16 March 1996: Coutts, J., 'Drug Giant Seeks to Delay Sale of Generic Prozac'.

Toronto Star
4 May 2000: Levy, Harold, 'Doctor Deemed Too Good to Fire for Harassment'.

USA Today
19 January 2000: Sternberg, Steve, 'Drug Firms Buy Results from Doctors'.

10 November 1999: Cauchon, Dennis, 'Americans Pay More – Here's Why'.

Vancouver Sun
15 August 1997: Pharmaceutical Industry Job Vacancies Ad.

Wall Street Journal
6 July 2000: Harris, Gardoner, 'Drug Firms Stymied in the Lab, Become Marketing Machines'.
24 May 2000: Harris, G., 'Drug Makers Pair up to Fight Key Patent Losses'.
11 May 2000: Murray, S. and Lagnado, L., 'Drug Companies Face Assault on Prices'.
29 March 2000: 'Rezulin Proves the System Works'.
24 March 2000: Waldholz, Michael, 'Pfizer Weighs Requests to Cut Price of Drug'.
9 December 1999: Adams, Chris, 'A Determined Doctor Decides to Write a New Prescription for Drug Research'.
19 February 1999: 'Dose of Reality – Idea of Having Medicare Pay for Elderly's Drugs Is Roiling the Industry'.
2 February 1999: 'Medical Journals Rarely Disclose Researchers' Ties'.
16 November 1998: Langreth, R., 'Drug Marketing Drives Many Clinical Trials'.
16 November 1998: Tanouye, E., 'Drug Dependency – US Has Developed an Expensive Habit, Now, How to Pay for It?'
21 July 1997: Schatz, Tom and Paige, Leslie, 'Politics Trumps Science at the FDA'.
1 July 1997: Burton, T. M. and Ono, Y., 'Campaign for Prozac Targets Consumers'.
6 May 1997: Ingersoll, Bruce, 'American Home Products Gets a Boost as FDA Rejects Generics of Premarin'.
13 February 1997: Tanouye, Elyse, 'Prices of Drugs Increase Faster than Inflation'.

18 January 1996: Cohen, Laurie P. and Tanouye, Elyse, 'Bitter Pill'.

31 August 1995: Tanouye, Elyse, 'Drug Makers Seek Relaxed Restrictions on Marketing'.

12 August 1994: Tanouye, Elyse, 'Drug Marketers May Use Illegal Tactics to Sell'.

1 August 1994: Anders, George, 'Drug Resistance – Costly Medicine Meets Its Match, Hospitals Just Use Lower Doses'.

31 May 1994: Tanouye, Elyse, 'Owning Medco, Merck Takes Drug Marketing the Next Logical Step'.

27 April 1994: Miller, M. W., 'Creating a Buzz – With Remedy in Hand, Drug Firms Get Ready to Popularize Illness'.

5 April 1994: 'Druggist Payments Ending'.

10 September 1993: Anders, G., 'Managed Health Care Jeopardizes Outlook for Drug Detailers'.

3 August 1993: Gutfeld, R., 'FDA Attacks Drug Makers' Ads to Doctors'.

26 February 1993: Racz, G., 'Drug Companies' Profit Margins Top Most Industries, Study Says'.

22 January 1993: Rosewicz, Barbara, 'Science Posts Pose a Puzzle for President'.

26 May 1992: Waldholz, Michael, 'Stymied Science, New Discoveries Dim Drug Makers' Hopes for Quick AIDS Cure'.

14 November 1989: Ingersoll, Brice, 'Chief of FDA to Step Aside after 5 Years'.

22 October 1987: Waldholz, M., 'Merck, in Unusual Gesture, Will Donate Drug to Fight Leading Cause of Blindness'.

Washington Post

11 May 2000: Burgess, John, 'Africa Gets AIDS Drug Exception'.

23 March 1999: Schwartz, John, 'Is FDA Too Quick to Clear Drugs?'

15 February 1998: O'Harrow, R., 'Prescription Sales, Privacy

Fears – CVS, Giant Share Customer Records with Drug Marketing Firm'.

22 August 1997: Schering-Plough Is Told to Halt Clarintin TV Ads'.

16 April 1997: Weiss, Rick, 'Data on Drug's Generic Rivals Suppressed'.

30 January 1997: Baker, Donald P., 'Virginia Bill Would Bar Cash Incentives for Persuasive Druggists'.

26 March 1996: Auerbach, Stuart, 'Study Finds Cheap Drugs Can Be Costly in Long Run'.

10 December 1995: Sakson, Steve, 'Drug Discounts for HMOs May Shift Costs to Others'.

31 July 1990: Spolar, Chris, 'New Schizophrenia Drug Arouses Furor over Cost'.

MAGAZINES AND JOURNALS
Academic Medicine

December 1996: Frankel, Mark S., 'Perception, Reality, and the Political Context of Conflict of Interest in University–Industry Relationships'.

ACP-ASIM Observer (American College of Physicians – American Society of Internal Medicine)

July–August 1999: Maguire, Phyllis, 'Community-Based Trials under Scrutiny – Critics Worry about Conflicts of Interest and Quality of Research'.

September 1995: Wiebe, Christine, 'Drug Representatives and Residents – Dangerous Liaison?'

Alive – Canadian Journal of Health and Nutrition

March 1998: Wolfson, Richard, 'Pharmaceutical Money Drives the Medical Profession'.

American Druggist
1 July 1999: 'Mail Order Drug Sales Leap 10 Percent'.
April 1996: Vaczek, David, 'The Rise of the Generic Drug Industry'.

American Economic Review
May 1996: Baker, Laurence C. and Corts, Kenneth S., 'HMO Penetration and the Cost of Health Care – Market Discipline or Market Segmentation'.
December 1994: Griliches, Zvi and Cockburn, Iain, 'Generics and New Goods in Pharmaceutical Price Indexes'.
May 1986: Grabowski, Henry and Vernon, John, 'Longer Patents for Lower Imitation Barriers – The 1984 Drug Act'.

American Journal of Medicine
July 1982: Avorn, J., Chen, M. and Hartley, R., 'Scientific versus Commercial Sources of Influence on the Prescribing Behavior of Physicians'.

American Medical News
11 October 1999: Greene, Jay, 'Policing CME. A Tough, Complex Job'.

American Prospect
Summer 1993: Love, James, 'The Other Drug War – How Industry Exploits Pharm Subsidies'.

Annals of Internal Medicine
15 August 1998: Shuchman, Miriam, 'Secrecy in Science – The Flock Worker's Lung Investigation'.
15 August 1998: Davidoff, Frank, 'New Disease, Old Story'.
15 August 1998: Kern, David G., et al., 'Flock Worker's Lung – Chronic Interstitial Lung Disease in the Nylon Flocking Industry'.
1 March 1996: Cho, Mildred and Bero, Lisa, 'The Quality of Drug Studies Published in Symposium Proceedings'.

1 June 1992: Wilkes, M. S., Doblin, B. H. and Shapiro, M. F., 'Pharmaceutical Advertisements in Leading Medical Journals – Experts' Assessments'.

Antitrust Report
September 1997: Bloch, Robert, Perlman, Scott and Hansen, Myles, 'Product Market Definition in Pharmaceutical Mergers'.

Applied Economics
August 1994: Alexander, Donald, Flynn, Joseph and Linkins, Linda, 'Estimates of the Demand for Ethical Pharmaceutical Drugs across Countries and Time'.
January 1992: Hudson, John, 'Pricing Dynamics in the Pharmaceutical Industry'.

The Atlantic
January 1991: Graham, Mary, 'The Quiet Drug Revolution'.

Best's Review
June 1996: Jones, John D., 'A Look at Formularies – Prescription for Success?'

British Medical Journal
8 January 2000: Editorial: 'Protecting Whistleblowers'.
23 October 1999: 'Study into Medical Errors Planned for the UK'.
9 October 1999: Ciment, James, 'Study Finds That Most Drug Donations to Developing Countries Are Appropriate'.
25 September 1999: Hopkins, Tanne J., 'Direct to Consumer Drug Advertising Is Billion Dollar Business in US'.
25 September 1999: 'American Medical Association Guidelines on Direct to Consumer Advertising'.
10 July 1999: Griffith, David, 'Reasons for Not Seeing Drug Representatives'.

17 January 1998: Letters: 'Regulating the Pharmaceutical Industry'.

13 February 1998: Smith, R., 'Beyond Conflict of Interest – Transparency Is the Key'.

20 December, 1997: Campbell, Duncan, 'Medicine Needs Its MI5'.

13 December 1997: Editorial: 'Hazardous Drugs in Developing Countries'.

15 June 1996: Shaughnessy, A. F. and Slawson, D. C., 'Pharmaceutical Representatives – Effective if Used with Caution'.

30 March 1996: Dyer, Owen, 'GP Struck off for Fraud in Drug Trials'.

20 January 1996: Roberts, John and Smith, Richard, Editorial: 'Publishing Research Supported by the Tobacco Industry, Journals Should Reverse Ban on Industry Sponsored Research'.

26 March 1994: Kingman, Sharon, 'Drug Companies Are Censured by Watchdog'.

Business & Health

March 1996: Gemignani, Janet, 'PBMs – Why This Exponential Growth?'

Business Week

31 January 2000: Capell, Kerry, Dawley, Heidi and Barrett, Amy, 'Deals – Burying the Hatchet Buys a Lot of Drug Research'.

31 January 2000: 'Year 2000 Pharmaceutical Sales'.

6 December 1999: 'R&D by the Numbers'.

6 December 1999: Barrett, Amy, Licking, Ellen, Carey, John and Capell, Kerry, 'Pharmaceuticals – Addicted to Mergers?'

30 November 1998: Weber, Joseph, 'The Doctor vs the Drugmaker'.

16 May 1994: Weber, Joseph, 'Drug-Merger Mania'.

Canadian Family Physician
June 1997: Lexchin, Joel, 'What Information Do Physicians Receive from Pharmaceutical Representatives?'
April 1997: Lexchin, Joel, 'Consequences of Direct-to-Consumer Advertising of Prescription Drugs'.
August 1991: Tong, K. L. and Lien, C. Y., 'Do Pharmaceutical Representatives Misuse Their Drug Samples?'

Canadian Medical Association Journal
25 January 2000: Hailey, David, 'Scientific Harassment by Pharmaceutical Companies – Time to Stop'.
18 May 1999: Lexchin, Joel, 'Rethinking the Numbers on Adverse Drug Reactions'.
9 February 1999: Shuchman, Miriam, 'Independent Review Adds to Controversy at Sick Kids'.
26 January 1999: Lexchin, Joel, 'Making Drug Data More Transparent'.
20 October 1998: Hoey, John, 'Placing the Ads'.
20 October 1998: Lexchin, Joel, 'Placing the Ads'.
20 October 1998: Phillips, Robert A. and Hoey, John, 'Constraints of Interest – Lessons at the Hospital for Sick Children'.
20 October 1998: Shuchman, Miriam, 'Legal Issues Surrounding Privately Funded Research Cause Furore in Toronto'.
1 April 1997: Lexchin, Joel, 'Can Drug Companies Have It Both Ways?'
1 February 1997: Desjardins, Jean G., 'The PMAC Code of Marketing Practices – Time for Improvement?
1 February 1997: Lexchin, Joel, 'Enforcement of Codes Governing Pharmaceutical Promotion'.
1 February 1997: Shapiro, Martin F., 'Regulating Pharmaceutical Advertising – What Will Work?'
15 November 1993: Lexchin, Joel, 'Interactions between Physicians and the Pharmaceutical Industry – What Does the Literature Say?'

Chemistry and Industry
18 January 1999: Gilvert, David, 'Drug Firms Promoting Choice?'

Chest
July 1992: Orlowski, J. P. and Wateska, L., 'The Effects of Pharmaceutical Firm Enticements on Physician Prescribing Patterns – There's No Such Thing as a Free Lunch'.

Chronicle for Higher Education
18 July 1997: Strosnider, Kim, 'Medical Professor Charges Brown U. with Failing to Protect His Academic Freedom'.
17 April 1997: Wheeler, David L., 'Journal Publishes Thyroid-Study Report That Had Been Blocked by Drug Company'.

Clinical Pharmacology and Therapeutics
June 1994: DiMasi, Joseph A., Seibring, Mark A. and Lasagna, Louis, 'New Drug Development in the United States from 1963 to 1992'.

Clinical Therapeutics
April 1992: Dickson, M., 'The Pricing of Pharmaceuticals – An International Comparison'.

Consumer Policy Review
June 1996: Gilbert, D. and Chetley, A., 'New Trends in Drug Promotion'.

Consumer Reports
October 1999: 'Relief for the Rx Blues'.
June 1996: 'Drug Advertising – Is This Good Medicine?'
July 1992: 'Wasted Health Care Dollars'.
February 1992: 'Pushing Drugs to Doctors'.

Disease Management Health Outcomes
5 May 1999: Lexchin, Joel, 'Direct-to-Consumer Advertising – Impact on Patient Expectations Regarding Disease Management'.

Drug Information Journal
May 1995: DiMasi, Joseph A., 'New Drug Development – Cost, Risk and Complexity'.

Drug Topics
5 April 1999: Glaser, M., 'Boom Year'.
16 March 1998: Gebhart, F., 'Annual Rx Survey – The New Golden Age'.
2 September 1996: Muirhead, Greg, 'Consenting Adults – PCS' Pilot Program for Rx Compliance Looks Promising'.
8 July 1996: Conlan, M. F., 'In-Your-Face Pharmacy'.
8 July 1996: Muirhead, Greg, 'Chain PBMs'.
24 June 1996: Sheetz, Patricia, 'Drug Compliance Program Can Boost Refills'.
4 September 1995: Muirhead, Greg, 'Discount Program Targets Patients without Rx Benefit'.
7 August 1995: Muirhead, Greg, 'Disease Management'.
24 July 1995: Muirhead, Greg, 'HMOs More Willing to Pay Pharmacists for Extra Services'.
10 July 1995: Conlan, Michael F., 'Prior-Authorization Programs Can Save Money – Sometimes'.
24 April 1995: Conlan, Michael F., 'Pharmacy and Manufacturers Spar over Drug Discounts'.
20 March 1995: Conlan, Michael F., 'Patent Law Changes Could Help or Hurt Drugmakers'.
7 November 1994: Muirhead, Greg, 'HMOs Are Controlling More and More Prescriptions'.
19 September 1994: Muirhead, Greg, 'Generics Market to Reach $5.9 Billion by 2000'.
25 July 1994: Ukens, Carol, 'Shaping the Future'.

23 May 1994: Ukens, Carol, 'Drug Switch Reimbursement – Really Pharmaceutical Care?'

25 April 1994: Ukens, Carol, 'Under Legal Fire, Miles Ends Drug Switch Payments'.

21 February 1994: Ukens, Carol, 'Buying Group Offers Consumer Discount Card'.

7 February 1994: Gebhart, Fred, 'New Pharmacist Pricing Suit Adds to the Turmoil'.

The Economist

22 January 2000: 'The New Alchemy – The Drug Industry's Flurry of Mergers Is Based on a Big Gamble'.

31 December 1999: 'A Dose of History'.

21 February 1998: 'Survey on the Pharmaceutical Industry'.

24 January 1998: 'Drug Mergers – Popping the Question'.

27 January 1990: 'The Doctors' Dilemma'.

Educational Health Professional

August 1988: Bowman, M. A., Pearle, D. L., 'Changes in Drug Prescribing Patterns Related to Commercial Company Funding of Continuing Medical Education'.

Families USA

November 1999: 'Hard to Swallow – Rising Drug Prices for America's Seniors'.

FDA Consumer

1 May 1999: Henkel, John, 'How TV Launched the Orphan Drug Act'.

January 1995: Special Report, 'New Drug Development in the United States'.

Food and Drug Law Journal

January 1997: Balto, David A., 'A Whole New World?'

Forbes
22 November 1993: Brimelow, Peter and Spencer, Leslie, 'Food and Drugs and Politics'.

Fortune
17 April 2000: 'How the Industries Stack up'.
March 1998: 'Fortune 500'.
30 March 1998: Guyson, Janet, 'A Mangled Merger'.
7 February 1998: 'The Mother of All Mergers'.
27 December 1993: Tully, Shawn, 'The Plots to Keep Drug Prices High'.

Gerontologist
April 1997: Rowgowski, J., Lillard, L. A. and Kington, R., 'The Financial Burden of Prescription Drug Use among Elderly Persons'.
March 1997: Lillard, L. A., Rogowski, J. and Kington, R., 'Long-Term Determinants of Patterns of Health Insurance Coverage in the Medicare Population'.

HAI News
June 1999: Sagoo, Kiran and Hayes, Lisa, 'Public Health First – Revised Drug Strategy Addresses Trade & Health'.
October 1998: Balasubramaniam, K., 'Impact of WTO on National Drug Policies'.
June 1998: Balasubramaniam, K., 'The Revised Drug Strategy'.
April 1998: Balasubramaniam, K., Lanza, O. and Kaur, S., 'Retail Drug Prices – The Law of the Jungle'.
December 1995: Balasubramaniam, K., 'Retail Drug Prices in the Asia-Pacific Region'.
December 1992: Balasubramaniam, K., 'Pharmacoeconomics'.

Harvard Business Review
January–February 1977: Brenner, S. N. and Molander, E.A., 'Is the Ethics of Business Changing?'

Health Affairs
18 January 1999: Davis, M., Poisal, J., Chulis, G., Zarabozo, C. and Cooper, B., 'Prescription Drug Coverage, Utilization, and Spending among Medicare Beneficiaries'.
May 1998: Smith, S., Freeland, M., Heffler, S., et al., 'The Next Ten Years of Health Spending – What Does the Future Hold?'
February 1994: Long, S., 'Prescription Drugs and the Elderly – Issues and Options'.

Health Care Financing Review
March 1999: Poisal, J. A., Murray, L. A., Chulis, G. S. and Cooper, B. S., 'Prescription Drug Coverage and Spending for Medicare Beneficiaries'.

Health Marketing Quarterly
Autumn 1997: Mehta, Subhash and Mehta, Sanjay, 'Strategic Options for Brand-Name Prescription Drugs When Patents Expire'.

International Journal of the Economics of Business
November 1997: Danzon, Patricia, 'Price Discrimination for Pharmaceuticals – Welfare Effects in the US and the EU'.
November 1997: Reekie, W. Duncan, 'Cartels, Spontaneous Price Discrimination and International Pharmacy Retailing'.
November 1997: Elzinga, Kenneth and Mills, David, 'The Distribution and Pricing of Prescription Drugs'.

International Journal of Pharmaceutical Compounding
8 October 1998: 'Proposed List of Agents Not to Be Compounded Due to Withdrawal for Safety/Efficiency Concerns'.

International Journal of Strategic Management
April 1999: Jones, J. and Pollitt, M., 'From Promise to Compliance – The Development of Integrity at SmithKline Beecham'.

Journal of the American Medical Association
19 January 2000: Wazana, A., 'Physicians and the Pharmaceutical Industry'.
16 April 1997: Rennie, Drummond, 'Thyroid Storm'.
16 April 1997: Dong, Betty J., et al., 'Bioequivalence of Generic Brand-Name Levothyroxine Products in the Treatment of Hypothyroidism'.
16 April 1997: Blumenthal, David, et al., 'Withholding Research Results in Academic Life Science – Evidence from a National Survey of Faculty'.
27 January 1997: Pécoul, Bernard, Chirac, Pierre, Trouille, Patrice and Pinel, Jacques, 'Access to Essential Drugs in Poor Countries. A Lost Battle?'
26 April 1995: Ziegler, M. G., Lew, P. and Singer, B. C., 'The Accuracy of Drug Information from Pharmaceutical Sales Representatives'.
2 March 1994: Chren, M. M. and Landefeld, C. S., 'Physicians' Behavior and Their Interactions with Drug Companies'.
3 October 1990: McKinney, W. P., Schiedermayer, D. L., Lurie, N., Simpson, D. E., Goodman, J. L. and Rich, E. C., 'Attitudes of Internal Medicine Faculty and Residents toward Professional Interaction with Pharmaceutical Sales Representatives'.

Journal of Business
July 1974: Cocks, Douglas and Virts, John, 'Pricing Behavior of the Ethical Pharmaceutical Industry'.

Journal of Commerce
2 March 1998: Sutter, Mary, 'US Drug Makers Fear Generics Law in Mexico – Brand-Name Sales Considered at Risk'.

Journal of Drug Issues
February 1992: Morris, L. A. and Griffin, J. P., 'The Evolving Role of FDA in Prescription Drug Promotion'.
February 1992: Basara, L. R., 'Direct-to-Consumer Advertising – Today's Issues and Tomorrow's Outlook'.

Journal of Economic Literature
September 1986: Comanor, William S., 'The Political Economy of the Pharmaceutical Industry'.

Journal of Economics and Management Strategy
Spring 1997: Frank, Richard G. and Salkever, David S., 'Generic Entry and the Pricing of Pharmaceuticals'.
Fall 1994: Cockburn, Iain and Henderson, Rebecca, 'Racing to Invest? The Dynamics of Competition in Ethical Drug Discovery'.

Journal of the Family Practitioner
January 1992: Brotzman, G. L. and Mark, D. H., 'Policies Regulating the Activities of Pharmaceutical Representatives in Residency Programs'.

Journal of General Internal Medicine
13 March 1998: Gibbons, R. V., Landry, F.J., Blouch, D. L., Jones, D. L., Williams, F. K., Lucey, C. R. and Kroenke, K., 'A Comparison of Physicians' and Patients' Attitudes toward Pharmaceutical Industry Gifts'.

November 1996: Wolfe, Sidney, 'Why Do American Drug Companies Spend More Than \$12 Billion a Year Pushing Drugs? Is It Education or Promotion?'

11 October 1996: Stryer, D. and Bero, L. A., 'Characteristics of Materials Distributed by Drug Companies – An Evaluation of Appropriateness'.

September 1994: Shaughnessy, A. F., Slawson, D. C. and Bennet, J. H., 'Separating the Wheat from the Chaff – Identifying Fallacies in Pharmaceutical Promotion'.

May 1990: Lurie, N. and Rich, E. C., 'Pharmaceutical Representatives in Academic Medical Centers – Interaction with Faculty and Housestaff'.

January 1986: Davidson, R. A., 'Source of Funding and Outcome of Clinical Trials'.

Journal of Healthcare Marketing

Spring 1995: Williams, James and Hensel, Paul, 'Direct-to-Consumer Advertising of Prescription Drugs'.

Journal of Health Economics

February 1997: Garber, Alan and Phelps, Charles, 'Economic Foundations of Cost-Effectiveness Analysis'.

July 1991: DiMasi, Joseph and Hansen, Ronald, 'Cost of Innovation in the Pharmaceutical Industry'.

Journal of Industrial Economics

September 1987: Jensen, Elizabeth J., 'Research Expenditures and the Discovery of New Drugs'.

March 1978: Reekie, W. Duncan, 'Price and Quality Competition in the United States Drug Industry'.

Journal of the Institute for Fiscal Studies

March 1999: Bloom, N. and Van Reene, J., 'Regulating Drug Prices – Where Do We Go from Here?'

Journal of Law and Commerce
Fall 1995: Davis, Melissa K., 'Monopolistic Tendencies of Brand-Name Drug Companies in the Pharmaceutical Industry'.

Journal of Law and Economics
April 1997: Manning, Richard L., 'Products Liability and Prescription Drug Prices in Canada and the United States'.
October 1992: Grabowski, Henry G. and Vernon, John M., 'Brand Loyalty, Entry, and Price Competition in Pharmaceuticals after the 1984 Drug Act'.
April 1989: Dranove, David, 'Medicaid Drug Formulary Restrictions'.
October 1988: Hurwitz, Mark and Caves, Richard, 'Persuasion or Information? Promotion and the Shares of Brand Name and Generic Pharmaceuticals'.
April 1981: Leffler, Keith B., 'Persuasion or Information? The Economics of Prescription Drug Advertising'.

Journal of Research in Pharmaceutical Economics
July 1996: Kucukarslan, Suzan, 'In Search of an Understanding of Pharmaceutical Prices'.
July 1996: Pathak, Dev and Escovitz, Alan, 'Managed Competition and Pharmaceutical Care – An Answer to Market Failure?'
July 1996: Shah, Hemant K., 'Redefining the Pharmaceutical Industry'.
July 1996: Bobula, Joel D., 'A New Era in Pharmaceutical Pricing'.
July 1996: Cohen, Kenneth R., 'Managed Competition – Implications for the US Pharmaceutical Industry'.
June 1995: Kolassa, E. M., 'Physicians' Perceptions of Prescription Drug Prices – Their Accuracy and Effect on the Prescribing Decision'.
June 1995: Mullins, C. Daniel, 'Toward an Understanding

of Pharmaceutical Pricing Strategies through the Use of Simple Game Theoretic Models'.

Lancet
30 October 1999: 'NEJM Conflict-of-Interest Policy under Scrutiny'.
30 October 1999: 'Spain Investigates "Bribery" of Doctors'.
23 October 1999: 'Canadian Universities Go Shopping for Research Scientists'.
10 October 1998: Editorial: 'A Meeting too Many'.
28 March 1998: Editorial: 'Pushing Ethical Pharmaceuticals Direct to the Public'.
7 June 1997: Editorial: 'Good Manners for the Pharmaceutical Industry'.
26 April 1997: Firshein, J. 'Drug Firm Buys up Chain of US Cancer Clinics'.
9 January 1993: Sheldon, T. A. and Smith, G. D., 'Consensus Conferences as Drug Promotion'.

Managing Intellectual Property
May 1995: Wild, Joff, 'Pharmaceutical Trademarks in a Hostile World'.

Marketing Intelligence and Planning
October 1992: Blackett, Tom, 'Branding and the Rise of the Generic Drug'.

Medical Care
September 1999: Lillard, L. A., Rogowski, J. and Kington, R., 'Insurance Coverage for Prescription Drugs, Effects on Use and Expenditures in the Medicare Population'.
February 1998: Stuart, B. and Grana, J., 'Ability to Pay and the Decision to Medicate'.
May 1995: Stuart, B. and Grana, J., 'Are Prescribed and Over-the-Counter Medicines Economic Substitutes? A Study of

the Effects of Health Insurance on Medicine Choices by the Elderly'.

Medical Marketing and Media
April 1997: Goldberg, Gene L., 'Problems Ahead in Generic Marketing'.
November 1995: Hodnett, J., 'Targeting Consumers'.
September 1995: Gray, Michael, 'PBMs – Can't Live with 'Em, Can't Live without 'Em'.
January 1995: Castagnoli, William G., 'Is Disease State Management Good Therapy for an Ailing Industry?'
May 1994: Matalia, N., 'Journal Advertising Works! Three Studies Say So!'
April 1994: Goldberg, Gene L., 'Will There Be a Generic Industry Five Years from Now?'
October 1993: Paul, C. Marshall, 'Time to Cut back on Detailing'.

Mergers and Acquisitions
September/October 1994: Harrison, Joan, 'Going Upstream in Drug Marketing'.

Money Magazine
December 1998: Rock, Andrea, 'A Dose of Trouble'.
June 1997: Keating, Peter, 'Drugmakers Pressuring Medical Pros to Prescribe Their Products'.
June 1997: Keating, Peter, 'Why You May Be Getting the Wrong Medicine'.

The Nation
21 February 2000: Finkelstein, Katherine Eban, 'Medical Rebels – When Caring for Patients Means Breaking the Rules'.

Nature

21 October 1999: 'Dangers of Over-Dependence on Peer-Reviewed Publication'.

21 October 1999: 'US Guidelines Widen the Net on Scientific Misconduct'.

October 1998: Bonetta, Laura, 'A Duty to Publish'.

New England Journal of Medicine

22 June 2000: Angell, Marcia, 'The Pharmaceutical Industry – To Whom Is It Accountable?'

18 May 2000: Angell, Marcia, 'Is Academic Medicine for Sale?'

18 May 2000: Bodenheimer, Thomas, 'Uneasy Alliance – Clinical Investigators and the Pharmaceutical Industry'.

13 August 1998: Olivieri, N. F., Brittenham, G. M., McLaren, C. E., et al., 'Long-Term Safety and Effectiveness of Iron-Chelation Therapy with Deferiprone for Thalassemia Major'.

8 January 1998: Stelfox, H. T., Chua, G., O'Rourke, K. and Detsky, A. S., 'Conflict of Interest in the Debate over Calcium-Channel Antagonists'.

10 July 1997: Letter to the editor – 'Pfizer Night at Boston Billiards'.

3 October 1996: Angell, M. and Kaassirer, J. P., 'Editorials and Conflicts of Interest'.

8 February 1996: Rosenberg, Steven A., 'Secrecy in Medical Research'.

6 April 1995: Olivieri, N. F., Brittenham, G. M., Matsui, D., et al., 'Iron-Chelation Therapy with Oral Deferiprone in Patients with Thalassemia Major'.

17 November 1994: Kessler, David, Rose, Janet, Temple, Robert, Schapiro, Renie and Griffin, Joseph, 'Therapeutic-Class Wars – Drug Promotion in a Competitive Marketplace'.

8 September 1994: Brennan, T. A., 'Buying Editorials'.

New Medicine
January 1997: Nader, François, 'When Should Pharmaceutical Companies Be Involved in Disease Management Programs?'

New York Times Magazine
5 November 1989: Wilkes, M. S. and Shuchman, M., 'Pitching Doctors'.

Our Times Magazine
June–July 1994: Nore, Gordon, 'Pop Goes Education – No Choice for a New Generation of Students'.

Outlook on Science Policy
21 October 1999: 'UK Government Use of Science and Technology'.
21 October 1999: 'Report Assesses Australia's R&D Policy'.
21 October 1999: 'New Zealand's Blueprint for Science and Technology'.

Perspectives in Biology and Medicine
Winter 2000: Laver, G., Bischofberger, N. and Webster, R., 'The Origin and Control of Pandemic Influenza'.

Pharmacoeconomics
February 1999: Lyles, A. and Palumbo, F., 'The Effect of Managed Care on Prescription Drug Costs and Benefits'.
May 1998: Dickson, M. and Redwood, H., 'Pharmaceutical Reference Prices – How Do They Work in Practice?'
October 1996: Towse, A., 'The UK Pharmaceutical Market'.
October 1996: Le Pen, C., 'Drug Pricing and Reimbursement in France – Towards a New Model?'
August 1995: Denig, P. and Haaijer-Ruskamp, F. M., 'Do Physicians Take Cost into Account when Making Prescribing Decisions?'

Pharmacy Times
January 1994: Salmo, Rose, 'Market Forces Usher in a Golden Age of Generic Drugs'.

Policy Studies
March–April 1997: Earl, Slater, 'A Study of Pharmaceutical Policies in the EU'.

Prescrire International
1997: Becel, B., Bardelay, D. and 't Hoen, E., 'A French Physician's Network Monitoring Medical Representatives'.
May 1996: 'Calcium Antagonists – Overused and Inadequately Assessed'.
April 1995: Bardelay, D., 'Visits from Medical Representatives – Fine Principles, Poor Practice'.

Psychiatric News
7 June 1996: 'Ethics of Pizza, Prozac, and Profits Challenge Residents to Think Twice'.

Psychiatric Times
June 1997: Klein, Donald F., 'Current Obstacles to Drug Development'.

Public Citizen Magazine
March–April 1991: Atkinson, Carla and Geiger, John, 'Just Say No? When Drug Companies Make Offers Doctors Can't Refuse'.

Public Interest
Summer 1993: Weidenbaum, Murray, 'Are Drug Prices Too High?'

Report on Business Magazine
June 1998: 'Ivy-League Hustle'.

Review of Economics and Statistics
February 1998: Lu, Z. John and Comanor, William, 'Strategic Pricing of New Pharmaceuticals'.

Risk Management
February 1996: Jones, John D., 'Easier to Swallow'.

Royal College of General Practitioners International Newsletter
June 1999: Hickey, Kevin, 'MaLAM – An End to Exaggerol?'

Science
15 October 1999: 'A Misconduct Definition That Finally Sticks?'
8 October 1999: 'Philanthropy's Rising Tide Lifts Science'.
28 August 1998: Marshall, Eliot, 'NIH, DuPont Declare Truce in Mouse War'.
6 June 1997: Cohen, Jon, 'Exclusive License Rankles Genome Researchers'.
25 April 1997: Marshall, Eliot, 'Secretiveness Found Widespread in Life Sciences'.
25 April 1997: Pennisi, Elizabeth, 'Merck Gives Researchers Knockout Deal'.
25 April 1997: Vogel, Gretchen, 'Long-Suppressed Study Finally Sees Light of Day'.
25 April 1997: Roush, Wade, 'Secrecy Dispute Pits Brown Researcher against Company'.
8 March 1996: Holden, Constance, 'Company Secrets Don't Stop Science'.
23 June 1995: Cohen, Jon, 'Share and Share Alike Isn't Always the Rule in Science'.

Science and Public Affairs
October 1999: 'A Glimpse of the Future'.
October 1999: 'Taking Part in the Political Process'.

Science, Technology, and Human Values
Spring 1985: 'Secrecy in University-Based Research – Who Controls? Who Tells?'

Scientific American
January 1999: Laver, G., Bischofberger, N. and Webster, R., 'Disarming Flu Viruses'.
March 1995: Kessler, David A. and Feiden, Karyn I., 'Faster Evaluation of Vital Drugs'.

The Scientist
24 May 1999: Gwynn, Peter, 'Corporate Collaborations – Scientists Can Face Publishing Constraint'.
23 June 1997: Kreeger, Karen Young, 'Industry Support of Societies under Fire'.
1 April 1996: Benowitz, Steven, 'Is Corporate Research Funding Leading to Secrecy in Science?'
2 October 1995: Watanabe, Myrna E., 'Merger Mania among Drug Firms Raises Concern about Commitment to Discovery'.
2 October 1995: Watanabe, Myrna E., 'The Urge to Merge'.
26 June 1995: Benowitz, Steven, 'Wave of the Future, Interdisciplinary Collaborations'.
11 July 1994: Kahn, Robert L. and Prager, Denis J., 'Interdisciplinary Collaborations Are a Scientific and Social Imperative'.

Scrip
September 1999: Saunders, Philippa, 'It's Time to Call a Halt to Poor Drug Donation Practice'.

December 1997: 'Troglitazone Suspended in UK after More Adverse Events'.

3 June 1997: 'UK Pilot Disease Management Scheme'.

27 May 1997: 'Self-Medication Increasing in India'.

23 May 1997: 'WHO to Look at Internet Pharmaceuticals Trade'.

20 May 1997: 'EC Commission to Revisit DTC Advertising Ban'.

8 April 1997: 'New US Direct-to-Consumer Campaigns'.

28 February 1997: 'PhRMA to Continue Ad Campaign'.

21 February 1997: 'US DTC Campaigns – Caverject, Effexor'.

4 February 1997: 'US DTC Advertising Spend Tops $700 Million'.

February 1997: 'Evaluating Marketing Measures in Eastern Europe'.

June 1995: Mansfield, Peter, 'Pharmaceutical Customers – Prey or Partners?'

March 1995: Branthwaite, A. and Downing, T., 'Marketing to Doctors – The Human Factor'.

Social Science Medicine

April 1997: Grabowski, H. and Mullins, C. D., 'Pharmacy Benefit Management, Cost-Effectiveness Analysis and Drug Formulary Decisions'.

October 1985: Leibowitz, Arleen, Manning, Willard and Newhouse, Joseph, 'The Demand for Prescription Drugs as a Function of Cost-Sharing'.

Southern Economic Journal

October 1992: Frank, Richard and Salkever, David, 'Pricing, Patent Loss and the Market for Pharmaceuticals'.

This Magazine

September–October 1998: Schmidt, Sarah, 'The University of Toronto Is Selling Its Classrooms, Its Programs, Even Its

Washrooms, to the Highest Bidder – But the Corporate Takeover of the Academy Goes Much Further'.

Time
26 January 1998: Several authors, 'Swallowing Bitter Pills. Fake and Adulterated Medicines Are Posing Health Risks Greater Than the Diseases They're Meant to Cure'.
29 April 1996: Purvis, Andrew, 'The Goodwill Pill Mess – Eli Lilly and Other Firms Give away Medicine to Places like Rwanda. Trouble Is, It's Not Always of Use'.
30 June 1997: Gorman, C., 'Oh, My Aching Head!'
8 March 1993: Greenwald, John, 'The Pain of Pricey Pills'.
8 January 1990: Gorman, Christine, Cronin, Mary and Shaw, Peter, 'The Price Isn't Right. Drug Firms Start to Feel the Heat as the Cost of Medication Spirals'.

University of Cincinnati Law Review
Summer 1995: Dodd, Christine, 'Comments: The Merck–Medco Merger – An Isolated Incident or a Catalyst for the Transformation of an Industry?'

US News & World Report
29 March 1993: Podolski, D. and Newman, R., 'Prescription Prizes'.

MONOGRAPHS AND SPEECHES
Association of the British Pharmaceutical Industry, Code of Practice Authority, *Code of Practice Review*, London, May 2000.
Association of the British Pharmaceutical Industry, Code of Practice Authority, *Code of Practice Review*, London, February 2000.
Association of the British Pharmaceutical Industry, Code of Practice Authority, *Code of Practice Review*, London, November 1999.

Association of the British Pharmaceutical Industry, Code of Practice Authority, *Code of Practice Review*, London, August 1999.

Association of the British Pharmaceutical Industry, Code of Practice Authority, *Code of Practice Review. The Internet and the Code of Practice for the Pharmaceutical Industry*, London, May 1996.

Bond, Ronald and Lean, David, *Sales, Promotion and Product Differentiation in Two Prescription Drug Markets*, United States Federal Trade Commission, Bureau of Economics Staff Report, Washington DC, 1977.

Chetley, A. and Mintzes, B., eds., *Promoting Health or Pushing Drugs? A Critical Examination of Marketing of Pharmaceuticals*, Health Action International, Amsterdam, 1992.

Eastman, H. C., *Report of the Commission of Inquiry on the Pharmaceutical Industry*, Commission of Inquiry on the Pharmaceutical Industry, Ottawa, 1985.

Eastman, H. C., *The MRC of Canada and the Pharmaceutical Patent Legislation*, Medical Research Council of Canada, Ottawa, 1987.

Edwards, Charles C., *The Competitive Status of the US Pharmaceutical Industry*, Economic Report to the President of the United States, Washington DC, 1998.

Generic Pharmaceutical Industry Association, *Facts and Figures*, Washington DC, 1998.

Gibson, M., Brangan, N., Gross, D., et al., *How Much Are Medicare Beneficiaries Paying Out-of-Pocket for Prescription Drugs?* American Association of Retired Persons, Washington DC, 1999.

Gluck, M., *A Medicare Prescription Drug Benefit*, National Academy of Social Insurance, Washington DC, 1999.

International Federation of Pharmaceutical Manufacturers' Associations, *Code of Pharmaceutical Marketing Practices*, Geneva, 1994.

Jacobzone, S., *How Can Pharmaceutical Policy Reconcile Social*

Objectives and Industrial Efficiency? A View from the Recent Experience of OECD Countries, Organisation for Economic Co-operation and Development (OECD), Paris, 1999.

Kern, David G., *A Recent Case Study*, MIT, Cambridge, MA, 29 March 1999.

Kessler, David A., Commissioner of Food and Drugs, Speech before the FDLI Annual Meeting, Washington DC, 13 December 1994.

Kessler, David A., Commissioner of Food and Drugs, Speech before the National Food Editors and Writers Association, Washington DC, 3 October 1991.

Levy, Roy, *The Pharmaceutical Industry – A Discussion of Competitive and Antitrust Issues in an Environment of Change*, Bureau of Economics, Federal Trade Commission, Washington DC, 1999.

Medical Research Council of Canada, Natural Sciences and Engineering Research Council of Canada, Social Sciences and Humanities Research Council of Canada, Tri-Council policy statement, *Ethical Conduct for Research Involving Humans*, Ottawa, 1998.

Morrison, Sylvia, *Prescription Drug Prices – the Effects of Generics, Formularies, and Other Market Changes*, Congressional Research Service, Washington DC, 17 August 1993.

Naimark, Arnold, *Clinical Trials of L1 (Deferiprone) at the Hospital for Sick Children – A Review of Facts and Circumstances*, Hospital for Sick Children, Toronto, December 1999.

National Institutes of Health, *Estimates of National Support for Health Care R&D by Source of Funds*, Washington DC, 1999.

National Pharmaceutical Council, *Pharmaceutical Benefits under State Medical Assistance Programs*, Virginia, 1998.

National Wholesale Druggists' Association (NWDA), *Industry Profile and Health Care Fact Book*, Washington DC, 1999.

Novartis, *Pharmacy Benefit Report Facts and Figures*, New Jersey, 1999.

Organisation for Economic Co-operation and Development (OECD), *Social and Health Policies in OECD – A Survey of Current Programmes and Recent Developments*, Paris, 1998.

Parke-Davis, 'Dear Healthcare Professional Letter – Important Drug Warning', 28 October 1997.

Parke-Davis, 'Dear Healthcare Professional Letter', 1 December 1997.

Pharmaceutical Manufacturers' Association of Canada, *Towards a Better Informed Consumer of Prescription Medicines*, Toronto, 1997.

Pharmaceutical Research and Manufacturers' Association (PhRMA), *Corporate Welfare and the Pharmaceutical Industry*, Washington DC, 1996.

Pharmaceutical Research and Manufacturers' Association (PhRMA), *Pharmaceutical Industry Profile*, Washington DC, 1999.

Pharmaceutical Research and Manufacturers' Association (PhRMA), *Pharmaceutical Industry Profile*, Washington DC, 1998.

Pharmaceutical Research and Manufacturers' Association (PhRMA), *The Drug Development and Approval Process*, Washington DC, 1996.

Reich, Michael R., ed., *An Assessment of US Pharmaceutical Donations – Players, Processes and Products*, Harvard School of Public Health, Boston, 1999.

Rose, Eric, *Pharmaceutical Marketing in the United States – A Critical Analysis*, Seattle, 1997.

Sasich, Larry, *False and Misleading Promotion of the Nonsteroidal Anti-Inflammatory Drug (NSAID) Nabumetone (Relafen). Worst Pills Best Pills News*, Public Citizen, April 1997.

Sasich, Larry and Torrey, E. Fuller, *International Comparison of Prices for Antidepressant and Antipsychotic Drugs*, Public Citizen, Washington DC, 1998.

Schondelmeyer, Stephen, *The Cost of Bill C-91 – An Economic Analysis of the Elimination of Compulsory Licensing of Pharma-*

ceuticals in Canada, PRIME Institute, University of Minnesota, Minneapolis, 1993.

Shimm, David, 'Attitudes towards Industry Capitation Payments for Entering Patients into Clinical Trials', 39th Annual Meeting of the American Society for Therapeutic Radiology and Oncology, Florida, October 1997.

Smith, M., *Patent Protection for Pharmaceutical Products*, Library of Parliament Research Branch, Ottawa, 1993.

United Kingdom, Department of Health, *Pharmaceutical Price Regulation*, London, 2000.

United Kingdom, House of Commons, Science and Technology Committee, *Fifth Report, British Biotech, Volumes I and II*, London, August 1998.

United Nations, *The Trips Agreement and Developing Countries*, New York, 1996.

United States Bureau of Labor Statistics, *Producer Price Index Revision – Current Series for Pharmaceutical Preparations, Prescriptions*, Washington DC, 1999.

United States Central Intelligence Agency, *National Intelligence Estimate – The Global Infectious Disease Threat and Its Implications for the United States*, Washington DC, 2000.

United States Congress, Office of Technology Assessment, *Drug Labeling in Developing Countries*, Washington DC, 1993.

United States Congress, Office of Technology Assessment, *Pharmaceutical R&D – Costs, Risks and Rewards*, Washington DC, 1993.

United States Congress, Office of the Budget, *How Health Care Reform Affects Pharmaceutical Research and Development*, Washington DC, June 1994.

United States Congress, Office of the Budget, *How Increased Competition from Generic Drugs Has Affected Prices and Returns in the Pharmaceutical Industry*, Washington DC, 1998.

United States Department of Health and Human Services, Food and Drug Administration, *FDA Talk Paper – Rezulin Labeling Changes*, 3 November 1997.

333

United States Department of Health and Human Services, Food and Drug Administration, *FDA Talk Paper – Patient Testing and Labeling Strengthened for Rezulin*, 1 December 1997.

United States Department of Health and Human Services, Food and Drug Administration, *Code of Federal Regulation – Prescription Drug Advertising*, Washington DC, 1996.

United States Department of Health and Human Services, Food and Drug Administration, Center for Drug Evaluation and Research (CDER), *Report to the Nation – Improving Public Health through Human Drugs*, Washington DC, 1998.

United States Department of Health and Human Services, Food and Drug Administration, Center for Drug Evaluation and Research (CDER), *Approved Drug Products with Therapeutic Equivalence Evaluations*, Washington DC, 1998.

United States Department of Health and Human Services, Office of Inspector General, *Experience of Health Maintenance Organizations with Pharmacy Benefit Management Companies*, Washington DC, 1997.

United States Department of Health and Human Services, Office of Inspector General, *Special Fraud Alert – Prescription Drug Marketing Schemes*, Washington DC, 1994.

United States General Accounting Office, *Pharmacy Benefit Managers – FEHBP Plans Satisfied with Savings and Services, but Retail Pharmacies Have Concerns*, Washington DC, 1997.

United States General Accounting Office, *Pharmacy Benefit Managers – Early Results on Ventures with Drug Manufacturers*, Washington DC, 1996.

United States General Accounting Office, *Prescription Drug Benefits – Implication for Beneficiaries of Medicare HMO Use of Formularies*, Washington DC, 1999.

United States General Accounting Office, *Prescription Drug Pricing – Implications for Retail Pharmacies*, Washington DC, 1996.

United States General Accounting Office, *Prescription Drugs –*

Companies Typically Charge More in the United States Than in the United Kingdom, Washington DC, 1994.

United States General Accounting Office, *Prescription Drugs – Companies Typically Charge More in the United States Than in Canada*, Washington DC, 1992.

United States General Accounting Office, *Prescription Drugs – Spending Controls in Four European Countries*, Washington DC, 1994.

United States House of Representatives, Committee on Government Reform, Minority Staff, *Prescription Drug Pricing in the United States – Drug Companies Profit at the Expense of Older Americans*, Washington DC, 9 November 1999.

United States House of Representatives, Committee on Government Reform and Oversight, *Prescription Drug Pricing in the US – Drug Companies Profit at the Expense of Older Americans*, Washington DC, February and October 1998.

United States House of Representatives, Committee on Government Reform and Oversight, Minority Staff Report, *Prescription Drug Pricing in the United States – Drug Companies Profit at the Expense of Older Americans*, Washington DC, 1998.

United States House of Representatives, Committee on the Budget, *Testimony of Ralph Nader*, Washington DC, 30 June 1999.

United States House of Representatives, Prescription Drug Task Force, *Affordable Medications for Americans – Problems, Causes and Solutions*, Washington DC, 1999.

United States House of Representatives, Subcommittee on Courts and Intellectual Property of the Committee on the Judiciary, *Testimony of Andrew M. Berdon*, Washington DC, 1 July 1999.

United States House of Representatives, Subcommittee on Courts and Intellectual Property of the Committee on the Judiciary, *Testimony of Gordon Binder*, Washington DC, 1 July 1999.

United States House of Representatives, Subcommittee on

Courts and Intellectual Property of the Committee on the Judiciary, *Testimony of Richard P. Burgoon, Jr*, Washington DC, 1 July 1999.

United States House of Representatives, Subcommittee on Courts and Intellectual Property of the Committee on the Judiciary, *Testimony of Peter Barton Hutt*, Washington DC, 1 July 1999.

United States House of Representatives, Subcommittee on Courts and Intellectual Property of the Committee on the Judiciary, *Testimony of Maura Kealey*, Washington DC, 1 July 1999.

United States House of Representatives, Subcommittee on Courts and Intellectual Property of the Committee on the Judiciary, *Testimony of Gerald F. Meyer*, Washington DC, 1 July 1999.

United States House of Representatives, Subcommittee on Courts and Intellectual Property of the Committee on the Judiciary, *Testimony of Dr. Richard F. Selden*, Washington DC, 1 July 1999.

United States House of Representatives, Subcommittee on Courts and Intellectual Property of the Committee on the Judiciary, *Testimony of Jonathan Spicehandler MD*, Washington DC, 1 July 1999.

United States House of Representatives, Subcommittee on Courts and Intellectual Property of the Committee on the Judiciary, *Statement of Congressman Pete Stark*, Washington DC, 1 July 1999.

United States House of Representatives, Subcommittee on Courts and Intellectual Property of the Committee on the Judiciary, *Statement of Congressman Henry A. Waxman*, Washington DC, 1 July 1999.

United States House of Representatives, Subcommittee on Regulation, Business Opportunities and Technology of the Committee on Small Business, *Testimony of James P. Love, Director, Consumer Project on Technology – Comments on the*

Need for Better Federal Government Oversight of Taxpayer Supported Research and Development, Washington DC, 11 July 1994.

United States House of Representatives, Subcommittee on Regulation, Business Opportunities and Technology, Committee on Small Business, *Pricing of Drugs Codeveloped by Federal Laboratories and Private Companies*, Washington DC, 25 January 1993.

United States Senate, Committee on Labor and Human Resources, Hearings before the Committee on Labor and Human Resources of the United States Senate, *Examining Practices of United States Pharmaceutical Companies and How Drug Prices and Prescriptions Are Affected*, Washington DC, 11–12 December 1990.

United States Senate, Committee on the Judiciary, Subcommittee on Antitrust, Monopolies and Business Rights, *Anticompetitive Abuse of the Orphan Drug Act – Invitation to High Prices*, Washington DC, 21 January 1992.

United States Senate, Special Committee on Aging, *Federally Funded Pharmaceutical Inventions, Testimony of Ralph Nader and James Love*, Washington DC, 24 February 1993.

World Health Organization, *Clinical Pharmacological Evaluation in Drug Control*, Copenhagen, 1993.

World Health Organization, *Globalization and Access to Drugs – Perspectives on the WTO/TRIPS Agreement*, Geneva, 1999.

INDEX